Proceedings
Series

Emerging Perspectives on Services Marketing

Edited by: Leonard L. Berry
Texas A&M University

G. Lynn Shostack
Bankers Trust Company

Gregory D. Upah
Young and Rubicam

AMERICAN
MARKETING
ASSOCIATION

250 South Wacker Drive   Chicago, Illinois 60606   (312) 648-0536

Cover Design by Cory DeLacey

LIBRARY OF CONGRESS CATALOGING IN PUBLICATION DATA

Main entry under title:
Emerging perspectives on services marketing.
(Proceedings series/American Marketing Assn.)
1. Service industries. 2. Marketing. I. Berry, Leonard
L. II. Shostack, G. Lynn III. Upah, Gregory D.
IV. Title: Services marketing. V. Series: Proceedings
series (American Marketing Association)
HD9980.5.E45 1983   658.8   82-20676
ISBN 0-87757-161-9

271/1000/483

TABLE OF CONTENTS

v

PREFACE

Today, out of every dollar consumers spend in America,
about $.47 goes for services. In addition, vast sums
are spent by businesses and institutions for services.
Nearly three out of every four workers on non-farm
payrolls work for service organizations. The "services
economy" is no longer a thing of the future; the services economy is here.

In America, and elsewhere in the world, interest in
services marketing is rising. Most observers now
believe there are key differences in marketing tangi-
bles and intangibles that warrant far more thought and
study than has been the case heretofore. Accordingly,
a small but growing number of academicians are devoting much of their research time to issues related to
the marketing of services. Also, more marketing executives
in such industries as communications, transportation,
hospitality, health care, professional and financial
services are beginning to think of themselves as "services
marketers" rather than as "marketers."

In recognition of these developments, the American Marketing Association has now sponsored two major conferences on
services marketing. The first one, held in Orlando,
Florida in February 1981, resulted in the publication of
a proceedings Marketing of Services edited by James H.
Donnelly and William R. George. The second conference was
held in West Palm Beach, Florida in November 1982. The
presentations given at this conference are published in
the present volume.

The AMA conferences on services marketing have been unusual -- perhaps unique-- events. They have been lively,
intense, exploratory and provocative. They have emphasized theory and practice rather than one or the other.
The 1982 conference was designed to encourage cross-
fertilization, and was structured topically rather than
by industry or specific service. We sought diversity and
were pleased that a superb mix of academics and executives, Americans and overseas professionals participated.
Because the calibre of participation at the 1982 Conference was a principal factor in its success, we have listed
in this volume each person in attendance. In addition,
we have listed all of the reviewers for the competitive
paper sessions.

There is nothing quite so exciting as participating in the
building of a new field. We believe that the 1982 Conference opened many new vistas for future exploration, yielded
new insights into concepts and practices relevant to services and confirmed the unique nature of services marketing and the marketer's role therein. We hope the readers
of this volume will sense some of the dynamism and growth
that lie ahead in service marketing, and we are proud to
have played a role in helping to move toward that goal.

Leonard L. Berry   G. Lynn Shostack   Gregory D. Upah
Texas A&M University Bankers Trust Company   Young & Rubicam
College Station, Texas New York City   New York City

Jeri S. Adleman	American Express Company, Great Neck, NY
Alan R. Andreasen	University of Illinois, Urbana, IL
John Bateson	London Business School, London NW1, ENGLAND
Douglas Bell	Holiday Inn, Memphis, TN
Kenneth Bernhardt	Gorgia State University, Atlanta, GA
Ann Berry	Lake City Madical Center, Lake City, FL
Leonard L. Berry	Texas A&M University, College Station, TX
Mary J. Bitner	University of Washington, Seattle, WA
Barry Blackman	Blackman Marketing Group, Seattle, WA
Thomas M. Bloch	H&R Block, Inc. Kansas City, MO
Bernard Booms	Seattle, WA
Maureen Broderick	Price Waterhouse, San Francisco, CA
Irwin Broh	Irwin Broh & Assoc., Inc., Des Plaines, IL
Laurie J. Budd	University of Southern Florida, Tampa, FL
Anthony J. Calabro	Itran Corporation, South Plainfield, NJ
Jim Cammisa	James V. Cammisa, Inc., New York, NY
Cathi Campbell	Price Waterhouse, Miami, FL
Steve Carter	Bozell & Jacobs, Inc., Dallas/Fortworth Airport, TX
Richard B. Chase	University of Arizona, Tucson, AZ
Michael Cleary	Wright State University, Dayton, OH
Carole Congram	Touche Ross & Co., New York, NY
William Crosby	American Airlines, Dallas/Fort Worth Airport, TX
Steve Curtis	The Marketing Institute, Newport Beach, CA
John A. Czepiel	New York University, New York, NY
Gilles de Courtivron	Novotel, Inc., Scarsdale, NY
Linda Delene	Western Michigan University, Kalamazoo, MI
Carl J. Demery	Blue Cross Blue Shield, Jacksonville, FL
Marshall S. Dickman	Warwick Advertising, New York, NY
Donald F. Dixon	Temple University, Philadelphia, PA
William T. Douton	Chase Manhatan Bank, New York, NY
Ruth J. Dumesic	Williams, Young & Associates, Madison, WI
Robert F. Dyer	George Washington University, Washington, D.C.
Leif Edvinsson	Dovelkns 6.64, SWEDEN
Adel El-Ansary	Bethesda, MD
Bob Fane	Young & Rubicam, Inc., New York, NY
Gail Farkas	Merrill Lynch Commodities, Inc., New York, NY
Mitchell S. Farkas	Merrill Lynch Commodities, Inc., New York, NY
Sandra Fiebelkorn	Citibank, New York, NY
P. Filiatrault	University of Quebec, Montreal, CANADA
Sidney H. Firestone	Young & Rubicam Inc., New York, NY
Raymond Fisk	Oaklahoma State University, Stillwater, OK
Jean-Paul Flipo	York University, Downsview, Ontario, CANADA
Neil M. Ford	University of Wisconsin, Madison, WI
Zane Fractor	GECU, San Antonio, TX
Bill George	Phialdelphia, PA
Peter Gillett	University of Central Florida, Orlando, FL
Emily Green	Beverly Enterprises, Rockville, MD
Christian Gronroos	Swedish School of Economics and Bus. Adm. FINLAND
Stephen J. Grove	University of Baltimore, Baltimore, MD
Jon Gutman	University of Southern California, Los Angeles, CA
Evert Gummesson	Stockholm Consulting Group AB, SWEDEN
Sven-Eric Hallbeck	Securitas, SWEDEN
Nancy Hansen	University of New Hampshire, Durham, NH
Phil Heeg	Mor ale, Welfare & Recreation, Randolf AFB, TX
Garl G. Gellman	Hellman, Werneckl & Assoc., Millwakee, WI
Peter M. Horowitz	Coopers and Lybrand, North York, Ontario, CANADA
Jenny Johnson	Satellite TV Corp./Comsat, Washington, D.C.
Henry C. Joyner	American Airlines, Dallas/Fort Worth Airport, TX
Eugene Kelley	Pennsylvania State University, University Park, PA
J. Patrick Kelly	Institute of Business Management, Provo, UT
Sally J. Clock	Lake County Office on Aging, Painesville, OH
Don Klug	AT&T, Parsippany, NJ
Candi Dramer	Palm Beach Gardens Comm. Hosp., Palm Beach Garden, FL
Jean-Jacques Lambin	Louvain University, BELGIUM
Eric Langeard	IAE Aix, FRANCE
Len Larson	Campbell-Mitchum, Minneapolis, MN
Margaret E. Lavin	GTE Satellite Communications Corp., Stamford, CT
William Lazer	Michigan State University, East Lansing, MI
Jarmo R. Lehtinen	Service Management Institute Finland Oy, FINLAND
Robert R. Lemoi	FinanceAmerica Corporation, Allentown, PA
Michael Leven	Americana Hotels, Chicago, IL

Robert Lewis	University of Massachusetts, Amherst, MA
Ronny Linser	Civilekonom, SWEDEN
Ted Livingston	Continental Cablevision, Inc., Boston, MA
Anthony S. Luciano	Chase Manhattan Bank, New York, NY
Larry Litten	Consortium on Financing, Cambridge, MA
Christopher Lovelock	Harvard Business School, Boston, MA
Lou Mahoney	Western Electric Company, Newark, NJ
Robert Malte	Loyola University, Maywood, IL
Claudia Marshall	Chase Manhattan Bank, New York, NY
Rita Martenson	University of Gotherburg, SWEDEN
Patricia L. Matosic	Arthur Andersen & Co., Chicago, IL
Sarah Maxwell	ARA Coffee Systems, Philadelphia, PA
Archie McGill, Jr.	American Telephone & Telegraph, Basking Ridge, NJ.
Wendy McQuillan	Avis Rent-A-Car, Garden City, NY
Dick Moberg	Campbell-Mitchum, Minneapolis, MN
Charles Moldenhauer	Lefkowith, Inc., New York, NY
Dory Munder	American Express - Travel Division, New York, NY
Sheri Nadel	Ted Bates Advertising, New York, NY
Torgny Nandorf	Dobelns G. 64, SWEDEN
Louis I. Nzegwu	Alcorn State University, Lorman, MS
John D. O'Brien	The Chase Manhattan Bank, New York, NY
Gerry O'Connor	Connecticut General Life, Bloomfield, CT
Samuel G. Offen	American Automobile Assoc. Dearborn, MI
Laurie Pamenthal	Susquehanna University, Selinsgrove, PA
Sara J. Parks	Pennsylvania State University, University Park, PA
Jim Peckham	A.C. Nielsen Co., Northbrook, IL
Gunnar Hihlgren	Maria Trappgrand 5, SWEDEN
Julie Pollack	University of Baltimore, Baltimore, MD
Clive H. Porter	Marketing Science International, AUSTRALIA
Virginia P. Quarti	Connecticut General, Bloomfield, CT
Jane Redfern	AT&T, Basking Ridge, NJ
Thomas Reynolds	University of Texas at Dallas, Richardson, TX
Jim Rice	Western Electric, Rolling Meodows, IL
Richard K. Robinson	Marquette University, Milwaukee, WI
Frank Rothman	General Electric, Bridgeport, CT
Peter M. Sanchez	Villanova University, Villanova, PA
Louis E.S. Santamaria, II	MIICORP, Washington, D.C.
Diane Schmalensee	Marketing Science Institute, Cambridge, MA
Russ Schmuhl	Polaroid Corporation, Cambridge, MA
Robert Shulman	Clancy, Shulman Associates, Inc., New York, NY
Lily T. Seymour	Southwestern Bell, St. Louis, MO
Jim Shanahan	American Express Co., New York, NY
Hank Sherowski	Wendy's International, Blacklick, OH
Michael Smith	Temple University, Philadelphia, PA
Ruth A. Smith	University of Wisconsin, Madison, WI
Mike Spindler	A.C. Nielsen Company, Northbrook, IL
Ronald Stiff	University of Baltimore, Baltimore, MD
Alexander Stone	TRW, Miami, Florida
Arne Svensson	Statskonsult Organisation AB, SWEDEN
Brynjulf Tellefsen	The School of Marketing, NORWAY
Bruce Thorsen	The Gillette Co., Boston, MA
Frank Tiedemann	Community Hospital, Watervliet, MI
Phillips L. Tracy	GTE Satellite Comm. Corp, Stamford, CT
J. Don Trotter	AT&T, Soverset, NJ
Gregory Upah	Young & Rubicam, New York, NY
M. Ven Venkatesan	Wright Stat University, Dayton, OH
Stu Berge	Bell Canada Intl., CANADA
Perry Verille	Walker Research, Inc., Indianapolis, IN
Alan N. Vinick	Connecticut General Life Insurance Co., Hartford, CT
Julian W. Vincze	Rollins College, Winter Park, FL
Kathleen B. Wagner	AAA - Michigan, Dearborn, MI
H. Brant Wansley	Merrill Lynch Pierce, Fenner & Smith, New York, NY
A. Watt	University of Strathelyde, Glasgow, Scotland
Don R. Webb	University of Missouri, Columbia, MO
C.R. Westphal	PT&T, San Francisco, CA
Dr. Leif Widman	University of Stockholm, SWEDEN
Paul F. Wilchek	Carrier International Corporation, Syracuse, NY
Edward D. Wirth Jr.	American Tel. & Tel. Co., Orlando, FL
Valarie A. Zeithaml	Texas A&M University, College Station, TX

REVIEWERS FOR COMPETITIVE PAPER SESSIONS

Alan Andreasen	University of Illinois, Champaign, IL
Eric Berkowitz	University of Minnesota, Minneapolis, MN
Ken Bernhardt	Georgia State University, Atlanta, GA
Mary Bitner	Washington State University, Seattle, WA
Barry Blackman	Blackman Marketing Group, San Antonio, TX
Bernard Booms	Washington State University, Seattle, WA
Stephen Brown	Arizona State University, Tempe, AZ
Richard Connor	Springfield, VA
James Cox	Illinois State University, Bloomington, IL
James H. Donnelly	University of Kentucky, Lexington, KY
Robert F. Dyer	George Washington University, Washington, D.C.
Penny Erickson	Young & Rubicam, New York City
William George	Villanova University, Philadelphia, PA
Peter Gillett	University of Central Florida, Orlando, FL
Christian Gronroos	Swedish School Of Economics, Helsinki, Finland
Brian F. Harris	University of Southern California, Los Angeles, CA
Babette Jackson	J. Walter Thompson, New York City
Robert C. Judd	Governor's State University, Park Forest, IL
Eric Langeard	Universite Aix-En-Provence, Marseille, France
Charles W. Lamb, Jr.	Texas Tech University, Lubbock, TX
John H. Lindgren	University of Virginia, Charlottesville, VA
William Locanber	University of Houston, Houston, TX
Debra Low	Arizona State University, Tempe, AZ
John Martin	Boston University, Boston, MA
Ian MacFarlane	MacFarlane and Co., Atlanta, GA
Jon Millenson	Young & Rubicam, New York City
William Mindak	Tulane University, New Orleans, LA
Mel Moyer	York University, Toronto, Ontario
Jack Nevin	University of Wisconsin, Madison, WI
Steven E. Permut	Yale University, New Haven, CT
Ken Roering	University of Minnesota, Minneapolis, MN
Robert Schulman	Clancy-Schulman, New York City
James Shanahan	American Express, New York City
Terence Shimp	University of South Carolina, Columbia, SC
Ronald Stiff	University of Baltimore, Baltimore, MD
M. Venkatesan	Wright State University, Dayton, OH
Edward Wheatley	University of Miami, Miami, FL
Charles Weinberg	University of British Columbia, Vancouver, B.C.
Valarie A. Zeithaml	Texas A&M University, College Station, TX

SERVICES MARKETING IN EUROPE AND THE USA

Eric Langeard, Institut d'Administration des Entreprises, Université Aix-Marseille III

INTRODUCTION

The case of services marketing in the USA and in Western Europe provides interesting insights about the impact of the environment on the diffusion of innovative research and innovative practice.

Part one is devoted to the environment of services, and to the similarities and differences existing between Western Europe and the USA.

Part two is attempting a broad assessment of the practice of services marketing. Maintaining a good level of service development requires an understanding of the key factors.

The focus of part three is on Services Marketing Research: how research is done on both parts of the atlantic ocean and a brief presentation of three marketing research directions.

THE ENVIRONMENT OF SERVICES IN WESTERN EUROPE AND THE USA

A few facts and figures should be introduced before any assessment of international similarities and differences.

Services: a Neglected Sector.

All the countries with a service or a post-industrial economy have inadequate and unereliable statistics under-estimating service figures. International comparisons are difficult according to the following example. The USA are well known for the reliability of their statistics, however foreign revenues of the US services in 1980 are 100 billions dollars, according to OECD, or 60 billions dollars, according to the US trade representative for services, who offers the following comment "our trade statistics do not reflect data in services in the precise way that they reflect it in goods. This is something that we are doing a good deal of research on right now".

The service sector is generally not a national economic priority. Among the European countries having an economic planning system, none has included a major service industry as a key priority. For example, Table 1 shows the evolution of the workforce in France from 1959 to 1979. The growth of 46 % of the service workforce has been obtained without any help from the French economic planning system

TABLE 1

France 1959-1979: Evolution of the workforce

Agriculture	- 2 500 000	- 43 %
Manufacturing	+ 550 000	+ 8 %
Services	+ 3 800 000	+ 46 %

(source INSEE)

Services: a major share share of the gross domestic product

Table 2 shows services as a percentage of the GDP of a few countries for 1980. Again one should be aware of the diffi-culties when comparing figures from different countries. At best they provide us with a broad indication : we have a cluster of countries between 60 % and 65 % and three exceptions Italy, West Germany and Japan. Leaving aside,

momentarily, the analysis of this minority group, we shall recognize that for all these countries services are a major share of GDP. It has two consequences in relation with the economic crisis: one, rather negative, which is a common fear of industrial collapse and expensive initiatives for the sake of re-industrialisation. The other one is rather constructive, it is a pledge for a combined agricultural-industrial-service approach. Instead of opposing "unproductive services" to industrial wealth, it supports a realistic view of developed economies: the search for added value depends on the ability to develop packages of related services and agricultural or industrial products.

TABLE 2

Services as a percentage of 1980 Gross Domestic Product for ten industrialized countries

Canada	63	France	61
U.S.A.	63	W. Germany	49
Japan	53	Italy	50
Belgium	61	Nederlands	59
Sweden	65	U. K.	62

(Source OECD)

Services: a Major Share of the Workforce.

Table 3 shows two clusters of countries. Services as a percentage of total civil employment is at a very high level (between 59 and 66 %) for six countries. The second cluster is made of Japan, West Germany, Italy and France with service employment between 48 and 55 %. For both groups of countries the leading activities have been very much the same in terms of employment growth: social services, financial services, business to business services. Unfortunately all these countries foresee that the level of service employment will be stable with the possible exception of the communication industry. Services are not anymore "natural" providers of jobs to the idle workforce of countries with a post-industrial economy.

TABLE 3

Services as a percentage of 1980 total Civil Employment for ten industrialized countries

Canada	66	Japan	54
U.S.A.	66	France	55
Belgium	62	W. Germany	49
Sweden	62	Nederlands	62
U. K.	59	Italy	48

(source OECD)

Services: a Growing Share of International Trade

It is estimated that one third of the worldwide interna-tional trade comes from service activities. Table 4 shows a diversity of cases: a cluster of four countries with a very similar situation. For them, services represent already between 23 and 28 % of their total export receipts. Two countries, Japan and West Germany are at a lower level, respectively 16 and 18 %. The USA are a well established leader with 32 %.

TABLE 4

Services exports as a percentage of total export receipts
1980 - per country

U.S.A.	32	France	26
Canada	11	Italy	23
Japan	16	Nederlands	23
W. Germany	18	U. K.	28

(source OECD)

With the help of Table 5, it is possible to reduce the
diversity of cases by looking at the evolution over ten
years of services surplus or deficit. Two countries, Japan
and West Germany, are increasing their deficit against a
majority group which is increasing its services surplus.
For this last group of countries services play a major
role as a competitive force. However, services exports
are extremely vulnerable to political factors and the lack
of a GATT services agreement is a major weakness which
could jeopardize existing levels of services exports.

TABLE 5

Services surplus or deficit
(billions dollars)

West Germany	- 2.2	- 8	- 13.6
Japan	- 1.8	- 7.4	- 11.3
France	+ 0.6	+ 5.5	+ 8.4
Italy	+ 1.3	+ 3.7	+ 5.3
U. K.	+ 2.4	+ 7.7	+ 8.3
U.S.A.	+ 3	+ 24.6	+ 36.1

(source OECD)

Three Environmental Similarities.

These similarities are shared by all developed countries
with two major exceptions: Japan and West Germany. These
two countries have shown a distinct pattern through the
sample of indicators which has been used. It could be
related to their strong industrial culture, it could also
be related to a different breakdown of statistics. More
comparative research on data collection is needed before
reaching a meaningful explanation.

The environmental similarities are the following:
a) more than 55 % of the working force is in the service
sector and service employment growth is leveling off.
b) more than 50 % of household consumption is spent on
services and services expenditures suffer less rapidly
than goods expenditures from economic stagnation.
c) service exports are a key element of balance of
payments equilibrium and uncertainties exist about future
development.

Three environmental differences between Western Europe and
the U.S.A.

Table 6 summarizes these differences ; the following
remarks should be added:
a) The extent of regulation. In Western Europe, it is
common practice that countries are shifting from one
political side to another, and they usually make contradictory moves. Public policies have a strong impact on
regulation, therefore it is difficult to offer a global
diagnosis about the extent of regulation. It is unlikely
that deregulation should reach in any country of Europe
the American level. Overall stability of service regulation
at a fairly high level seems a reasonable prediction.
b) The diversity of culture. The countries of Western
Europe are by and large a common market for many consumer

and industrial goods. It is far from being true when
dealing with services. Cultural traits influence interactions between service organizations and their clients.
c) The size of the public sector. The difference is
obvious. Public services have grown rapidly in the U.S.A.
but it is still a limited public sector compared to
Western Europe.
d) The main consequences of these combined differences.
- Service efficiency is more likely to be achieved in the
U.S.A. due to the existing competitive pressure related to
deregulation and the limited size of the public sector.
- Service diversity and invention will reach a higher
level of occurrence in Western Europe because so many
different settings exist and exchange information.
- Mass markets for services are more easily developed in
the U.S.A. The country will maintain a strong stream of
consumer service innovations.
- Professional and business to business services could
find a favorable climate for innovation in Western Europe
due to the diversity and the overall quality of human
resources.

TABLE 6

Environmental differences

	Western Europe	U.S.A.
The extent of regulation	Overall stability at a high level of regulation	Declining
The size of the public sector	Big	Limited
The diversity of culture	A growing lack of consensus	A widely accepted rule of the game

-:-:-:

THE PRACTICE OF SERVICES MARKETING: AN ASSESSMENT

Both in the U.S.A. and Western Europe, the development of
a service economy has provided exciting growth opportunities to service firms. Catching up with the market rate
of growth has been the main challenge of the 60's and the
early 70's. The challenge of the 80's is to develop a
marketing understanding of technological and societal
innovations capable of strenghtening the competitiveness
of service networks.

The Life Cycle of Service Networks.

Huge domestic networks have been developed during the
last thirty years both in the private and public sector.
The marketing skills of shrewd entrepreneurs have been
very effective at creating brand new service organizations
or at developing an innovative redesign of a conservative
existing service firm. Services marketing success stories
exist ; looking back at the Seventies, Fortune Magazine
selected six service organizations among the ten success
stories of the decade, among them Merril Lynch, Federal
Express, McDonald's and Baker. From the financial super-
market to oil services through parcel service and fast
food, it is a large sample of service industries.
A similar selection could be made of Western Europe
service entrepreneurs : Club Méditerranée, holiday and
leisure, IKEA, home equipment chain store, ISS, cleaning
and security, Comex, deep sea diving, Laker, airline.
At one point or another several of them have had severe
problems which have to do with a lack of managerial
control expertise or a highly regulated environment protecting conservative competitors, or maybe a combination
of the two.

Many large service networks have reached in 1982 the maturity or even the decline stage of their life cycle. The struggle of many post-office networks, the dramatic changes in the American gas service-station and super-market networks, the unability of European retail bank networks to cope with excess capacity and geographic saturation are a few examples of that situation. A shift is needed from both ends of the spectrum: some service firms are too entrepreneurial and refuse to recognize the inherent complexity of mature networks ; others are too bureaucratic and afraid of reallocating resources.
A managerially sophisticated approach of marketing has to overcome three widespread difficulties:
- regulation creates inertion and has a strong negative impact on innovative marketing
- marketing knowledge at the general management level is low
- marketing specialists working in large service networks cannot stimulate the handling of the marketing function throughout the network.
- an innovative environment within the service firm.

Large service networks cannot develop an innovative environment without being able to control or influence three key areas:
- the technological evolution of key equipments
- the potentialities for societal changes
AN INNOVATIVE ENVIRONMENT WITHIN THE SERVICE FIRM.

The European airline companies provide us with the example of an industry which has almost no control over these key areas and great difficulties to adjust to a depressed mass market and an economy crisis.

Airport logistics and the manufacturing of airplanes are beyond their influence. Airline companies provide inaccurate estimates of their long-term needs because they are accustomed to a high level of air transport regulation. As a consequence wide-body jets have often been used at the expense of non-stop flights and high frequencies.

Societal changes are usually slow when they meet a dominant profession. This is the case of most European pilots' unions ; well organized, they have a powerful influence on the management of airlines. Inertia is a major caracteristic of the decision-making process in the area of personal management.

A complex network of bilateral commercial agreements leaves most European airlines with no freedom of marketing action. Any change in the pricing structure or in the delivery of in-flight services has to be negotiated with partners-competitors.

The case of the European airline industry is not an exception. Many service firms have to implement a much better control over these 3 key areas.

The Development of New Services.

At the maturity stage where many large service networks are in 1982, the capacity to act innovatively in three key areas is not enough. It is necessary to manage changes in a systematic and managerial way. A service approach of the management of research and development shall be based on the recognition that service innovations are a mix of technological and societal factors.

Too many large service firms in the U.S.A. and Western Europe do not manage a R & D function and do not allocate financial and human resources to a R & D program. They expect that suppliers of equipments will do the job and they are wrong. A few service leaders and writers have recognized the diversity of hard and soft technologies available and that success is often dependent on hybrid technologies. This delicate balance of hard and soft technologies cannot be obtained and tested by a single

supplier. It requires the cooperation of many different suppliers on a long-term program, preferably under the leadership of the service firm sponsoring it or at least with its active participation. The discovery and development of successful new service formula take time and some formal R & D planning would help.

How to organize a R & D taskforce in a large service firm is not an easy question to answer. It is not only a techni-cal lab, in most cases it is also a social laboratory. Many services such as professional require an under-standing of highly complex human relationships. An investi-gation of successful new consumer services in France has shown that the background of the initiators were unusually related to political and social issues on which they had taken a strong stand and that experience had an influence on their business career. For the years to come, more and more service firms will need a marketing management approach of service delivery and offering systems. The marketing inertia of large service bureaucracies and the the marketing intuition of service entrepreneurs were appropriate to the economic prosperity of the sixties. In 1982 it is not enough, marketing skills have to be improved without losing contact with the field. Both American and European service managers will welcome the help of marketing researchers willing to spend time and effort on meaningful conceptual and methodological issues.

SERVICES MARKETING RESEARCH IN WESTERN EUROPE AND THE USA

On each side of the Atlantic Ocean, the research environ-ment is different in many ways that will be described before introducing a few directions for research and action.

The American Marketing Research Environment.

The academic community produce a steady stream of research through reputable journals. The community is well-organized and large. It has developed a set of unwritten rules which are well understood by the junior researchers. It is reasonable to practice self-limitation because new areas are dangerous and to do empirical research which is more easily accepted than conceptual research. The American marketing scholars have been fighting hard for gaining scientific recognition to our field of research. Many of them are suspicious that multidisciplinary research pojects would cause a reduction of marketing science standards and identity. The organization of publications influence the choice of short projects managed by a limited number of co-authors. All these traits probably explain the relative lack of enthusiasm for the exploration of new applied domains. With about 80 % of the active m arketing researchers working in the U.S.A., no more than 50 % of the services marketing researchers work in this country. This subgroup could grow rapidly because research has well organized channels. One example is the Marketing Science Institute which is updating its research priorities on service marketing.

The European Marketing Research Environment.

The research community is small. It has no mobility. The pressure to publish is low and there are only a few reputable journals. It does not exist any specific pressure for empiricism. The national group of marketing scholars have a diversified set of research value systems. For example, the Scandinavian community gives high marks to clinical research, and the German researchers are giving a high value to conceptual frameworks. Therefore, the small size of the community and the diversified research environments force into the conceptual level these resear-chers who are willing to work together. Many European countries are having their first generation of marketing scholars, and the organization for research is weak. Such

an organization does not exist at a European level, no
European MSI is available. A significant exception is
Sweden with the MIC in Stockholm which has sponsored
research projects on services marketing with the full
support of a group of Scandinavian firms. In most other
countries companies would not commit both data and money
to the development of marketing science without an
intimate knowledge of the program and a close relationship
with the team members.

This environment has encouraged researchers to be in
charge of promoting their areas of expertise, of diffusing
knowledge through workshops, of implementing multidisciplinary projects. This is precisely how services marketing
research has been managed for the last ten years by an
international network of scholars exchanging ideas and
contacts.

The American and the European research environment have
different resources which have been randomly used for the
development of services marketing as an applied domain.

Before 1972, a few individuals here made significant
contributions attempting to attract attention from the
research and the business community. Rathmell, Regan,
Johnson within the marketing community, Fuchs, Lefton,
Rosengren outside the marketing group belong to this first
generation of research discoverers.

During the last ten years, thanks to their efforts and
because the time was ripe, research projects have been
stimulated and junior members of our academic community
are less reluctant than before to join a research track
which offers at least as much opportunities than industrial
on international marketing.

Much more has to be done. At the present stage we offer
useful or not so useful bits and pieces which cannot be
qualified as a school of thought. The momentum exists for
a quality development of services marketing research.
Such a goal would be more easily reached if research
priorities are clarified and we would like to suggest three
directions.

Services Marketing Directions for Research and Action.

Three areas deserve a special treatment by marketing
researchers. One is the development of a combined marketing
operations management approach.

Another is the management of customer participation. At
last, one is the implementation of international marketing
strategies for services. None of these areas can be studied
without integrating existing marketing research methodo-
logies with inputs from other disciplines.

A better management of customer participation requires an
understanding of how to adjust to a diversity of cultural
environments, of personal management policies, of regulated
operating procedures, and an ability to identify different
kinds of service organizations-clients relationships. The
work done by sociologists and psycho-sociologists should
help the marketing scholars.

What degree of environmental sensitivity should influence
international strategies ? Is the world service in the
hotel industry or in consulting activities as significant
as the concept of the world car or the world camera ? What
major role can play a dominant culture in the successful
implementation of an international marketing strategy for
services ?

Probably the most critical area has to do with the
development of a combined marketing-operations management
approach. Large service networks have to fight several

vicious circles. It is natural and unfortunate to go from
a clear specialization to an excessive diversification of
the delivery system, to go from the simplicity (associated
with a growth period) to the complexity (associated with
the maturity stage) of the managing procedures, to go from
reliable quality levels to unpleasant surprises. Marketing
should be recognized as one of the critical factors which
create vicious circles and more research should investigate
the compatibility of the marketing function with the
operations of the service firm.

Many more research suggestions will be made during the
Conference and these concluding remarks about key research
areas are brought to your attention only as an example of
a selective approach of a research program. The coming
sessions will bring more contributions and it is the
"raison d'être" of such a Conference to stimulate exchanges
between service managers and researchers, American and
European on how to do a better job in managing and
studying services marketing.

INNOVATIVE MARKETING STRATEGIES
AND ORGANIZATION STRUCTURES FOR SERVICE FIRMS

Christian Grönroos, Swedish School of Economics,
Helsinki, Finland

INTRODUCTION

In the literature on marketing and marketing management,
the marketing department is generally suggested as the
most developed way of organizing for modern marketing
(Kotler 1980, p. 581-583). It is also suggested that such
organizational principles will work in many service
industries, like retailing, insurance, banking, mass
transit, and health maintenance (Kotler 1980, p. 581).
On the other hand, there are a large number of marketing
managers and marketing directors, who feel very frustrated with their role as heads of marketing departments in
service companies. Moreover, there are remarkable examples
of small and large service firms, which do not have any
marketing department or any single organizational unit
that is responsible for handling the marketing activities.
At AMA's first special conference on service marketing in
1981, Mr. Thomas J. Fitzgerald of the ARA Services, Inc.,
gave a talk on how to develop service marketing. His
company, a gigantic multi-service organization, seems to
be a successful example of such firms.[1]

Hence, the marketing department stage, which may be quite
common in many service industries today (Donelly & Berry
1981, p. 68-69), may be an unnecessary and even dangerous
era for many service firms. The purpose of the present
report is to analyze the potential problems caused by
traditional marketing department solutions, and to develop innovative and more service-oriented organizational
structures for service companies. The empirical material,
which this analysis is based on, is gathered in Sweden
and Finland. However, published reports on problems connected with organizing marketing in the service sector as
well as pilot case observations in the U.S. suggest that
the results put forward here are relevant outside these
Nordic countries, too.

HOW AND WHERE ARE SERVICES MARKETED?

In order to be able to explore how the organization of
service firms should be developed, we must have a clear
picture of how and where services are marketed. Unless we
know this, we will not be able to develop organizational
solutions, which are truly service-oriented. We will give
an answer to the question by presenting three models from
the so-called Nordic School of Services Marketing.[2] In
doing so we divide the overall question into three parts:
(1) How is the total quality of service perceived by a
customer?, (2) how can the firm influence this perceived
service in the long run?, and (3) what determines the outcome of the buyer-seller interactions, where a service
is simultaneously produced and consumed?

Figure 1 shows a model of the Perceived Service Quality.
According to this model the total service quality is perceived by the customer as a comparison between the expected service, which he or she expects to get, and the perceived service, which the customer feels he or she in
fact has received (Hansen 1972, p. 165 and 179, Bettman
1972, p. 272, Swan & Comb 1976, p. 25, and Grönroos 1982a
and 1982b, p. 60-61.) This means that the provider of a
service will have to match the expected service and the
perceived service to each other, so that customer satisfaction is achieved.

Clearly, the expectations are influenced by traditional
marketing activites, such as advertising, field selling
on industrial markets, PR activites, sales promotion and
pricing, and moreover, by previous contacts with the service, previously perceived services, as well as by traditions, ideology and word-of-mouth. On the other hand, the
perceived service is only marginally influenced by traditional marketing activities. The contacts between the customer and the service firm and its contact personnel,
physical/technical resources and its other customers during the buyer-seller interactions are much more important.
In these interactions the service is rendered to the customer, and the service is perceived by him or her. The
service can be broken down into two quality dimensions:
technical quality and functional quality. Both dimensions
are important to the customer. For example, a bank's customer expects that invoices are paid promptly, that money
is transfered from one account to another, but on the
other hand, any bank can do this. The bank which is chosen
by the customer is the one that has good functional quality, too. As Figure 1 demonstrates, the functional quality of a service is influenced by the accessibility and
appearance of the bank office, of long run customer contacts, internal relations in the firm, and the attitudes,
behavior and service-mindedness of the contact personnel.

Figure 1   Managing the perceived service quality

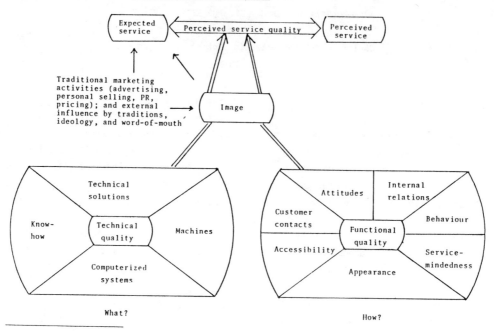

What?   How?

Source: Grönroos, Christian (1982): Strategic Management and Marketing in the Service
Sector, Helsingfors, Finland: Swedish School of Economics and Business Administration, p.79.

The image of the firm, or of a branch office in some cases, is a result of how the customers perceive the technical and the functional quality dimensions. This model
seems to be equally valid for industrial services as for
consumer services.

As the next purchase, obviously, depends on how the service quality was perceived, managing the perceived service quality is a major part of the marketing function of
a service firm. Figure 2 illustrates how the perceived
service quality can be influenced by the service firm,
and thus, how repeat purchases and enduring customer
contact can be achieved. This Figure illustrates the
Customer Life Cycle Concept. The customer contacts of a
transportation company offering conference services at
sea are used as an example.

As can be seen from the model, the interest of a potential customer, or segment of customers, has to be created
at the first stage of the life cycle, the initial stage.
At this stage, traditional, marketing activites, as well
as traditions, rumor and word-of-mouth, are important
means of competition. At the second stage, the purchase
process, promises for the third stage, the consumption
process, should be given so that they are accepted. At
this stage, traditional marketing activities are still

most important, although other contacts, such as those
related to booking routines and control visits onboard the
ship, may be important to the purchase decision, too.

At the third stage the customers next move is determined.
If the firm fails to render an acceptable total service
offering, the perceived service quality may not be good
enough, and the customer does not return. On the other
hand, a customer-oriented and successful management of the
contacts during this third process of the customer relation life cycle may lead to repeat purchases, enduring
customer contacts, increasing cross-selling opportunities,
and moreover, to improved internal relations. During the
consumption process the technical quality is transfered
to the customer, and the functional quality is produced
and felt by the customer, which frequently is even more
important as a means of competition. As can be seen from
Figure 2, the contacts between the firm and the customer
involve personnel, physical/technical resources and operational routines which are not under the control of a traditional marketing department. Nevertheless, these resources and activites performed by these are critical to long
run success and important means of competition. As an
overall term for these resources and activities, the interactive marketing concept has been introduced as a complement to the traditional marketing activities (Grönroos
1979).

10

Figure 2.   <u>The marketing circle and the customer relation life cycle of the transportation company</u>

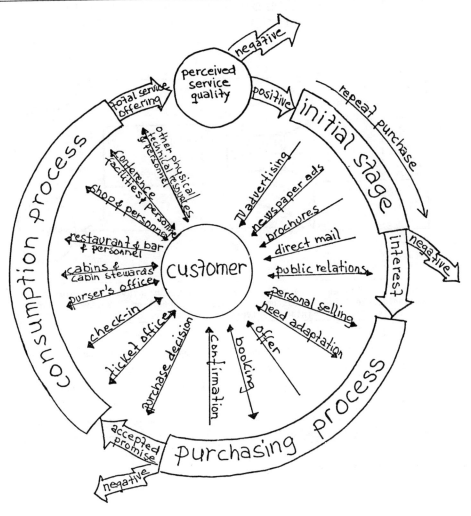

Source: Grönroos, Christian (1982): Strategic Management and Marketing in the Service Sector, Helsingfors, Finland: Swedish School of Economics and Business Administration, p. 159.

Successful interactive marketing means good functional quality and, among other things, more cross sales and less expensive market shares. Figure 3 illustrates how the functional quality is produced in the buyer-seller interactions of the consumptions process in most cases (Lehtinen 1982). As can be seen from the illustrations of the contacts between the firm and its customer during the consumption process in Figure 2, three main cathegories of resources are involved: the <u>contact personnel</u>, the <u>customer</u> and his or her fellow customers, and <u>physical resources</u> and technology. The outcome of the contacts depends on the customer-consciousness and service-mindedness of the contact person, as well on his or her technical abilities and know-how. The performance of the contact person, the <u>style of performance,</u> has to be geared to the expectations and behavior of the customer,

i.e., to the <u>style of consuming</u> of the customer. Moreover, the <u>physical resources</u> and the technology used, such as conference facilities, cabins, restaurant milieu and computerized cash registers, should support the customer-orientation of the contacts between the personnel and the customer and not counteract it as too often seems to be the case today.

The better the outcome of these contacts, the better the functional quality, and the higher the possibility that the customer will return.

Obviously, marketing must not stop when promises have been given and a customer perhaps has made a first purchase decision. Marketing will have to continue to be responsible for how the promises are backed up by the

Figure 3. The nature of the buyer-seller interactions during the
consumptions process of the customer relations life cycle.

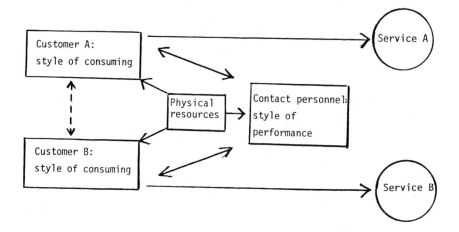

Source: Lehtinen, Jarmo (1982): Asiakasohjautuva palveluiden
tuotantojärjestelmä (Customer-oriented production systems for
services), Tampere, Finland: University of Tampere, p. 115

total service offering, so that an acceptable perceived
service quality is achieved. This means that the marketing function also involves managing, motivating and planning the resources and activities which are part of the
customer relation at the third stage of this life cycle.
This makes the interactive marketing function an important part of the total marketing function of service
firms.[3] Moreover, the traditionel marketing activites
cannot do much more than create interest and give promises in such a manner that they are accepted. The activities and resources of the interactive marketing function
do, however, influence the perceived service quality and,
therefore, the long run consumption behavior of the market.

CONSEQUENCES FOR ORGANIZATION

As we have noticed in the previous section, traditional
marketing activities, such as advertising, PR activities,
sales promotion and pricing, and field selling on industrial markets, are only part of the total marketing function of service firms. In order to get repeat sales and
enduring customer contacts and to develop cross-sales
oppurtunities, the interactive amrketing function must be
recognized and developed in a customer-oriented manner.

In the context of professional services Gummesson (1979,
p. 309) observes that "the person who is a marketer of
the service usually must also be prepared to take part in

the operations of assignments" (see also Wilson 1972).
The situation is the same in most service businesses.
Figure 4 illustrates the situation in a bank.

Lovelock and others have studied the perceived importance
of various functional responsibilities among field managers of service firms. They report that the field managers in the companies involved in the study in general almost always are responsible for marketing and customer
relations as well as for management of personnel and operations. Moreover, the importance of the marketing responsibilities are perceived to be at least equally important
as the responsibilities for personnel and operations
(Lovelock & al. 1981, p. 171). It is not, however, quite
clear from their study what is meant by marketing and customer relations. It may perhaps be reasonable to believe
that marketing refers to traditional marketing activities,
whereas customer relations to a greater extent is related
to the interactive marketing function.

Booms and Bitner (1981, p. 51) suggest that better communication has to be encouraged between marketing, operations and personnel. Lovelock and others (1981, p. 171)
conclude that "service marketers must develop organizational structures and procedures that establish a better
balance between marketing and other management functions -
especially operations - than currently exists". In both
cases the term marketing seems to be used as an equivalent to the traditional marketing function.

12

Figure 4. The simultaneous responsibility for operations and marketing among the personnel in a service organization

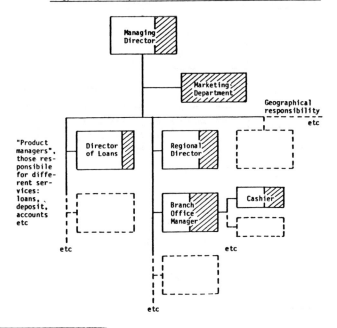

Source: Gummesson, Evert (1981): Marketing Cost Concept in Service Firms,
Industrial Marketing Management, No. 3, p. 177.

As a conclusion, we may state that service firms need an
organizational structure, which supports the development
of the traditional marketing activities as well as of
interactive marketing activities in connection with, for
instance, operations and personnel in a customer-oriented
direction, and which makes it possible to coordinate all
marketing activities, traditional as well as interactive,
so that the company becomes market-oriented on an overall
basis. The different business functions are much more interrelated in a service firm than in a firm manufacturing
consumer goods.[4] Therefore, the organizational structure
must not become an unnecessary burden to co-operation
between various functions and activites.

In general, service firms are personnel intensive.
Because the service, especially the functional quality of
the service, is not preproduced, but turned into a concrete service offering in the presence of the customer,
every situation is unique. Consequently, a large amount
of flexibility is needed in the buyer-seller interactions.
The organizational structure must not become a burden to
flexibility and ad hoc customer-oriented behavior. Therefore, the organization should be more organic than mechanistic in nature (Lindell 1981, p. 32).[5]

PROBLEMS WITH TRADITIONAL ORGANIZATIONAL STRUCTURES

In the industrial sector the responsibility for various
business functions has normally been delegated to separate
departments and the different departments have got their
own managers with the general manager on the top of the
organization. This kind of traditional organizational
structure is schematically, and in a hihgly simplified
way, illustrated in Figure 5.

Production, personnel, finance and accounting, and marketing, as well as other functions, are separated from each
other. This general model has been adapted by growing
firms in the service sector, too. The responsibility for
various functions have been delegated to different departments with their own heads. Normally, marketing is the
newest and weakest department in the organization. This
kind of organizational solution may work as long as the
marketing department can initiate, plan and implement all
or at least most marketing activities. In a typical firm
in the consumer goods sector this is also the case, as can
be seen from the left part of Figure 6. Only a few marketing tasks, such as sales negotiations performed by the
general manager, etc. are located outside the marketing

13

Figure 5. <u>A traditional organizational solution</u>

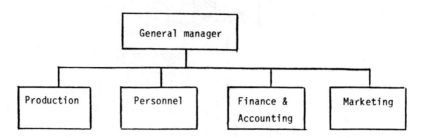

department, which is indicated by the small unshaded area of the total marketing function in the Figure. Hence, the traditional marketing department can handle, and therefore be responsible for, most of the total marketing function.

Unfortunately, a service firm faces quite another situation, because of the presence of the interactive marketing function. As the right part of Figure 6 demonstrates, only part of the total marketing function can be managed by a traditional marketing department, namely, the traditional marketing activites such as advertising, PR activities, sales promotion and pricing. The important interactive marketing activities are most frequently outside

the control of the marketing manager and the marketing department, which is indicated by the large unshaded area of the right part of the Figure. Nevertheless, the marketing manager is expected to be responsible for the customers and their long term satisfaction. If the firm loses customers, the marketing department is expected to do something about it.

The traditional marketing department is, however, in an <u>off side</u> position in the organization. Production, personnel, finance, and even the general manager often expect the marketing manager to be responsible for something he does not have power or an organizational position to do. If such an off side marketing manager wants to influence

Figure 6. <u>The relationship between the marketing function and the marketing department</u>

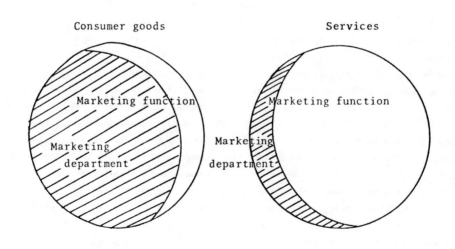

Source: Grönroos, C. (1980): Designing a Long Range Marketing Strategy, Long Range Planning, April, p. 40.

14

Table 1. Effects of separate marketing departments

	Percentage agreeing strongly or partly with item								
Type of respondent		Position in organization			Structure of operations		Structure of customers		
Item	Total	Top man-agement	Market-ing	Other	Net-work	Single outlet	Indus-trial	House-holds	Both
1. A separate marketing department may widen the gap between marketing and operations	66.7%	72.8%	53.9%	77.4%	67.1%	65.8%	68.1%	64.7%	63.9%

	Percentage agreeing strongly or partly with item								
Type of respondent	Industry								
Item	Bank & fi-nance	Hotel & restau-rant	Trans-porta-tion	Travel agency	Profes-sional services	Cleaning, security etc.	Public sector	Insur-ance	Misc.
1. A separate marketing department may widen the gap between marketing and operations	57.5%	100.0%	62.9%	25.0%	73.4%	75.1%	62.5%	84.6%	86.7%

	Percentage agreeing strongly or partly with item					
Type of respondent	Size (employees)					
Item	Less than 11	11 - 50	51 - 200	201 - 501	501 - 1000	More than 1000
1. A separate marketing department may widen the gap between marketing and operations	67.6%	85.2%	90.9%	76.7%	90.0%	76.6%

the ways of thinking or performance of the head of production and operations or the heads of personnel or technological development, the internal climate easily suffers. The marketing manager has too weak a position and too short traditions.

The potential danger in introducing traditional marketing departments as a means of managing service marketing was tested in a survey of executives representing various private and public service firms and institutions in 1981 in Sweden (Grönroos 1982b). The respondents represented top management and marketing as well as other positions, such as production, personnel and internal training. The total number of respondents was 219. The results are shown in Table 1, which gives the proportions of respondent[5] in various categories agreeing strongly or partly with the following item: "A separate marketing department may widen the gap between marketing and operations." This item is, of cource, only part of a much larger questionnaire. The answers were given on a Likert-type scale with five points ranging from agreeing strongly to disagreeing strongly.

The figures in Table 1 indicate clearly that executives involved in various service industries consider the use of marketing departments rather dangerous. One interesting detail is the observation that marketing executives are less inclined to agree with the item (53.9%) than top management and other respondents (72.8% and 77.4% respectively). This may be a defence reaction by the marketing people, although the percentage is very high all the same. It may, on the other hand, also illustrate a frustration among top management and other executives concerning the usefulness of the marketing department.

In conclusion we may say that a traditional marketing department usually cannot be responsible for the total marketing function of service companies. The introduction of such marketing departments does, however, easily influence the organization in an unfavorable direction. People working in other departments performing, for instance, operations or personnel tasks, stop worrying about their customer-related responsibilities and totally concentrate on just handling operations or personnel tasks for their own sake. The reason for this is clear. The firm now has marketing specialists in their marketing department, why should we bother any longer. The results is an increasing production-orientation and resource-orientation and a less market-oriented performance.[6]

CASES: SUCCESSFUL ORGANIZATIONAL DEVELOPMENT IN THE
SERVICE SECTOR

In order to develop some general guidelines to be used in
developing the organizational structure in a market-oriented direction, we have studied the development of the
organizational structure of successful service firms in
Finland and Sweden. Because of the nature of the research
problem, a case study approach was used. Three typical
cases are illustrated and analyzed in this context.

The bank case

The bank is one of the largest in the country and operates all over the country. Some twelve years ago the bank
suffered from low profitability and production-oriented
attitudes among its personnel including branch managers
and other middle management executives. The marketing
function was handled by a large marketing department on
the head office level. In order to turn the bank to a
market-oriented and profitable firm, it was decided that
the bank should concentrate on profitable services and
profitable market segments. Moreover, an organizational
development process was initiated. This process included
several stages, where each stage was caused by problems
in relation to the market orientation of the bank perceived at the previous stage.

At the first stage, the central marketing department was
closed down. Instead a customer contact development office
was established. This office included only a few people,
and it was reporting directly to the President. The bank
was divided into regional banks, and the responsibility
for marketing, including field selling on industrial markets, was given to local branch managers. Marketing consultants were located at the regional level. Their duty
was to give marketing assistance to the local managers.
At the same time the bank stopped all nation-wide advertising, because the people in charge felt that purchase
decisions are made locally and are influenced by the performance of the local branch office.

However, the local branch offices remained quite production oriented, and they did not actively take over marketing tasks. When the branch manager felt he ought to do
some marketing, he called the regional marketing consultant. When the regional marketing consultant left, the
interest in market-oriented activities decreased again on
the local branch level. Nevertheless, the situation was

better than before, because the customer contact development office created guidelines for local advertising and
especially for training employees in how to handle customer contacts in a marketing-like manner.

In order to improve the market orientation on the local
level, the regional marketing consultants were taken away,
and the total marketing responsibility was delegated to
the local branch manager. At the same time the bank started to turn the local bank offices to profit centers one
by one. When the regional marketers were removed, and
there was no central department implementing marketing
activities, the market-orientation and customer-consciousness among the branch managers started to increase. The
profit center responsibility accompanied by a very large
decision-making freedom obviously supported this tendency.
The customer contact development office supported the
branch office managers in training their personnel and in
developing advertising and field selling activites. Slowly,
the market orientation and sales-mindedness among the personnel increased. The bank has been one of the most profitable ones for many years now.

The shipping case

The shipping company is located in a Nordic country. It is
divided into four divisions, which operate lines in four
different parts of the world. The company is one of the
largest in its country. Up to the mid-70's the operations
were planned and implemented by the four divisions, the
heads of which reported to a transportation manager,
whereas marketing including sales was planned and implemented by a separate marketing department. However, there
were continuous conflicts between the marketing department
and the operational divisions, as the marketers either
promised too much or the wrong things, according to the
operations people, and as operations were not able to perform in a market-oriented manner according to the marketing and sales people. In fact, those responsible for marketing and sales did not know enough obouth operations,
and those responsible for operations did not care enough
about the customers.

In order to cope with the problems, the central marketing
department was closed down. The responsibility for marketing including sales was delegated to the divisions, and
the division heads were made responsible for this function.
Sales representatives reporting to the division managers
were located in each division. The gap between the promi-

ses given by marketing and sales and the real services rendered by operations diminished, but instead differences in marketing policies, such as differing prices and terms, between the divisions emerged. Moreover, the operations did not become more customer-conscious and market-oriented to any considerable extent. As many of the customers of the shipping firm experienced the services of two or more of the divisions, the overall image became unclear.

In order to coordinate the policies of the divisions and to improve the market orientation of the operations, the shipping company moved into a third stage. The responsibility for sales and market-oriented performance of the contact personnel and operational routines was left with the divisional heads, but a marketing planning office reporting to the transportation manager was established. This office is very small, and its duties are to coordinate the traditional marketing activities of the divisions, such as sales, pricing and sales promotion, and to support the development of market-oriented performance in each division, for instance by creating customer-oriented production routines, developing internal training programs and other internal marketing activities. The market planning office only implements some corporate advertising and public relations activities. The responsibility for marketing, traditional as well as interactive marketing activities, is given to the division managers, who also have profit center responsibility.

The cleaning company case

The cleaning company is very large and operates all over the country. In the beginning of the 70's no marketing was needed. The only thing that was needed was somebody who answered the telephone, when potential customers called. However, in the mid-70's competition increased, and some active marketing had to be done. The company, therefore, established a marketing department responsible for marketing planning, sales, advertising and sales promotion. The company also had a operations department divided into several regional organizations, a personnel department and a finance department. All departments were on the same hierarchical level.

Fortunately, the company got a marketing manager, who realized that the marketing department was in an off side position and that the firm would remain production-oriented, if marketing and sales activities were expected to be implemented by the people in the marketing department. Therefore, the marketing manager kept his department very small. Because of his personal qualifications, he succee-

ded in developing such informal contacts with people in the operations department on the regional level, which gave him much more authority than the formal organizational structure did. This was possible, because the marketing manager, although he formally was in an off side position, was supported by the President.

The regional managers were made responsible for sales, advertising and public relations on the regional level. The central marketing department did not include any salespeople. Only corporate advertising and sales promotion material were developed and to some extent implemented by the central department. The marketing department also started to develop internal marketing programs and internal training programs, which were to be used locally, in order to support the market orientation and customer-consciousness among the contact personnel and the supervisors.

During the last few years the firm has also developed some new service businesses outside the cleaning area. This year (1982) the organization has been developed further. The marketing department has been removed from the organization, and the firm has been divided into three divisions, one for the traditional cleaning business, and the two other for two different lines of new service business. The division managers are made responsible for operations, personnel, and marketing and sales, including the traditional marketing function as well as the interactive marketing function. They are expected to perform the same marketing and sales tasks as the former marketing manager as well as to be in charge of operations. They are also responsible for internal marketing. They report directly to the President. On the same hierarchical level there are a personnel support department and a financial department.

The cleaning division for example, is divided into regional organizations, which operate as profit centers. The regional managers have a responsibility for sales and traditional marketing and for interactive marketing as well as for operations and personnel. They are also free to develop new services, which can be marketed regionally. Marketing is implemented on the regional level, whereas the division manager only develops and gives external and internal marketing support. He is also responsible for service development on the divisional level.

The cleaning company has been very successful and profitable.

The three cases presented in the previous section represent only a sample of similar organizational development cases. There are some general tendencies, which can be observed. First of all, the marketing department may, at some stage in the process, be useful, although this in not quite clear, but in the long run the seperate marketing department easily becomes a burden, which hinders market-orientation efforts in the firm. As long as there are mar-keting specialist somewhere in the organization, they are expected to implement marketing, whereas the others do something else. Only if the marketing manager is such a personality that he manages to overrun the formal organization, a customer-oriented development can be expected. Otherwise the marketing manager is likely to be overrun by the organizational constraints. The result is bad or non-existent interactive marketing and bad functional quality, and in the long run, bad image and lost customers.

Figure 6.   A customer-oriented organizational structure for services

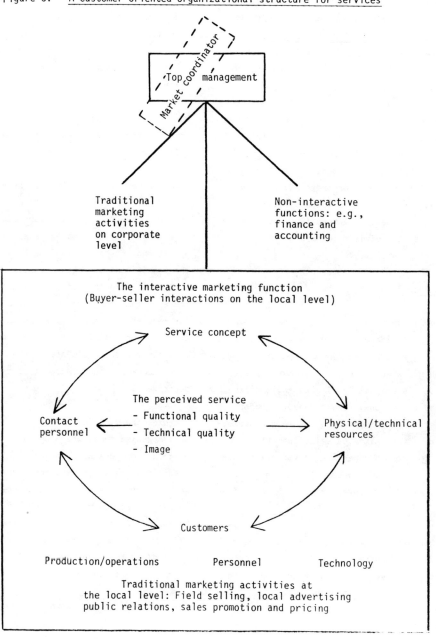

Secondly, the responsibility for planning and implementing both the traditional marketing function and the interactive marketing function should be delegated down in the organization as much as possible to, for example, a regional manager or a branch manager, who also is responsible for operations. It seems reasonable to give such a person responsibility for the management of personnel on his level. Such a regional or local unit could be a profit center.

Thirdly, on the head office level some kind of marketing coordination, and marketing planning and support may be needed. In the bank case there is the customer contact development office, in the shipping case the marketing planning office, and in the cleaning case the division manager. These offices are in all cases extremely small, including only a few persons. Their main duty is to give assistance in marketing planning, plan corporate advertising and public relations activities, help the regional or local managers to develop and implement their own traditional marketing activities, and assist them in developing the interactive marketing performance on the local level. Internal marketing planning may also belong to their duties. This office could be labeled the market coordinator, or the marketing and customer contact coordinator.

Finally, as the market coordinator supports all kinds of marketing activities on the local level and coordinates the traditional and interactive marketing functions as well as internal marketing throughout the organization, he is actually planning the total performance of the firm. As we have noticed, the interactive marketing concept requires that marketing on the interactive level is not separated from operations and the use of technology and other physical resources. Consequently, no limited marketing plans, which are accompanied by operational plans or other subplans, are needed in a service firm. Instead, the marketing coordinator can be responsible for developing market-oriented corporate action plans, which cover traditional marketing as well as interactive marketing, and which therefore, also takes into account operations, personnel, internal marketing, and new technology.

This customer-oriented organizational structure for services is schematically illustrated in Figure 6. In the Figure the functions of the firm are divided into three categories: traditional marketing function, interactive functions and non-interactive functions. In order to develop a customer-oriented organizational structure, the non-interactive functions, such as finance and accounting, can be left aside. The interactive functions, however,

include operations and production, personnel and technology on a local level. Starting from the service concept of the firm and its local unit, the contact personnel and the physical/technical resources must be developed and used in contact with the customers, so that an acceptable perceived service quality is achieved. If the firm is successful in this respect locally, the interactive marketing is good. The interactive marketing activities must, however, be coordinated with the traditional marketing activities, most of which are planned and implemented locally, but some of which may be implemented on the head office level. This means that the local manager is responsible for total marketing on the local level.

On the corporate level, only the top manager can be responsible for total marketing, in principle. In a growing company a market-coordinator may be needed, who coordinates all marketing activities throughout the company. Moreover, this office or person can be responsible for internal marketing, market analysis, service development, etc.

BIGNESS VS. SMALLNESS

Organizational structures which have been successfully applied in the industrial sector seem to be a potential danger to growing service firms. Various activities are much more interrelated in a service firm than in a company producing consumer goods. Therefore, an organizational innovation seems to be needed. In this study, a customer-oriented organizational structure for services has been developed. This structure is based on the perceived service quality concept and on the Service Quality Model and other models of the Nordic School of Service Marketing. It is, therefore, geared to the characteristics of service quality and the nature of the buyer-seller interactions of service production and consumption.

In conslusion, it could be argued that a service firm, which is relatively small on the local level, frequently is more market-oriented than a big firm. In a smaller organization decisions are made faster and closer to the market. It is easier to develop good interactive marketing performance and to give a more competitive functional quality in such a situation. Internal marketing is less time-consuming and troublesome. On the other hand, there is a potential strength in the fact that a service firm is large, too. In a bigger company more resources can be used in order to develop the technical quality dimension in most cases. It is also sometimes easier to attract better trained persons to leading positions in a larger organization. Moreover, economies of scale can be achieved in such functions related to production, administration, finance, etc. which are invisible to the market.

Figure 7. The strength of bigness vs. the strength
          of smallness

  1. The strenght of smallness

     - decisions are made near the market
     - decisions are made quickly
     - better knowledge of the desires of the
       customers
     - good interactive marketing performance is
       easier to achieve
     - internal marketing is easier
     - quality control, technical as well as func-
       tional, is easier to handle

  2. The strength of bigness

     - economies of scale can be achieved in func-
       tions which are invisible to the customers
     - more resources, personnel and technology as
       well as financial, available for developing
       technical quality
     - easier to attract personnel to the organi-
       zation (at least to some jobs)

Therefore, as Figure 7 illustrates, one may argue that a growing service firm, in order to remain market-oriented and be successful, will have to be able to combine the strength of being small in a local perspective with the strength of belonging to a large organization. However, there are a wide range of cases that demonstrate that this may be difficult to do. As a company grows and tries to achieve the advantages of bigness, far too often it destroys the potential strength of being small locally.

Of source, no general model can be suggested. The structure put forward in this report seem, however, to be of some general relevance, also outside the Nordic countries. More research, especially from other countries, is needed, because today far too little is known abouth how to organize for services.

FOOTNOTES

1. On the other hand, there are examples of successful service companies, which have introduced marketing departments into their organizations.

2. See Grönroos, Christian (1982): Strategic Management and Marketing in the Service Sector, Helsingfors, Finland: Swedish School of Economics and Business Administration.

3. Compare the definition of marketing management in Grönroos, Christian (1982): Strategic Management and Marketing in the Service Sector, p. 32.

4. Business functions are interrelated in a very similar way in companies producing producer goods and systems (Webster 1978).

5. About mechanistic and organic organization, see, for instance, Burns & Stalker (1961, p. 120 ff.). See also Shepard (1965). Using the terminology of Thompson (1967), the technology of the organization of many service firms can be labeled mediating.

6. Of cource, no organization works exactly according to its formal structure. In reality informal relations between inidividuals, informal communication patterns and co-operative efforts may be far more important (Engwall 1982, p. 125). This probably explains why some service firms are successful, in spite of their organizational structures and marketing departments.

REFERENCES

Bettman, J.R. (1969): An Information Processing Theory of Consumer Choice, Reading, Mass.: Addison-Wesley

Booms, B.H. & Bitner, M.J. (1981): Marketing Strategies and Organization Structures for Service Firms. In Donnelly, J.H. & George, W.R. (eds.): Marketing of Services, Proceedings Series, Chicago, Ill.: American Marketing Association.

Burns, T. & Stalker, G.M. (1961): The Management of Innovation, London: Tavistock

Donnelly, J.H. & Berry, L.L. (1981): Bank Marketing - Past, Present, Future. In Donnelly, J.H. & George, W.R. (eds.): Marketing of Services

Engwall, L. (1982): Organization Theory: Where Are You? Omega, No. 2

Grönroos, C. (1979): Marketing Services, Ann Arbor, Mich.: University Microfilms

Grönroos, C. (1980): Designing a Long Range Marketing Strategy for Services, Long Range Planning, April

Grönroos, C. (1982a): A Service Quality Model and Its Management Implications, Research Report, Workshop on Research into the Management of the Service Businesses, EIASM/London Business School, London

Grönroos, C. (1982b): Strategic Management and Marketing in the Service Sector, Helsingfors, Finland: Swedish School of Economics and Business Administration

Gummesson, E. (1979): The Marketing of Professional Services - An Organizational Dilemma, Industrial Marketing Management, No. 5

Gummesson, E. (1981): Marketing Cost Concept in the Service Firm, Industrial Marketing Management, No. 3

Hansen, F. (1972): Consumer Choice Behavior. A Cognitive Theory, New York: The Free Press

Kotler, P. (1980): Marketing Management. Analysis, Planning, Control, 4th edition, Englewood Cliffs, N.J.: Prentice-Hall

Lehtinen, J. (1982): Asiakasohjautuva palveluiden tuotantojärjestelmä (Customer-oriented production systems for services), Tampere, Finland: University of Tampere

Lindell, M. (1981): Affärsidéns uppbyggnad inom tjänste-
företag (Development of business concepts in service firms), Helsingfors, Finland: Swedish School
of Economics and Business Administration

Lovelock, C. & al. (1981): Some Organizational Problems Facing Marketing in the Service Sector. In
Donnelly, J.H. & George, W.R. (eds.): Marketing
of Services

Shepard, H.A. (1965): Changing Interpersonal and Inter-
group Relations in Organizations. In March, J.G.
(ed): Handbook of Organizations, Chicago, Ill.

Swan, J.E. & Comb, L.J. (1976): Product Performance
and Consumer Satisfaction: A New Concept, Journal
of Marketing, April

Thompson, J.D. (1967): Organizations in Action, New
York: McGraw-Hill

Webster, Jr., F.E. (1978): Management Science in Industrial Marketing, Journal of Marketing, January

Wilson, A. (1972): The Marketing of Professional Services, London: McGraw-Hill

INNOVATIONS IN SERVICES MARKETING

Thomas M. Bloch, H & R Block, Inc., Kansas City

I appreciate the privilege of addressing you this morning. I am quite sure that over the next few days each of you will have ample opportunity to discuss and learn many ways to improve and examine services marketing and will translate this information to your own business or field.

The story of H & R Block is truly without parallel in American commerce. Consider a service business that had never been proven, for which no precedents had been established, for which little perceived need existed, and which operated fully only 105 days each year -- a very seasonal business indeed. Yet my father, Henry Bloch, and his brother, Richard, faced all these disturbing prospects. The Block story is one of imagination, instinct, management skill, and the ability to recognize opportunity when it presented itself. Let me briefly discuss the development of H & R Block and discuss some important marketing innovations that have contributed to our company's growth.

It all began in 1946. To Richard, who graduated from the Wharton School of Finance, and Henry, who graduated from the University of Michigan and later attended Harvard Business School, a financial service business seemed an altogether natural choice. As they considered various types of businesses, they wisely sought the counsel of, among others, General Omar Bradley and Henry Wallace, who was at that time Secretary of Commerce. One sagely advised them to start the business in the attic, the other suggested the basement.

The result was the formation of the United Business Company, a bookkeeping service for small companies who wanted their books kept. The method of marketing this service was simple and direct; they knocked on doors. At first, they offered to keep books for free in order to display their talents. The only trouble with that approach was that Henry was heard to remark much later that some firms thought "free" meant "forever." But prosper they did, and by 1954, a year that was to become another turning point in their lives, they had become the largest bookkeeping service in Kansas City.

They realized that the most important marketing technique in a service business is customer service. They attempted to keep their customers happy in every possible way, which included preparing income taxes for their clients without charge. This created a good problem because their clients began telling all their friends about the Bloch's tax service. As more people began to seek them out for the tax help they began to charge for it. By 1954, the brothers were working seven days and nights a week to keep up with the tax and bookkeeping business. Something obviously had to give. To the dismay of their customers, they decided to give up the tax business. When their clients started protesting loudly, the Blochs gave in again, but it started them thinking.

By late 1954, Dick and Henry decided to stake their futures entirely on the tax business. On January 25,

1955, the United Business Company was dissolved and H & R Block was born. On that day, at the insistence of an ad salesman for the Kansas City Star, two small newspaper ads ran which read, "Income Taxes Prepared, $5 and Up." They sharpened their pencils and waited, but they didn't have to wait long before clients began appearing in droves. The $5 tax return was born. That was an important marketing or pricing decision which continues today. The fee for an income tax return prepared by H & R Block is based solely on the complexity of that return without regard for the client's income, refund, or the time spent to prepare the return and the fee is a reasonable one.

Henry and Richard didn't just go into business when they started H & R Block; they created an industry, and the response to this new kind of service business -- one that only prepared income tax returns -- was overwhelming. Their first tax season in 1955 produced a volume equal to one-third of the total business volume done by United Business Company in the preceding nine years. In 1956 they opened two more offices in Kansas City. And because of federal budget cuts and the closing of the IRS taxpayer assistance center in New York City, seven offices were opened there. In 1957 the company expanded to 17 offices in three states, an achievement that rightfully entitled them to boast that H & R Block was "America's largest tax service."

An innovative marketing decision for a service business was made in 1958 to expand through the concept of franchising, allowing rapid expansion with limited capital. And although we were not the first to offer franchises, we were certainly among the pioneers. Oil companies and automobile manufacturers had employed franchising since the early 1900's. We were among the first service businesses to franchise, and we did so without the benefit of the knowledge we have today. In fact, we didn't even refer to the process as franchising. H & R Block had a very unique approach to franchising -- we gave them away. In the early days, licensing agreements were granted for entire states. Today these Major Franchises, as we refer to them, account for a total of over 1,700 tax offices, which is about 19 percent of all H & R Block offices.

By 1960, H & R Block offices were in most major markets in the United States. However, there was a lot of business to be had between these big cities, and it was decided the best way to reach these remote smaller markets economically was to create the "satellite franchise," a franchise arrangement in which Block trained local businesspeople to prepare tax returns in their own communities. Once again, these franchises, in towns with a population under 20,000, were given away. This time, however, rather than charging a modest royalty fee and providing little else than the H & R Block name, the satellite franchisee received virtually everything needed to run the business short of an office, furniture, and labor, in exchange for an ongoing royalty fee based on the gross volume of the office. Today, 3,011 offices in the U.S. and Canada are operated as satellite franchises and make a significant contribution to the company's total profits.

In 1965, the year the company first prepared a million tax returns in a single season, it was decided to use television as the primary advertising medium. John Cameron Swayze became the company spokesman. He had credibility with the American public as both an announcer and newscaster. It worked. Two years later, one million new customers came to Block in a single tax season.

As the number of offices grew, the off-season expenses grew as well. The major cause for these off-season expenses was the amount of rent that was being paid on offices that were not productive eight months of the year.

An important marketing innovation occurred when office expansion took place with our entry into 147 Sears stores, all identified with the H & R Block name. Through Sears, H & R Block has had the opportunity of operating in a highly visible location with much traffic, and our rental expense is limited to the tax season period only. It has proved to be a successful marketing decision, and not surprising when one considers the high degree of similarity in the demographics of the Sears customer and the Block customer. H & R Block was the first concessionaire in Sears to use a company name other than Sears. Today, we operate in 867 Sears locations and 402 offices are located in other department stores, including J.L. Hudson, the May Company, and Hudsons Bay and Woodwards in Canada. Convenience is a very important reason why H & R Block has succeeded. In fact, most people will travel a maximum of three miles from their home to come to us. That's why H & R Block operates 9,350 tax preparation offices in the U.S., Canada, and in 10 foreign countries. The majority of the locations are storefronts where, as I mentioned, rent is paid 12 months each year. In every city, though, we staff some offices on a year-round basis to provide off-season service to our customers.

As the company grew, so did its need for qualified individuals to prepare income tax returns. In the early days of the company, my father used to teach a 40-hour class between Christmas and New Year's to train his staff. He offered the course for free and consequently ran into trouble with the Wage & Hour Division of the Department of Labor. They insisted that the course was a requirement for employment and therefore would require that the students be paid for attending.

To overcome this obstacle, Henry and Richard made another important innovative decision. Rather than offer the course for free and have to pay the students for attending, they opened the class to the public and charged tuition. This not only satisfied the Wage and Hour Division but opened a new source of profit. Last year the tuition tax school produced $6.8 million dollars in revenues from 102,000 enrolled students.

The fact that our business is seasonal presents an obstacle that we are constantly trying to overcome. We want our customers to view H & R Block as a year-round tax service. We are therefore available 12 months a year to assist with last year's return, tax planning, and answering tax questions. In addition, years ago we introduced the Taxsaver. Very simply, this is an envelope for the taxpayer in which an entire year's worth of receipts are kept. It serves two important functions. It not only helps organize our client's receipts, making our job easier and the tax preparer's time more productive at tax time, but it keeps the name of our company in full view of our customers 12 months a year. Our tax record books for business, farm, rental, and automobile expenses perform a similar function. We distribute millions of these items each year and, in a sense, it provides for some of our least expensive advertising.

As with any service industry, marketing plays an all important role in establishing and maintaining a solid customer base. At H & R Block, we are constantly testing new ideas to increase our share of the paid preparer market. We also strive to tap the self-preparer sector, a group that has grown larger in recent years.

Our commitment to marketing and advertising in Company-owned areas totalled $18.8 million in fiscal 1982. Much of our advertising budget goes to TV and newspaper. Many of you may have seen our commercials. Last year, we returned after a 3-year hiatus with our ever popular and successful 17 Reasons campaign, featuring Henry Bloch as the spokesman. Our earlier campaigns were not as successful as the 17 Reasons. For example, in 1971, we produced a campaign that was one of our first attempts directed at the non-user or self-preparer market. And although the commercials won a lot of impressive advertising awards, they did little for our business. We learned a very valuable lesson, however. In order for a commercial to be successful in our business it has to be serious and not humorous. The public perceives taxes as serious business, and our advertising campaign has changed accordingly.

Not all of our marketing innovations have been successful. For example, a few years ago we tested a program we called Phone Power. We called every one of our clients, 10 million of them, to offer them appointments. Prior to that time, we were strictly a walk-in, non-appointment type service. We felt that this direct marketing approach would increase our repeat customer business which accounts for over 70 percent of our business annually. The program was one of our biggest mistakes. For although our clients had always been willing to wait in line for however long it took to get served, a client with an appointment at 1:00 expected service by 1:00. And though when we got behind and offered the analogy of the doctor's office, thinking it would be an acceptable excuse, we were dead wrong. More importantly, most of our clients prefer to visit our office whenever they want, and an appointment was not perceived by most to be an attractive additional service.

Each and every detail of our office procedures is carefully designed to provide comfort for our clients and staff and to ensure an efficient and cost effective operation. Our policy and procedure manual spans 14 volumes and contains nearly 2,000 pages, each written to allow our field management personnel and our franchises to successfully operate according to our system. Above all else, we emphasize customer service. Therefore, training is a key ingredient in our success. Even though we deliver a tangible product to our clients, what we sell is a feeling -- a feeling that begins to develop from the time a client walks in the door of our office until the completed tax return is signed and dropped in the mail. It begins with a friendly greeting by our receptionist, a cup of fresh coffee, and a complete and thorough interview by a trained pre-parer. It includes the peace of mind offered by our guarantee and the assurance that at H & R Block, we stand behind our work and our clients.

Our service must constantly improve, in large part because customers expect more today than they used to. Like most businesses, the company's product begins to decline if efforts are not made to im-prove it. Our procedures, therefore, are constantly changing. In the early years, we used a "take a number" system. A client often waited an hour or more before being recognized by a member of our staff. Today we offer appointments, drop-off service, or at-home or office preparation, all for a modest fee. We also give instant client recog-nition so as soon as a customer opens our door, he is greeted and the waiting period is substantially shorter. And our delivery system has been expanded, too. We now offer other companies the opportunity to offer tax preparation as an employee benefit through our Group Tax programs.

Through all our efforts, we have sought to demystify and take the anxiety out of income tax preparation. Taxes, like tooth decay, won't just go away. In fact, as Benjamin Franklin said so many years ago, "there is nothing certain except death and taxes." We bring a needed service to individuals who are confused by the complex tax laws and forms and who might otherwise pay more money in taxes than is required because they are unaware of legitimate deductions and credits.

Let me turn briefly to the newest operating division of our company. Following the 1977 U.S. Supreme Court decision that permitted lawyers to advertise, several national publications and law journals asked, "Who will become the H & R Block of the legal services industry?" We think we have the answer. And we think we also have the answer to the question: How can we make use of our tax offices during the off-season?

Block Management Company was formed in 1980 to provide administrative, marketing, and management services to Hyatt Legal Services. Hyatt started in Cleveland and, at the time Block Management Company was formed, had nine offices in Cleveland and Toledo. These were storefront legal offices of-fering at affordable prices legal counsel for a selected menu of problems typically encountered by middle income families and individuals, such as wills, uncontested divorces, adoptions, bankruptcies, and similar matters.

Based on the fact that legal help for the average person in traditional law offices was all too often expensive and the surroundings too intimidating,

Block Management Company and Hyatt Legal Services joined together whereby the new law offices established by Hyatt Legal Services would share facilities with H & R Block income tax operations.

Today, Hyatt has expanded to 110 offices in 12 states. We believe that Hyatt Legal Services very closely adheres to the basic business principles on which H & R Block was founded -- namely, that of providing a much needed service at an affordable cost to the mass market. We look forward to seeing Hyatt Legal Offices expand nationwide. Block Management Company's mission is to support that growth.

All divisions of H & R Block have a record of accomplishment of which we are very proud. Al-though we at H & R Block may fondly remember the past, we are constantly examining results and events with a view toward the future. We continue to be strong believers in the entrepreneurial spirit, not only within our company and its sub-sidiaries but also within our numerous franchised operations. All signs pointed to a business that wouldn't work, that would at best be limited in profitability and demand. Through imagination, skill, important marketing innovations, and a little luck, Henry and Richard Bloch have proved the early critics wrong. That's what makes the past fun to remember. And with the same imagina-tion and skill of the Company founders along with the marketing innovations that are unknown to us today but will pave the way for new business op-portunities, the future promises to be exciting.

RELATIONSHIP MARKETING

Leonard L. Berry, Texas A&M University

ABSTRACT

Many service firms are vulnerable to customer loss due to
increasing intratype and/or intertype competition. Discussed in this paper is the importance of formal marketing
programming not only to attract new customers but also to
keep and improve existing customers. This approach is referred to as "Relationship Marketing." Specific relationship marketing strategies--and examples of firms using
them--are presented.

INTRODUCTION

When it comes to marketing, many service firms devote most
of their resources to attracting new customers. Efforts
to retain existing customers are minimal, at least insofar
as formal marketing programming is concerned. This view
of marketing is needlessly restrictive and potentially
wasteful.

It is needlessly restrictive because firms benefit by
keeping valued customers as well as by attracting new customers. Assuming equality in customer attractiveness, the
firm that attracts 100 new customers and loses 20 existing
customers for a net gain of 80 customers is better off
than the firm attracting 130 new customers but losing 60
for a net gain of 70 customers.

The "new customer only" approach to marketing can also be
wasteful since it conceivably may cost more to acquire new
customers than retain or build up existing ones. For example, a firm spending $1 million in advertising to at-
tract new customers may experience less of a gain in net
business than if it were to spend $750,000 divided among
new customer advertising, direct mail to existing customers promoting additional services, and staff training to
improve service quality.

Thinking of marketing in terms of having customers, not
merely acquiring customers, is crucial for service firms.
The combined impact of low growth rates in many service
industries and deregulation--which has centered on service industries--is resulting in "everyone getting into
everyone else's business." Securities brokerage companies
have attracted billions of deposit dollars from banking
and thrift institutions through money market mutual funds.
Sears, which announced the acquisition of the nation's
largest real estate company (Coldwell-Banker) and fifth-
largest securities firm (Dean Witter) within the span of
one month in 1981, is gearing up to become the United
States' largest department store of financial services.
The discount brokerage sector of the securities industry
is emerging as a significant competitive influence and
will become a major factor now that banks are entering
this business. The Airline Deregulation Act has resulted
in intense competition--and price cutting--on popular
routes. Consumers can now select from among multiple
suppliers of long-distance telephone service. Clearly,
marketing to protect the customer base is becoming ex-
ceedingly important in a wide variety of service industries.

This paper introduces the concept of "Relationship Marketing" and discusses some of the principal relationship
marketing strategies available to service organizations.
The theme is that relationship marketing is an appropriate and useful approach for many service firms.

WHAT IS RELATIONSHIP MARKETING

Relationship marketing is attracting, maintaining and--in
multi-service organizations--enhancing customer relationships. Servicing and selling existing customers is viewed
to be just as important to long-term marketing success as
acquiring new customers. Good service is necessary to retain the relationship. Good selling is necessary to enhance it. The marketing mind-set is that the attraction of
new customers is merely the first step in the marketing
process. Cementing the relationship, transforming indifferent customers into loyal ones, serving customers as
clients--this is marketing too.

For such a basic idea, there has been relatively little attention paid it in the services marketing literature.
As Schneider (1980, p. 54) writes:

> What is surprising is that (1) researchers and
> businessmen have concentrated far more on how
> to attract consumers to products and services
> than on how to retain those customers, (2) there
> is almost no published research on the retention
> of service consumers, and (3) consumer evaluation
> of products or services has rarely been used as a
> criterion or index of organizational effectiveness.

Although smaller than one would expect, a body of literature relating to the idea of relationship marketing is
developing. Levitt (1981) emphasizes the need for firms
marketing intangible products to engage in constant reselling efforts. Ryans and Wittink (1977) have categorized services based on the degree of differentiation of
competing service offerings and the ability of consumers
to change suppliers and have suggested that many service
firms pay inadequate attention to encouraging customer
loyalty. Gronroos (1981), Berry (1980, 1981), George
(1977) and others have stressed improving the performance
of service personnel as a means of retaining customers.
Berry and Thompson (1982) have applied relationship marketing to the banking industry, claiming the concept
"...will dominate retail bank marketing practice and
thought throughout the 1980's."

The practice of relationship marketing is most applicable
to a service firm when each of the following conditions
exists:

1. There is an ongoing or periodic desire for the
   service on the part of the service customer,
   e.g., telephone or janitorial service versus
   funeral home service.
2. The service customer controls selection of the
   service supplier, e.g., selecting a dry
   cleaner or dentist versus entering the first
   taxi in the airport waiting line.
3. There are alternative service suppliers and
   customer switching from one to another is common, e.g., patronizing various restaurants or
   airlines versus buying electricity from the
   one electric utility serving a community.

These conditions are actually quite prevalent. Relatively
few service firms sell "one-time" services and in most service situations the customer both controls the choice process and has alternatives from which to choose. When these
conditions do exist, the opportunity to not just attract
customers but to build relationships with them is present.
Required are specific strategies that differentiate the

service from competitive offerings on dimensions that are meaningful to customers and difficult for competitors to duplicate (Ryans and Wittink, p. 314).

RELATIONSHIP MARKETING STRATEGIES

There are a number of possible relationship marketing strategies to be considered in the development of a relationship marketing plan. Discussed in this paper are five such strategies:
1. Core Service Strategy
2. Relationship Customization
3. Service Augmentation
4. Relationship Pricing
5. Internal Marketing

These strategies are not totally independent of one another and can be used in combination. A firm might use all five simultaneously.

Core Service

A key strategy in relationship marketing is the design and marketing of a "core service" around which a customer relationship can be established. The ideal core service is one that attracts new customers through its need-meeting character, cements the business through its quality, multiple parts, and long-term nature, and provides a base for the selling of additional services over time (Berry and Thompson). Core services are directed toward central rather than peripheral target market needs.

An example of a core service is the "Individual Financial Services" program offered through the trust department of Wachovia Bank and Trust headquartered in Winston-Salem, North Carolina. In this program customers select those specific services they wish from a package of services including tax preparation, cash flow analysis, budget assistance, insurance analysis, investment analysis, purchase and safekeeping of securities, financial record keeping, bill paying, asset management, and estate planning. Customers pay only for those services they select. The Individual Financial Services program addresses affluent consumer needs that many banks fail to address, has multiple parts, is long-term in nature, and offers a platform from which other financial services can be sold.

Merrill-Lynch's Cash Management Account also illustrates the concept of a core service. Introduced in 1977, the Cash Management Account is a $20,000 minimum balance margin account that automatically sweeps money from stock or bond sales into a money market fund. Consumers can access the dollars in their money fund account by writing a check or using a Visa debit card. If the balance in the money fund account is insufficient to cover such transactions, credit collateralized by securities is automatically extended.

By the fall of 1982, Merrill-Lynch had more than 750,000 Cash Management Account customers with an average account balance of about $67,000. The appeal of this service to upscale consumers has recently prompted other securities firms and, increasingly, commercial banks to develop their own versions of the service. However, the lag time of several years between when Merrill-Lynch launched the service and when similar services began appearing from competitors allowed Merrill-Lynch to attract many thousands of new clients who then became prospects for the firm's other service lines.

Customizing the Relationship

The nature of services affords many service firms the opportunity to customize the relationship. By learning about the specific characteristics and requirements of individual customers, and then capturing these data for use as needed, service firms can more precisely tailor service to the situation at hand. In so doing, they provide their customers an incentive to remain as customers rather than "starting over" with other suppliers.

The possibilities for relationship customization are considerable, especially when personal service capabilities are combined with electronic data processing capabilities. For example, Xerox has introduced a service system called "Field Work Support System" that involves keeping the history of a customer's equipment in a computerized data bank. When assistance is required, the customer calls a "work support representative" on a toll-free number. The representative can instantly access data concerning the customer's location, equipment, and its service record. If the problem cannot be worked out over the telephone using a computer checklist, a field service representative is sent to the customer's site.

American Express has recently run a print advertisement for the American Express Card with the headline: "When you have a question on a bill, you'll get some human understanding." The small copy then reads:

> This is not a recording. American Express Card customer service telephones are answered by real live people. Sure, the service centers are equipped with some amazing computers, but we count on our people to be equipped with brains of their own, as well. So they're expected and authorized to use their judgment and initiative to solve billing problems, and to explain the many services that go along the Cardmembership.

Free Spirit Travel, a Colorado-based travel agency with several outlets, assigns frequent traveler commercial clients a specific travel agent to coordinate all travel arrangements. The travel consultant develops a personal profile card on each business traveler in a company and records such information as preferred form of payment, secretary's name, and seating preferences in computerized reservation system client files. Clients receive personalized baggage tags with the travel consultant's business card on one side (in case of emergency) and the traveler's own business card on the other side.

Automotive Systems, a foreign car repair firm near Atlanta, provides explicit notes on customer service bills specifying the work that still needs to be done on the car and the time frame within which it should be done.

Whereas goods are manufactured, services are performed. Frequently they are performed by people who are in the position to custom-fit the service to the customer's particular requirements. If the customer receives custom service from company A but not from company B--and if receiving custom service is valued by the customer--then the customer is less likely to leave company A for B than would otherwise be the case.

Service Augmentation

Another relationship marketing strategy is service augmentation. Service augmentation involves building "extras" into the service to differentiate it from competitive offerings. For meaningful service differentiation to occur, the extras must be genuine extras--that is, not readily available from competitors--that are valued by customers. When this is the case, customer loyalty is encouraged. As Levitt writes (1974, pp. 9-10): "Having been offered these extras, the customer finds them beneficial and therefore prefers doing business with the company that supplies them."

One practitioner of service augmentation is the Fairfax Hotel in Washington, D.C. The Fairfax attempts to differentiate itself with its upscale target market by providing concierge service, night butler and 24-hour room service, a multi-lingual staff, a morning newspaper delivered to all guest rooms, a mint and cognac with the evening turn-down service, and room amenities including terry-cloth robe, linen laundry bag and bathroom telephone. More than 60 percent of the Fairfax Hotel guests have stayed there previously (Gates 1982).

A totally different application of service augmentation in the same industry in Holiday Inn's "No Excuses" room guarantee program. Holiday Inn places the following written guarantee in each room:

> •Your room will be right. It will be clean, everything will work properly, and you'll have enough of everything you need.
> •Or we will make it right.
> •Or we will refund the cost of your room for that night.

One form of service augmentation becoming more prominent is the "preferred customer club." By inviting priority customers to join a company-sponsored club, the service company augments the offer with special services and added prestige while establishing a vehicle to stay in touch with these customers through promotional mailings, newsletters and the like. Marriott's Club Marquis provides still another example from the hotel industry. There is no membership fee to belong to Club Marquis. To qualify for membership, an individual must stay at Marriott hotels on five separate occasions and have their visits validated. Members receive the following services:

> •Express reservation service through a toll-free number.
> •Reservations automatically guaranteed for late arrival.
> •Pre-registration.
> •Most deluxe accommodations in the rate category requested.
> •Check-cashing privileges.
> •Complimentary Wall Street Journal delivered to the room each morning.
> •Express check-out.
> •Semi-annual newsletter.

Members also receive an identification card and personalized luggage tags. Club Marquis memberships are honored at all Marriott properties.

The three hotel examples used demonstrate the inherent flexibility of service augmentation. The "extras" can be anything so long as they are valued by the target market and not easily matched by competitors. The use of hotel examples does not mean, however, the concept is applicable only to hotels. The real estate company that spends a portion of an anticipated listing commission to cosmetically upgrade a home prior to marketing it is using service augmentation. So is the car rental company that provides time-saving services to members of a preferred membership club and the bank that conducts business management seminars for its small business clients.

Relationship Pricing *Value or Volume Pricing*

An old marketing idea--a better price for better customers--forms the basis of relationship pricing, another strategy option available to service companies pursuing customer loyalty. Relationship pricing means pricing services to encourage relationships. In effect, customers are given a price incentive to consolidate much or all of their business with one supplier.

Although the concept of quantity discounts is not new, some service companies are applying the concept in innovative ways. The "frequent flyer" programs of various airlines, which offer travelers upgrades to first class seating and free trips if they fly a certain number of miles on a given carrier, are an attempt to build brand loyalty in what many regard as a commodity business. An April 1982 poll of more than 6,000 frequent flyers indicated that 77% of the respondents were participating in an airline frequent flyer incentive program (Frequent Flyer 1982).

Transamerica Corporation sponsored a program during 1982 in which passengers on its airline could receive first day car rental free when renting from Budget Rent a Car for three or more days. Citibank was one of the first banks to offer consumers reduced installment and mortgage loan rates in return for their checking and savings account business.

As with the other relationship marketing strategies presented, relationship pricing can be implemented in various ways in various service industries. For example, a sports team could package a third or one half its home games for a reduced per game price to encourage fans who cannot afford or do not want season tickets to attend more games. A university could offer reduced tuition for each additional family member enrolling. A movie theater could sponsor a "Tuesday Night at the Movies Club" with participants buying a ticket packet including five regularly priced tickets, five reduced priced tickets, and two free tickets. Regardless of the form relationship pricing takes, the objective remains the same: to encourage customer loyalty by rewarding it.

Internal Marketing

A pivotal relationship marketing strategy for many service firms is internal marketing. There are several forms of internal marketing. What all forms have in common is the "customer" is inside the organization. The usage in this paper is the employee as the customer and the job as the product.

The people who buy goods and services in the role of consumer are the same people who buy jobs. What is known in marketing about selling and reselling them goods and services can also be used in selling and reselling them jobs. The stress placed on customer satisfaction in external marketing is just as appropriate, just as necessary, in internal marketing.

Internal marketing is relevant to virtually all organizations. It is especially important, however, for labor-intensive service organizations. In these organizations, the quality of services sold is determined in large measure by the skills and work attitudes of the personnel producing the services. To the extent that labor-intensive service firms can use marketing to attract, keep, and motivate quality personnel, they improve their capability to offer quality services. Offering services that consistently meet the quality requirements of target markets is clearly an important factor in building strong customer relationships in many service industries.

The processes one thinks of as marketing--for example, marketing research, market segmentation, product modification, and communications programming are just as relevant to internal marketing as to external marketing. Just as marketing research procedures can be used to identify needs, wants, and attitudes in the external marketplace, so can they be used for the same purposes in the internal marketplace. Marriott Corporation, for instance, annually surveys employees at each of its hotels about their jobs. Survey results are discussed with the management of the hotel property and shared with upper management at Marriott headquarters. Minnesota Power and Light and GEICO are

27

among the service companies that have regularly used small group meetings between senior management and employees to encourage dialogue and feedback (Business Week 1979). If employee needs and wants are to be satisfied, they must first be identified. The tools and techniques of marketing research can help.

To combat high turnover rates for bank tellers, which averaged 40% in 1979 (Zweig 1980), a growing number of banks are implementing teller accreditation/career advancement programs. Generally, these programs are designed to raise the stature of the teller position while allowing promotion and personal growth opportunities within it. In-bank and non-bank courses, examinations, time-in-grade, and favorable job performance evaluations are typical requirements for becoming certified. First Interstate Bank of Arizona lowered its teller turnover rate from 42% in 1979 to 35% in 1980 after instituting a teller certification program (American Banker 1981). In effect, banks developing such programs are modifying the teller job-product for a market segment willing to take on extra assignments and tasks to move forward in their jobs.

The growing number of service companies instituting "flexible work hour" or "cafeteria benefit" programs are also responding to the heterogeneity of the work force by segmenting the market and modifying the job-product to better fit the requirements of different segments.

Formal communications programming designed to shape work attitudes and behavior can also be an important element of an internal marketing strategy. For example, a service company's advertising directed to the external customer can often be designed in such a way that it motivates and/or educates employees as well. Indeed, employees are an important "second audience" for a company's advertising (George and Berry 1981). Recent Delta Airline advertising making repeated references to Delta employees as "professionals" and including pictures of actual employees is an example of advertising to external and internal audiences simultaneously.

In essence, internal marketing involves creating an organizational climate in general, and job-products in particular, that lead to the right service personnel performing the service in the right way. In consumption circumstances in which the performance of people is what is being sold, the marketing task is not only that of encouraging external customers to buy but also that of encouraging internal customers to perform. When internal customers perform, the likelihood of external customers continuing to buy is increased.

CONCLUSION

Relationship marketing concerns attracting, maintaining and--in multi-service firms--building customer relationships. The relationship marketing firm invests in formal marketing programming not only to attract new customers but also to keep and improve existing customers. Attracting new customers is viewed as an intermediate objective.

Relationship marketing is applicable when there is an ongoing or periodic desire for the service and when the customer controls the selection of a service supplier and has alternatives from which to choose. The concept is critical for those service firms vulnerable to customer loss due to intensifying intratype and/or intertype competition.

Discussed in this paper were the five relationship marketing strategies of core service marketing, relationship customization, service augmentation, relationship pricing, and internal marketing. These strategies can be used in combination and in fact a service firm might use all five simultaneously. The common element in all relationship

marketing strategies is the incentive the customer is given to remain a customer. The incentive may be extra service (service augmentation) or a price break (relationship pricing) or something else but in each case the customer is given one or more reasons not to change suppliers.

REFERENCES

American Banker (1981), "Incentives Lower Teller Turnover in Arizona," (March 6), 2.

Berry, Leonard L. (1980), "Services Marketing Is Different," Business, (May-June), 25-26.

_____ (1981), "The Employee as Customer," Journal of Retail Banking, (March), 33-40.

_____ and Thomas W. Thompson (1982), "Relationship Banking: The Art of Turning Customers into Clients," Journal of Retail Banking, (June), 64-73.

Business Week (1979), "Deep Sensing: A Pipeline to Employee Morale," (January 28), 124-128.

Frequent Flyer (1982), "The Frequent Flyer Poll," (September), 13.

Gates, Anita (1982), "Roots," Frequent Flyer, (July), 43.

George, William R. (1977), "The Retailing of Services: A Challenging Future," Journal of Retailing, (Fall), 85-98.

_____ and Leonard L. Berry (1981), "Guidelines for Advertising Services," Business Horizons, (July-August), 52-56.

Gronroos, Christian (1981), "Internal Marketing--An Integral Part of Marketing Theory," in Marketing of Services, James H. Donnelly and William R. George, eds., Chicago: American Marketing Association.

Levitt, Theodore (1974), Marketing For Business Growth, New York: McGraw-Hill Book Company, 9-10.

_____ (1981), "Marketing Intangible Products and Product Intangibles," Harvard Business Review, (May-June), 94-102.

Ryans, Adrian B. and Dick R. Wittink (1977), "The Marketing of Services: Categorization with Implications for Strategy," in Contemporary Marketing Thought, Barnett Greenberg and Danny Bellenger, eds., Chicago: American Marketing Association, 312-314.

Schneider, Benjamin (1980), "The Service Organization: Climate Is Crucial," Organizational Dynamics, (Autumn), 54.

Zweig, Phillip L. (1980), "Role of Tellers Reassessed; Banks Opening Career Paths," American Banker, (December 10), 17.

THE EXPORTING OF SERVICES: AN OVERVIEW AND PRESENTATION OF A CASE APPROACH

Leif Edvinsson, Consultus International AB, Stockholm, Sweden
Torgny Nandorf, Consultus International AB, Stockholm, Sweden

THE EXPORTING OF SERVICES

BACKGROUND

This paper is an abstract with some general highlights and aspects on the exporting of services as a separate business dimension. These aspects are drawn from:

- a research project at the Department of Business Administration, University of Stockholm, Sweden

- empirical action research from a project for the Ministry of Trade in Sweden and the Swedish Trade Council to promote service export from Sweden.

INTRODUCTION

The service areas covered in this research would mainly be professional services representing such services as engineering services, financial services, transport services, trading services, security services, computer software services, consultancy services and public services. The service concept is unfortunately not very strict and simple. Therefore the public statistics as well as the structuring of services will be problematic. From our viewpoint, we would like to regard services from the content of thoughtware. By doing that, we would also like to include in our presentation the so called industrial services or techno-services. That type of services is becoming more and more important but unfortunately not showing up at all in the public accounting systems for international trade of services. Only in Sweden the so called project export from the industrial sector is regarded to be 10% of the total trade and a major proportion of that is intangible thoughtware or so called industrial services.

In this paper we would like to highlight the foOllowing:

- an overview to the macro-level of international trade of services

- an approach and methodology regarding professional services to develop the service package as a basis for the customer interaction and transfer regarding professional services

- some critical aspects on international marketing of services.

AN OVERVIEW OF THE INTERNATIONAL TRADE OF SERVICES

The potential market for service trade has grown rapidly during the last years. Between 1969-1980 the growth of world invisible trade was more than 16% according to IMF (International Monetary Fund). Between 1979 and 1980 the trade rose by 20.3%. This means that the trade in services is growing much more rapidly than the international trade in goods. A new business dimension is being opened up for international business. This might be a revolution for some business areas with a traditionally more domestic approach, like education, security, catering, maintenance. Business that earlier might have been regarded as handicraft and small scale businesses will become internationally exposed. This will also cause an increase of competition over the borders.

This competition is also influenced by the growing amount of barriers to trade in services. Very many of these are related to subsidies, aspects and personnel regulations of the service sector in the various countries. Services are furthermore not a part of the consensus in GATT (General Agreement on Tariffs and Trade). This will however be a major topic in the coming talks in GATT this fall.

The service sector is for the moment very heterogeneous and the public accounting is very diverse between countries. A new international accounting and statistical system would be needed to register service activities rather than service companies to support any structuring of this heterogeneous sector.

These difficulties in the accounting will imply major statistical uncertainties. The official figures among others based on statistics from IMF are however said to be underestimated.

A rough indication based on statistics from IMF would indicate the world trade of services to be 25% of total trade or approximately $ 540 billion in 1980. With a growth of 20% that would give $ 1.090 billion service trade growth to be compared with an almost zero growth of global hardware trade. Out of the total estimated world trade in services 94% is coming from 35 countries.

In spite of being underestimated the world market for services is huge and in rapid growth.

The share of service trade of total export from the major industrial countries is as an average 26% among OECD-countries. The picture beneath will give some examples of the dependence on service trade out of total trade from the leading trade countries as well as the Nordic countries.

Fig 1

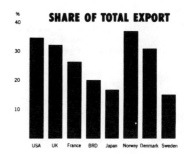

Looking into the top 35 countreis it could be seen that the leading countries in service world export by 1980 will be the following countries:

- USA   20%

- UK   9%

- France   9%

- BRD   8%.

Among the top four, France increased its share of world receipts strongly and the other three countries lost ground by 1980. Other growth countries would be Belgium/Luxemburg, The Netherlands and Japan.

Out of the top countries it is interesting to notice that the USA, UK and France are surplus countries but West Germany, Japan and the Nordic countries are deficit countries regarding service trade.

Sweden has a very small percentage of the total world trade of services, or only 1.3%. That could be compared with the Swedish share of the hard ware world trade, where Sweden has roughly 2%. This could indicate that Sweden ought to promote the service trade to reach a share of the service world trade of 2%, which would give roughly 3 billion dollars more in service export or 80.000 more jbs.

By looking into the service export promotion of GNP we would reach the following picture:

Fig 2

SERVICE EXPORT PROPORTION OF GNP (1980)

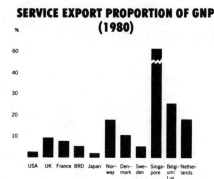

The service sector is taking a growing proportion of the GNP in the countries. More than 50% of the GNP is coming out of the service sector from these countries, but that sector is mainly so far domestically oriented. Only 5% of the GNP in the top 35 service trade countries is related to international service trade as an average.

For some countries, like Singapore, Belgium and The Netherlands as well as some of the Nordic countries it is a much higher proportion of international orientation of the service sector.

One implication of this picture is that the international competition will be growing as the major countries are becoming more international with their services, as well as an option for growth in service trade.

The major items in service trade are:

- transport   24%

- foreign travel   19%

- investment incomes   35%

- other services   22%.

By looking into the service trade from a portfolio viewpoint, the above mentioned items are very interesting. These are of course statistically uncertain, but will give a more operational basis for comparison between countries. Of a special interest is the tourism. It should be noticed that this sector is creating currency as receipts from foreign visitors by delivering the services on the domestic market.

US AND SWEDISH SERVICE EXPORT

Looking into the American service trade, we will have the following rough figure:

Fig 3

US SERVICE EXPORT

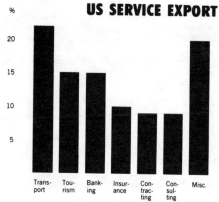

The American service export is estimated to be somewhere in the range between 60-100 billion dollars. The net value by 1981 of the service export was 40 billion dollars.

Out of the miscellaneous service export there are a lot of diverse sectors, such as motion pictures, franchising, helath, information.

The American service export is today estimated to be 2/3ds of the US mechanical export and roughly the same as US export of food products.

SWEDISH SERVICE EXPORT

As a comparison with the Swedish service epxort, we will have the following picture:

Fig 4

SWEDISH SERVICE EXPORT

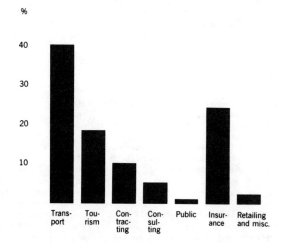

From both figures it could be seen that the major service export items in these two countries are in line with the average picture by showing transportation and tourism as the two major service export items.

Looking into, specifically, the US situation, the following picture will be coming through. What is less well known, is the degree to which the trade in services is supporting the US nation's overall trade position. The following picture shows the yawning dichotomy that has developed over the last dozen years regarding US overall trade balance.

Fig 5

U.S Balance of Payments Trade in Goods & Services

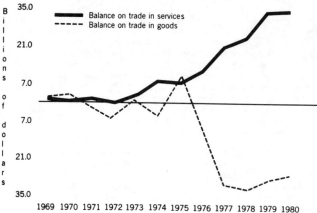

Source: U.S.Dept of Commerce, Bureau of Economic Analysis

In 1970 US export of goods and services succeeded such import by some $ 5.6 billion. By 1981, the same surplus was roughly $ 12 billion. This healthy picture changed however, dramatically without services. Without the service surplus, the deficit would be $ 27.8 billion by 1981. Evidently the service trade plays a crucial role in keeping the US trade balance in surplus. The trend is however to be flattening out. Protectionism is expected to grow in such transaction. To be pressing the course of service trade in Washington, there has recently been formed an organization called The Coalition of Service Industries.

The above mentioned trend of a service surplus and trade deficit on the good side could also be read regarding the UK. The importance of trade in invisibles to the UK:s balance and payment has been vital. It is estimated that in less than a dozen of the last 200 years or so the UK has exported more goods than she has imported. Further, the surplus on invisible earnings has usually made up the loss on visible trade. Currently, invisible trade accounts for about 1/3 of the total UK export earnings and import payments.

The Swedish situation is to some extent also perhaps following that development trend. 1980 seems to be a critical year. The deficit in trade of products starts to grow. The service trade is in balance from earlier being in a deficit. This picture does, however, not take into account the important industrial services or techno-services that go with turnkey- or project export from Sweden. Adding that to the earlier picture, the importance of invisible trade to Sweden is also becoming more and more apparent.

CONCLUSION

The conclusion from the development interview is that the services marketing overseas ought to gain more attention. The consequences for business are among others:

- large and growing export and business potential

- a new business dimension covering new potential entities to be traded

- new target groups such as foreign organizations aiming to start business of a similar type

- new packaging of hardware combined with software.

SOME CRITICAL EXPERIENCES

The international marketing of services is to a large proportion the same as that which is applied to the domestic marketing of services. However of larger importance are the situational and environmental contexts - social, political, economic, legal and cultural aspects to which the supplier has to adjust. The marketing of services is very much a highlight of the aspects of marketing management. This is even more stressed by going international.

Some of these international marketing aspects could be summarized into the following:

- internal marketing within the mother organization to get people to act

- interactive marketing with the foreign customer to get these people to buy both the idea and the service package

- interface marketing to create a bridge with a foreign environment to get a satisfactory relationship between people.

The above three critical aspects of international marketing of services could be used to initiate and support a positive development spiral of service export.

DEVELOPMENT OF THE MOTHER ORGANIZATION

To be able to develop international success, based on quality of the services and commercial efficiency, it has to start with an internal development program. The service know-how has to be packaged and a system developed to be able to deliver the services for reproduction on the foreign marekt. International commercial development of the staff and their know-how will be one of the first important steps.

The execution of services will often be a cahin of sub-activities. The key resources for performing these activities are the individuals. Therefore there will be an initial need for development of an "organizational know-how" of how to take care of the staff and their activities in an international environment, as well as the customer's involvement and participation.

The development of the know-how basis of the mother organization could consequently be grouped into the following areas:

- develop professional know-how to be able to solve the customer's problem

- develop organizational know-how to be able to handle various kinds of interactions with the customer, with the supplier, with local authorities

- develop commercial know-how to be able to package the services for the specific target group and to get paid for it.

DESIGNING OF THE SERVICE PACKAGE

One common denominator for a successful service exporter is that the company has taken a specific knowledge of the services, made an international packaging around it and developed a management philosophy to transfer this knowledge into an international market.

One format for this process of designing a service package which we have tested is the following service grid:

Fig 6

WORKING GRID – EXPORT OF SERVICES

Services Packages	Markets/Applications			
	I	II	III	Actions
A				1/ 2/ 3/
B				1/ 2/ 3/
C				1/ 2/ 3/
Actions	1/ 2/ 3/	1/ 2/ 3/	1/ 2/ 3/	

Partners

The philosophy behind this approach is to run an internal process with the involved carriers of the know-how to generate easily identifiable customer problems and possible problem solving actions. By having these individuals to participate through this process, they will start to think market-oriented and to focus customer problems as well as designing solution packages for these problems.

Based on this, the grid will take shape into:

- client related applications, i e customer problems or business areas

- service packages, i e modules with activities for the problem solving.

The service modules could also be regarded as delivery formats for the problem solving. The services could consequently be grouped into packages based on that. That grouping could also be done along a continuum showing an increasing interaction and involvement with the client such as from initial advisory services, through design and feasibility studies up to training and contracting.

Based on this service grid, it is possible to state the service package into clear figures and ambitions with clear assignments of responsibility and accomplishability.

Therefore it is also possible in the grid to state the actions to take, both regarding service packages as well as applications.

From the above grid it is also possible to develop clear descriptions and easily identifiable packages from the customer viewpoint, rather than traditional brochures and advertisements for services. It will rather show the services in a way what the service package can do for a customer.

CUSTOMER INTERACTION

From the Nordic School of Service Marketing we can learn the importance of so called interactive marketing. This implies the involvement of both the supplier and buyer into an interactive process to define the customer problem, to show how to solve the problem as well as the delivery of service activities to solve the customer problem in a satisfactory way.
One approach for that interaction which we have tested is to use a graphical dialogue approach or a checklist approach. This approach is aiming at reaching an explicit diagnosis of the customer's maturity and need situation as well as having a visual instrument for communication and involvement with the customer. This instrument will help the customer to identify relationship and ambition levels.

Based on such a graph, the buyer could identify his position today and aimed position in a 3-5 year period. From this the involved persons could discuss conclusions and consequences regarding what to do for the buyer as well as the supplier. Based on these consequences, various types of service packages could be used to solve the problem and transfer know-how from the supplier to the buyer.

This interactive marketing approach also aims at reaching an in-depth understanding of the customer at an early stage. By this it is possible to reach two important commercial dimensions of services marketing:

- pre-qualification of customer maturity for segmentation purposes and queuing purposes

- support the customer in becoming aware of needs as well as support the customer in problem formulation long before the traditional proposal competitive stage.

This interactive marketing approach is mainly based on experiences from professional service marketing and industrial service marketing. When talking about mass market interaction, other types of visual interactive tools could be used. It could perhaps be those used in the tourism and hotel services for showcase purposes, to give the customer an initial feeling of what kind of expoerience he will acquire. As a conclusion. it could be said that the interactive approach is used to give the customer the feeling of the show-how, based on the suppliers know-how.

SERVICE EXPORT SYSTEM

Successful service organizations are very much characterized by a way of performing, rather than producing. Based on earlier research and the research experience so far, the following export system description might be developed. It is based on three major components:

Fig 7

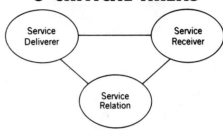

This system description could be used to focus three critical areas for export development of services. The restructuring of these components might result in:

- different business concepts and export potentials, e g industrial turnkey export or pure know-how export

- different service types, e g professional services, mass market services or public services

- different international approaches, e g joint venture, acquisition, franchising etc.

The service deliverer is very much characterized by:

- the service concept, e g road construction services

- the supporting services to reach a functional quality, e g traffic safety services.

The export development program will start with the know-how basis to be packaged for international launching. The company has to refine as well as re-define the service business formula for export articles.

The service receiver is very much characterized by:

- the consumer maturity level and his perception and acitivities within the decision making unit

- co-consumers and activities, i e business environment.

One of the largest obstacles of service export is related to the uncertainty of buying and consuming services. A lot of the need of the buyer is underperceived or hidden. The so called do-it-yourself syndrome will also advocate that the mature buyer will do it himself. An immature buyer, however, has difficulties in perceiving and specifying his needs. Therefore he will be interested in getting support e g system deliveries with a highly enhanced functional service package.

The service relationship is very much characterized by:

- accessability and convenience (legal, physical, human)

- staff interaction locally with the customer

- hardware support, e g desks, signs

- way of transfer to get people to act, e g directing a performance in a foreign environment.

This local interaction is often neglected in export discussions. This interaction, furthermore, often takes place in an unfamiliar foreign environment. The marketing management should therefore aim at training and guiding both the staff and the customers in their different roles and behavior for a successful interactive performance.

From the above export system description it might be possible to talk about three processes of international marketing of services:

- delivery process - packaging

- reception process - interaction

- relationship process - interface support.

THREE KEY AREAS

From our ongoing research projects in Sweden of professional service export, the following three key areas could be identified for service trade:

Internal marketing

The strength of the service organization is based on the know-how of the staff. The professional know-how of these people has to be packaged into some kind of thoughtware to be commercialized. Furthermore the personnel has to be stimulated to international initiatives, to a more commercial approach and to make them more internationally accessible. Therefore the attitude development is essential to secure the chain of functional subactivities. To reach a team of functional delivery it is essential with an internal marketing program for developing a script play and a rehearsal of roles for the involved people both regarding the commercial roles and the non-professional marketing roles. Experiences from the dramaturgy could here be applied to train each individual in the chain of executing service activities to be able to create income for the group as such through good market and customer relationships.

Interactive marketing

To reach a good customer contact and to get a confident relationship the company should start with developing instruments for a dialogue approach. This approach will be aiming at a show-how regarding the competence and professional know-how of the supplier. This approach could also be used to balance the expectations of the customer with his future perceptions. Another balance of critical importance is to balance the demand with the delivery capacity. Therefore it is of key importance to have a customer selection and pre-qualification based on a kind of need and maturity segmentation. This will give the company a number of specific target groups of a homogeneous segment type that is usually internationally spread around. This will also give the company a more firm base for readiness to serve and to secure a performance quality, i e balancing the operations with the marketing.

Another very important aspect of the interactive marketing is a customer follow-up to reach repeat business. This is a kind of relationship development based on the customer's experience with the supplier. As the image and confidence abroad for the foreign service supplier initially is very low, that would create an uncertainty with the buyer. Consequently after an initial order the gained experiences could be used as a leverage for follow-up. Especially as international marketing is very expensive, it is very important to think of how to maintain customer relationships and protect the customer base in a tough, international, competitive environment. Discontinuity could even be regarded as very annoying from the customer's viewpoint and could create a negative business spiral.

Interface marketing

A lot of service organizations sometimes expect their professional knowhow to speak for itself. To expect this to happen over the cultural barriers and borders between nations is not realistic, until the supplier has become famous and a confidence been established for his services. The softer the services, the more severe difficulties, due to the importance of a close interaction between the buyer and the deliverer of the services. That interaction is, furthermore, influenced by the cultural dimension. To bridge those cultural differences, it is important to think of an organizational approach such as a special interface function. The ambition behind this is to reach a platform to support the customer to buy and reduce the uncertainty. It is a kind of guidance for improved interaction. This interface action should aim at integrating the experience and solutions of the buyer into the cultural business environment. This is usually done by a local establishment or local support functions that will give identity, legitimacy and accessibility.

For the critical interaction with the customer regarding purchase, consumtion and delivery of the services, it is of key importance to have both legal, physical and human accessibility. Indirect representation such as agents or other types of intermediaries is usually complicating the interaction. Depending on the complexity of the services, different degrees of interactions might be required and. consequently, different degrees of accessibilities. One dimension of this interface marketing is, therefore, development of contact networks.

Another important dimension of the interface marketing is the organization of local performance and reproduction. This is based on the importance of getting a local profile to get around the trade barriers and gain an accreditation with key contacts on the market. To be able to handle the local delivery, it is important to have a satellite organization with local support resources. This will give the buyer the functional quality and also perhaps help the customer to acquire, perceive and appreciate the service package.

STRATEGY AREAS FOR INTERNATIONAL MARKETING OF THOUGHTWARE

Based on the above three key marketing areas for international marketing of services, it might be possible to establish a so called service export spiral. That could imply, for example, that an increased interest with the staff could give more international contacts, that would result in more inquiries that would further raise the level of fame as well as the level of confidence, which would further result in increased orders and experiences that would further give...............................

Based on the service export system it might also be possible to elaborate on two major dimensions:

- the interactive dimension, i e degree of activity to solve the customer's problem

- interface dimension, i e degree of mutual understanding/participation.

The following model could be drawn for analyzing the supplier engagement and the receiver involvement and adaption from those two dimensions:

Fig 8

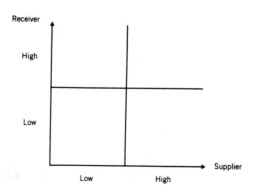

Modelling of International Marketing of Thought Ware

By using this model it might be possible to describe several different
strategy areas when going international with services:

- art of business (professional service or mass market service)

- service offering (problem solving package)

- delivery format (transfer package)

- network format (organizational relationship).

When going international it might be possible to select alternative strategies and make a detailed planning around the implications internally
and externally aorund these strategies to reach a positive export spiral.

International marketing of services could be viewed both from the macro
level regarding the role of services in the balance of payment situation
and economic development on the national level as well as at micro level
regarding the new business dimension for many organizations. On both
levels it is a fascinating dimension to do further research in, to gain a
more thorough understanding of the benefits that could be generated from
this growing sector of services.

REFERENCES

Barry, Leonard (1982), "Relationship Marketing," Texas A & M University

Cowell, Donald (1981), "International Marketing of Services", working
  paper, Loughborough University

Edvinsson, Leif (1982), "Some Aspects on Export of Services", Department
  of Business Administration, University of Stockholm

Grönroos, Christian (1979), "Service Oriented International Marketing
  Strategies: An Overview", Swedish School of Economics and Business
  Administration, Helsinki, Finland

Langueard, Eric (1982), "The Multinationalization Process of Service
  Firms", IAE, University of Aix, Marseilles, Fance

Leif Edvinsson
Torgny Nandorf
Consultus International AB
Döbelnsgatan 64
S-113 52 STOCKHOLM
Sweden

DIFFERENTIAL PERCEPTIONS OF SUPPLIERS AND CLIENTS
OF INDUSTRIAL SERVICES

A. Parasuraman, Texas A&M University, College Station
Valarie A. Zeithaml, Texas A&M University, College Station

ABSTRACT

What criteria are important to buyers of industrial services? Do industrial service suppliers know what these important criteria are? Suppliers and clients of marketing research services, a major category of "professional" industrial services identified by Gronroos (1980), were surveyed regarding issues such as the ones raised above. The survey results indicated substantial disagreement between the perceptions of suppliers and clients. The results have some important implications for industrial service marketers, as well as for researchers who have an interest in this area.

INTRODUCTION

Most of what is known about the evaluative criteria and processes used by consumers in selecting among industrial services pertains specifically to goods. Generalizing this knowledge to industrial services, under the assumption that services are similar enough in the consumer's mind to be chosen and evaluated in the same manner, has recently been criticized (Shostack 1977, Davis and Cosenza 1976, Weinberger and Brown 1977). Evidence suggests, for example, that the evaluative criteria used by buyers of services are more difficult to discern than criteria used by buyers of goods Guseman 1976, Zeithaml 1981, Fisk 1981). As a result, industrial service suppliers may need to exercise caution in using goods marketing tenets and research to understand their buyers. To the extent that they presently rely on goods marketing axioms, industrial service suppliers may not understand the criteria on which their offerings are evaluated and selected.

The criteria used to evaluate services are difficult to specify largely because services are intangible (Bateson 1979, Lovelock 1981). Intangibility precludes the use by buyers of well-defined and obvious cues such as style, weight, color, or feel on which to base evaluations prior to purchase. Instead, buyers rely on surrogate indicators of quality such as surroundings and equipment (Berry 1980, Upah 1980, Eiglier 1977, George 1977), service personnel (Rathmell 1974, Chase 1978, Gronroos 1980, Uhl and Upah 1978), and price (Booms and Bitner 1981, Berry 1980, Zeithaml 1981) when selecting services. An additional difficulty is comprehending the way buyers account for the heterogeneity (or nonstandardization) of services. The inability to depend on consistent service performance and quality may lead service buyers to experience greater perceived risk (Guseman 1976, 1981, Eiglier et al. 1977, Zeithaml 1981) which results in dependence on different types of prepurchase information (Czepial 1980, Kelly and George 1980, Zeithaml 1981). Since buyers experience more difficulty when evaluating services than when evaluating goods, evaluation processes for services may be more abstruse, more random, and more symbolic than with goods (Zeithaml 1981).

The main purpose of the research reported here was to compare the perceptions of suppliers and clients of one type of industrial service, namely the services offered by commercial marketing research firms. Among suppliers of different types of industrial services, marketing research firms should rank at or near the top in terms of understanding their clients. After all, a key function of marketing research firms is to aid client firms in clearly understanding the nature of their (the clients') own customers or markets. Therefore, commercial marketing research services were chosen as the focus of this study because client or customer orientation on the part of industrial service suppliers was expected to be most visible, and easiest to detect, among this category of firms.

RESEARCH DESIGN

Hypotheses

Three specific hypotheses related to perceptions about factors influencing the choice of commercial market research services were tested.

Hypothesis 1: Significant differences between suppliers and clients will exist regarding (a) the overall rankings of the factors based on perceived importance of the factors; and (b) the perceived importance of each individual factor. The basis for this hypothesis rests on recent evidence that service firms embrace narrower definitions of marketing and appreciate marketing skills less than their counterpart organizations offering goods (Lovelock 1981, Lovelock et al. 1981). Emphasis on operations rather than marketing, demonstrates a production orientation which is likely to result in greater concern for the supplier's own company and its services than for client needs.

Hypothesis 2: Greater agreement between suppliers and users than between suppliers and nonusers will exist on: (a) the overall importance rankings of the factors; and (b) the perceived importance of each individual factor. In this research, client firms that had purchased the services of marketing research firms during the last three years were classified as "users"; others were classified as nonusers." This hypothesis predicts that suppliers will better understand the perceptions of firms that are recent users of their services than those that are not. Presumably, working with recent users will provide suppliers with insights into their evaluative criteria and information sources. Suppliers are predicted to comprehend less about the needs of nonusers and their perceived importance of choice criteria, largely due to the suppliers' lack of interaction with these firms.

Hypothesis 3: Client will perceive personal sources of information to be more important than nonpersonal sources when evaluating services prior to purchase. Robertson (1970) claimed that personal influence becomes pivotal as product complexity increases and when objective standards by which to evaluate offerings decrease--two conditions which characterize most purchases of marketing research services. Eiglier and Langeard (1977) revealed that managers in four service industries believe word-of-mouth to have a strong influence in service purchases. Finally, many researchers (among them Perry and Hamm 1969, Cunningham 1967, Arndt 1967) confirmed that credibility of personal sources encourages their use in situations of high perceived risk. Given the intangible nonstandardized nature of most marketing research services, high perceived risk regarding outcomes and usefulness is expected to accompany their purchase.

Samples of Client and Supplier Firms

A group of 1,000 companies in the United States, chosen

randomly from Dun and Bradstreet's Million Dollar Directory (1980), constituted the sample of client firms. A questionnaire and cover letter were mailed to the marketing department of each firm. Three weeks later a follow-up post card was mailed to the entire sample. A total of 261 usable questionnaires were returned, for a response rate of 26.1%. Of the individuals filling out the questionnaires, 27% held the title of President or VP-Marketing, 29% held marketing titles such as Marketing Manager, Sales Manager, Advertising Manager and Marketing Research Director, while the rest held a variety of titles such as Owner, Assistant to the President and Management Trainee. Respondents and nonrespondents were considered to be similar, at least in terms of the size of the firms. The sales revenue distribution of the 261 responding firms was compared with the sales revenue distribution (obtained from Dun and Bradstreet's Directory) of the initial sample of 1,000 firms. A Kolmogorov-Smirnov test for the similarity between the two distributions failed to reveal a significant difference between them at the .05 level of significance.

A random sample of 500 commercial marketing research firms in the United States, chosen from the International Directory of Marketing Research Houses and Services (1979) constituted the sample of supplier firms. This directory contained approximately 1,200 listings, including about 200 foreign listings which were first removed from the sampling frame. Also removed were duplicate listings of branch offices of U.S. firms. Hence, the sample of 500 firms covered over 50% of the total population of marketing research firms in the U.S.

A questionnaire and cover letter were mailed to the president of each firm. Three weeks later a follow-up post card was mailed to the entire sample. A total of 150 usable questionnaires were returned, for a response rate of 30%. Of the individuals filling out the questionnaires, 68% held the title of President, 10% held the title of Vice President, 8% held the title of Director of Research, and the rest held a variety of titles such as Project Manager, Field Director, and Managing Partner.

Measurement Instruments

Respondents in the client and supplier firms were asked to evaluate a set of ten factors that were considered to be relevant in the purchase of marketing research services. The ten factors included seven evaluative criteria (research firm's reputation, expected quality of the research work, expected usefulness of the research results, research firm's understanding of the client's problem, qualifications of key employees of the research firm, and price of the research services), two personal information sources (referral by satisfied clients and personal solicitations from the research firms) and one nonpersonal information source (research firm's advertising). Respondents were instructed to rate the importance of each factor on a seven-point scale. The levels, "Extremely Important" (=7) and "Not at all Important" (=1) served as anchors for the importance scales.

RESULTS

Table 1 summarizes the perceptions of suppliers and clients regarding the relative importance of the ten factors considered relevant in the purchase of commercial marketing research services. The overall rankings of the ten factors for suppliers and clients disagree. The Spearman's correlation coefficient between the two sets of rankings was only 0.55, with an associated t-value of 1.86 (not significant at $p \leq 05$). This indicates disparity between the perceptions of suppliers and clients, as predicted in Hypothesis 1a. The results in Table 1 also demonstrate strong support for Hypothesis 1b--the differences between the mean ratings provided by suppliers and

clients are statistically significant (at $p \leq .05$) for seven of the ten factors. Furthermore, for the three remaining factors, t-values corresponding to the differences are close to the critical value of $t=1.96$.

Table 1

Perceived Relative Importance of Factors: Suppliers vs. Clients

Factor	Mean Ratings (Std. Deviations)		Overall Rankings[a]		T-value[b]
	Suppliers (n=150)	Clients (n=261)	Suppliers (n=150)	Clients (n=261)	
Research firm's reputation	6.67 (0.60)	6.03 (1.21)	1	4	6.82[c]
Quality of research	6.61 (0.80)	6.27 (1.11)	2	3	3.45[c]
Usefulness of research results	5.74 (1.41)	6.36 (1.11)	7	2	4.55[c]
Understanding client's problem	6.27 (1.04)	6.42 (1.02)	4	1	1.39
Qualifications of key employees	5.99 (1.25)	5.81 (1.17)	6	5	1.41
Personality of key employees	5.72 (1.22)	4.66 (1.47)	8	8	7.65[c]
Price of research services	4.91 (1.19)	5.23 (1.38)	9	7	2.39[c]
Referral by satisfied clients	6.58 (0.92)	5.67 (1.39)	3	6	7.71[c]
Personal solicitations	6.19 (1.49)	3.81 (1.69)	5	9	14.37[c]
Research firm's advertising	3.45 (1.68)	3.17 (1.55)	10	10	1.63

[a] Overall rankings are based on the mean ratings.

[b] Corresponds to the absolute difference between the mean ratings for suppliers and clients.

[c] Significant at $p < .05$ in a two-tailed t-test.

Comparisons of the importance ratings provided by suppliers with those perceived by "user" firms (i.e., firms purchasing commercial marketing research services during the last three years) are shown in Table 2. Similar information related to "nonusers" is shown in Table 3. Contrary to Hypothesis 2a, perceptions of suppliers do not agree with the perceptions of users more than with those of nonusers. The degree of correspondence between the overall rankings for suppliers and users ($r_s=0.54$), as well as for suppliers and nonusers ($r_s=0.55$), is equally weak. In fact, comparison of the importance rankings for the user and nonuser groups reveals almost identical rankings. The mean ratings obtained for each individual factor demonstrates little support for Hypothesis 2b. Signigicant differences exist between the mean importance ratings of suppliers and users for seven of the ten factors (Table 2). An equal number of significant differences exist between the perceptions of suppliers and nonusers (Table 3). Although the hypothesis predicts that service suppliers will understand recent service users better than nonusers, the results do not support this prediction.

As predicted by Hypothesis 3, clients perceived the importance of personal information sources (referral by satisfied clients and personal solicitations) to be greater than that of suppliers' advertising, which is a nonpersonal information source (Table 4). T-tests conducted to examine the differences between the ratings for the personal and nonpersonal sources confirmed that the mean differences were significantly greater than zero at $p \leq .01$.

Table 2

Perceived Relative Importance of Factors: Suppliers vs. Users

Factor	Mean Ratings (Std. Deviations)		Overall Rankings		T-value
	Suppliers (n=150)	Users[a] (n=80)	Suppliers (n=150)	Users (n=80)	
Research firm's reputation	6.67 (0.60)	6.20 (0.89)	1	4	4.12[b]
Quality of research	6.61 (0.80)	6.58 (0.57)	2	2	0.32
Usefulness of research results	5.74 (1.41)	6.60 (0.71)	7	1	6.14[b]
Understanding client's problem	6.27 (1.04)	6.51 (0.73)	4	3	2.02[b]
Qualifications of key employees	5.99 (1.25)	5.70 (1.05)	6	5	1.84
Personality of key employees	5.72 (1.22)	4.39 (1.33)	8	8	7.34[b]
Price of research services	4.91 (1.19)	4.99 (1.30)	9	7	0.45
Referral by satisfied clients	6.58 (0.92)	5.57 (1.33)	3	6	5.96[b]
Personal solicitations	6.19 (1.49)	3.39 (1.52)	5	9	13.18[b]
Research firm's advertising	3.45 (1.68)	2.61 (1.21)	10	10	4.26[b]

[a]Firms purchasing marketing research services during the last three years.

[b]Absolute difference between mean ratings for suppliers and users significant at p <.05, based on a two-tailed t-test.

Table 3

Perceived Relative Importance of Factors: Suppliers vs. Nonusers

Factor	Mean Ratings (Std. Deviations)		Overall Rankings		T-value
	Suppliers (n=150)	Nonusers[a] (n=181)	Suppliers (n=150)	Nonusers (n=181)	
Research firm's reputation	6.67 (0.60)	5.93 (1.34)	1	4	6.19[b]
Quality of research	6.61 (0.80)	6.10 (1.28)	2	3	4.16[b]
Usefulness of research results	5.74 (1.41)	6.22 (1.25)	7	2	3.12[b]
Understanding client's problems	6.27 (1.04)	6.37 (1.14)	4	1	0.80
Qualifications of key employees	5.99 (1.25)	5.87 (1.22)	6	5	0.84
Personality of key employees	5.72 (1.22)	4.79 (1.53)	8	8	5.87[b]
Price of research services	4.91 (1.19)	5.37 (1.40)	9	7	3.06[b]
Referral by satisfied clients	6.58 (0.92)	5.71 (1.43)	3	6	6.30[b]
Personal solicitations	6.19 (1.49)	4.01 (1.75)	5	9	11.64[b]
Research firm's advertising	3.45 (1.68)	3.42 (1.63)	10	10	0.16

[a]Firms not purchasing marketing research services during the last three years.

[b]Absolute difference between mean ratings for suppliers and nonusers significant at p<.05, based on a two-tailed t-test.

DISCUSSION AND IMPLICATIONS

The research results indicate that suppliers may not understand the relative importance which clients attribute to various factors used to evaluate and select marketing research services. There are major differences between the perceptions of the two groups, as shown by the importance ratings of individual factors, as well as factor rankings derived from the ratings. Notably, the factors "understanding the client's problem" and "usefulness of research results," which are client-centered and perceived to be most critical by the client group, are ranked as low as fourth and seventh respectively by the supplier group. Similarly, suppliers perceive "research firm's reputation," a firm-centered factor, to be most critical while clients rank it only fourth in terms of relative importance. These findings suggest that the philosophy of consumer orientation prescribed by the marketing concept may not be fully subscribed to by marketing research firms. Of greater concern is the possibility that other types of industrial service firms may possess even less understanding of customer needs and priorities than the supplier firms in this study. Marketing research firms, after all, should epitomize the understanding of customers, since one of their key functions is to help client firms comprehend their customers' needs and behavior.

Contrary to the second hypothesis, research suppliers do not appear to understand users better than they understand nonusers. While interaction with service users offers the opportunity for communication regarding client needs and evaluative criteria, the supplier firms in this study did not appear to benefit from this opportunity. Research suppliers in particular, and service suppliers in general, can make their interactions with clients more fruitful by making deliberate effort to seek client feedback and to pick up cues that reflect client concerns.

Comparison of the ratings provided by users and nonusers of marketing research services (Table 2 and 3) reveals several intriguing differences. First, only four of the ten factors were rated as more important by users than by nonusers: reputation of firm, quality of research, usefulness of results, and understanding of client problems. All four factors demonstrate a greater concern on the part of the users for the quality and relevance of the research. Experience with buying and using research service may have led them to place greater emphasis on the value of these factors, although the data do not reveal whether such emphasis is due to satisfaction or dissatisfaction with marketing research services. Second, users as a group appear to be more certain of their importance ratings than of nonuser ratings on all ten items. One possible explanation for this finding is that the relative importance of criteria on which marketing research services are evaluated are easier to discern after the services have been purchased, which is consistent with other recent research (Fisk 1981, Zeithaml 1981). With experience, buyers may become increasingly certain about which factors signify quality and satisfaction. This implies that research suppliers should recognize the importance of these factors and emphasize them in their marketing campaigns, especially in terms of generating repeat purchase and building client loyalty.

As past research has suggested, personal sources of information, including referral by satisfied clients and personal solicitation, were confirmed as being more pivotal than advertising, a nonpersonal source. Mass and selective media may not be capable of conveying credible information regarding the factors that clients consider to be most important (i.e., whether a research firm can understand the client's problem, whether research results will be useful, and what the quality of the research will be). Even a personal source that is supplier controlled (i.e., personal solicitation) appears to be unable to provide useful information to clients in selecting services.

It is notable that suppliers greatly overestimate the value of personal solicitation as an information source. While clients perceive its mean importance to be only 3.81, suppliers assess its mean importance value at 6.19, for a difference significant at $p \leq .001$. Furthermore, clients consider referral by satisfied customers to be more valuable than personal solicitation (significant difference at $p \leq .05$), perhaps because referrals can provide credible and specific information concerning the factors that most interest them (i.e., how well the firm understands clients' problems, and whether the research results are useful).

The low importance ratings assigned to advertising do not necessarily mean that marketing research fimrs shoudl stop using this form of promotion. In fact, advertising may be helpful in establishing and maintaining a good reputation, an attribute which is regarded as important by clients. However, marketing research firms should concentrate their advertising appeals on the factors most relevant to clients. Focus could be placed on evidence that the firm uunderstands clients and provides results that are useful. Testimonials from satisfied users, or case studies emphasizing the ways in which research has led to profitable changes in client strategies, are techniques which simulate word of mouth communications from peers, and may therefore be viewed as more credible. Suppliers might aalso want to encourage word of mouth communication by asking satisfied clients to tell others about their services, or perhaps by featuring the names of well known and satisfied clients in their advertising.

SUGGESTIONS FOR FUTURE RESEARCH

Research in other industrial service settings is needed to confirm the major findings of the study reported here: industrial service firms may not understand their clients' perceptions of the importance of criteria used in evaluating and selecting services.

Researchers have emphasized the salience of price as an indicator of quality in purchase situations where tangible criteria are not present. In the study reported here, however, price was not ranked as important (seventh out of ten) by clients. This may be due to the inability of the questionnaire to indicate whether price was being used in sense of cost (i.e., low price) or as a surrogate for quality. Future research studies in this area must explicitly state the two different connotations of price and obtain respondents' perceptions about each of them.

The factors "understanding client's problem," "usefulness of research results" and "quality of research" were ranked highest by clients in this study. Interestingly, all three factors can only be meaningfully evaluated _after_ the purchase of services. Hence one can hypothesize that critical or complete purchase evaluation by service clients may _follow_ (rather than precede) the purchase of services. This in turn lends tentative, and perhaps indirect, support to the hypothesis of researchers (Fisk 1981, Zeithaml 1981) that greater post-purchase evaluation may be associated with services than with goods. This finding may encourage further research related to understanding and confirming the differences between the evaluation process for goods and service purchases.

REFERENCES

Arndt, J. (1967), "Word-of-Mouth Advertising and Information Communication," in Risk-Taking and Information Handling in Consumer Behavior, D. F. Cox, ed., Boston, MA: Division of Research, Harvard University.

Bateson, John (1979), "Why We Need Services Marketing," in Conceptual and Theoretical Developments in Marketing Strategies and Organization Structures for Service Firms, in Marketing of Services, James H. Donnelly and William R. George, eds., Chicago: American Marketing Association, 47-51.

Chase, Richard B. (1978), "Where Does the Consumer Fit in the Service Operation," Harvard Business Review, (November-December), 137-142.

Cunningham, S. M. (1967), "Perceived Risk in Information Communications," in Risk Taking and Information Handling in Consumer Behavior, D. F. Cox, Ed., Boston, MA: Division of Research, Harvard University.

Czepial, J. A. (1980), "Managing Customer Satisfaction in Consumer Service Businesses," Cambridge, MA: Marketing Science Institute Report #80-107.

Davis, Duane, and Robert Cosenza (1978), "Differential Search Propensities and the Use of Marketing Offering in Service Context," in Proceedings, Southern Marketing Association, Robert S. Franz, et al., eds., Lafayette, LA: University of Southwest Louisiana.

Dun & Bradstreet's Million Dollar Directory--Volumes I&II (1980), New York: Dun & Bradstreet, Inc.

Eiglier, Pierre (1977), "A Note on the Commonality of Problems in Service Management: A Field Study," in Marketing Consumer Services: New Insights, Pierre Eiglier, et al., eds., Cambridge, Massachusetts: Marketing Science Institute, 59-82.

_____, and Eric Langeard (1977), "A New Approach to Service Marketing," in Marketing Consumer Services: New Insights, Pierre Eiglier, et al., eds., Cambridge Massachusetts: Marketing Science Institute, 31-58.

Fisk, Raymond P. (1981), "Toward a Consumption/Evaluation Process Model for Services," in Marketing of Services, James H. Donnelly and William R. George, eds., Chicago: American Marketing Association, 191-195.

George, William R. (1977), "The Retailing of Services: A Challenging Future," Journal of Retailing, 53 (Fall), 85-98.

Guseman, Dennis (1981), "Service Marketing: The Challenge of Stagflation," in Marketing of Services, James H. Donnelly and William R. George, eds., Chicago: American Marketing Association, 200-204.

Gronroos, Christian (1980), "Designing a Long-Range Marketing Strategy for Services," Long Range Planning, 13 (April), 36-42.

International Directory of Marketing Research Houses and Services (1979), New York: New York Chapter of the American Marketing Association, Inc.

Johnson, Eugene (1969), Are Goods and Services Different?: An Exercise in Marketing Theory, Ann Arbor, Michigan: University Microfilms.

Kelly, J. Patrick, and William R. George (1980), "Perceptions of the Personal Selling Function in Service Marketing: A Field Study," in Marketing in the 80's: Changes and Challenges, Chicago: American Marketing Association, 244-47.

Lewis, William (1976), "An Empirical Investigation of the Conceptual Relationship Between Services and Products in Terms of Perceived Risk," unpublished dissertation, University of Cincinnati, Ohio.

Lovelock, Christopher H. (1981), "Why Marketing Management Needs to be Different for Services," in Marketing of

Services, James H. Donnelly and William R. George, eds.,
Chicago: American Marketing Association, 5-9.

_____, Eric Langeard, John E. G. Bateson, and
Pierre Eiglier (1981), "Some Organizational Problems
Facing Marketing in the Service Sector," in Marketing
of Services, James H. Donnelly and William R. George,
eds., Chicago: American Marketing Association, 168-171.

Perry, M. and B. C. Hamm (1969), "Canonical Analysis of
the Relationship Between Socioeconomic Risk & Personal
Influence in Purchase Decisions," Journal of Marketing
Research, 6 (August), 351-4.

Rathmell, John S. (1974), Marketing in the Services Sector,
Cambridge, Massachusetts: Winthrop Publications, Inc.

Robertson, T. S. (1970), Innovative Behavior and Communication, New York: Holt, Rinehard and Wonston, Inc.

Shostack, Lynn G. (1977), "Breaking Free From Product Marketing," Journal of Marketing, 41 (April), 73-80.

Uhl, Kenneth P., and Gregory D. Upah (1978), "The Marketing
of Sciences: A Set of Propositions," in Macro-Market
ing: Distributive Processes for a Societal Perspective,
An Elaboration of Issues, Charles C. Slater and Philip
D. White, eds., Boulder, Colorado: University of
Colorado, 411-433.

Upha, Gregory D. (1980), "Mass Marketing in Service Retailing: A Review and Synthesis of Major Methods,"
Journal of Retailing, 56 (Fall), 59-76.

Weinberger, March G. and Stephen W. Brown (1977), "A Dif-
ference in Informational Influences: Services vs.
Goods," Journal of the Academy of Marketing Science, 5
(Fall), 389-402.

Zeithaml, Valarie A. (1981), "How Consumer Evaluation Processes Differ Between Goods and Services," in Marketing
of Services, James H. Donnelly and William R. George,
eds., Chicago: American Marketing Association, 186-90.

DEVELOPING IMAGES FOR SERVICES THROUGH MEANS-END CHAIN ANALYSIS

Jonathan Gutman, University of Southern California, Los Angeles
Thomas J. Reynolds, University of Texas at Dallas, Richardson

ABSTRACT

This paper will discuss an approach for the development of advertising strategy and will compare products and services in terms of the opportunities and problems they present for strategy development. First, advertising strategy will be defined in terms of its necessary components. Then, the types of knowledge of consumers necessary for strategy development will be discussed along with relevant theories of consumers' cognitive structures needed for gaining the appropriate understanding of consumers. Next, the relationship between image and advertising strategy will be specified.

At this point, the groundwork will have been laid for discussing differences between products and different types of services as to how strategies and images can be created. The authors feel that the traditional classifications for types of services, while useful, can be sharpened if one considers them in relation to the task of advertising strategy creation. To demonstrate these concepts, an example will be detailed.

DEFINING ADVERTISING STRATEGY

Advertising strategy may be thought of as specifying an approach for communicating to the consumer how the product or service helps the consumer reach his or her goals with respect to product usage. Strategy specification should act as a guide for determining the aspects of the product or service to be mentioned, and as a basis for determining the properties of the advertising that will best accomplish the strategic goals.

The preceding definition suggests that multiple decisions at many levels are involved in developing advertising strategy. To distinguish these multiple features of advertising strategy a bit more clearly, five broad characteristics of advertising strategy will be identified. The five levels of strategy development must fit together in a reinforcing way if the strategy is to be effective. The five levels of the advertising strategy model (Olson and Reynolds, in press) are listed below from the broadest, most general, to the most concrete level.

DRIVING FORCE -- the value orientation of the strategy; the end-level to be focused on in the advertising.

LEVERAGE POINT -- the manner by which the advertisement will "tap into," reach, or "activate" the value or end-level of focus; the specific way in which the value is linked to the specific features in the advertisement.

EXECUTIONAL FRAMEWORK -- the overall scenario or action plot, plus the details of the advertising execution. The executional framework provides the "vehicle" by which the value orientation is to be communicated, especially the Gestalt of the advertisement -- its overall tone and style.

CONSUMER BENEFIT -- the major positive consequences for the consumer that are to be explicitly communicated, verbally or visually, in the advertising.

MESSAGE ELEMENTS -- the specific attributes, consequences, or features about the product that are to be com-municated, verbally or visually.

KNOWLEDGE OF CONSUMERS NEEDED FOR STRATEGY DEVELOPMENT

One of the key factors in developing a useful understanding of consumers is their knowledge structures held in memory. Such structures encompass beliefs, attitudes, intentions, emotions, feelings, values, images, moods, representations of tastes and smells, and motor actions. It has become widely recognized that such memory structures exert a major influence on product purchase or usage of a service.

Interest lies in ascertaining what the contents of memory are in terms of, "What do people think about when they think about my product or service as well as that of my competitors?" It is also true that in addition to "contents," aspects of structure or linkages between content elements are of concern. That is, we need to understand the basis for the linkages or associations between specific concepts -- e.g., the types of associations that consumers make between a specific attribute of a product or service and the benefits implied by that attribute. This is of singular importance in that any single attribute representation has little or no meaning; its meaning is defined by the concepts with which it is associated, namely the more personal associations including benefits. Thus, content of memory cannot be studied independently of the structure of memory. Content is revealed through structure and vice versa.

Means-End Chain Theory

In order to develop a framework for studying the content and structure of consumers' knowledge about products and services, some theoretical perspective is necessary. The theory underlying the approach discussed in this paper is referred to a means-end chain theory (Gutman, 1982). The "means" can be thought of as services and the "ends" as values important to consumers. The "means-end chain" theory seeks to explain how a person's selection of a service enables him or her to achieve his or her desired end states. Such a model consists of elements that represent the major consumer processes that link values to behavior.

Two assumptions underlie the model: 1) all consumer action have consequences; and, 2) that all consumers learn to associate particular consequences with particular actions they may take. Consequences accrue to people from consuming products or services. Consequences may be desirable (benefits) or undesirable; they may occur directly from consuming the product or occur indirectly at a later point in time or from others' reactions to their consumption behavior. Relevant desirable consequences with respect to banking, for example, (accumulating funds, feeling comfortable, saving time and effort, providing for one's family) derive from the customer's doing business with a particular bank, savings and loan, or credit union. Undesirable consequences (feeling dehumanized, annoyed, uncomfortable, helpless) can also stem from the same source. The central aspect of the model is that consumers choose actions that produce desired consequences and minimize undesired consequences.

"Values" are held to provide consequences with their positive or negative valences. Values are important beliefs people hold about their views of themselves and about their feelings concerning others' beliefs about them. For banks, such feelings as satisfaction, security, pride in self, and independence are likely to be important. Therefore, it is important that the research procedure determine relevant values and consequences, and the relations between them.

Of course, one must consider the attributes these types of institutions possess (safety, liquidity, personal service). It is these attributes that produce the consequences, therefore we must make ourselves aware of attribute-consequence relations.

Overall, it is the attribute-consequence-value interrelations that are the focus of research. This is what constitutes a means-end chain. Values provide the overall direction, consequences select specific behaviors in specific situations, and attributes are what is in the actual products that produce the consequences. And of course, as consumers have different values, they will have different means-end chains (headed by these different values).

A total strategy is based on a clear understanding of the perceptual segment one is trying to reach. The means-end chain that represents how people in this segment structure their cognitions about the service (bank, airline, museum, etc.) becomes the basis for strategy development. Within this context the attributes at the bottom of the chain become the message elements, the consequences or benefits sought become the situations around which the advertising is developed, and the segment's values guide the executional tone of the advertising.

Procedures for Studying Cognitive Structure

As can be seen in retrospect, the means-end chain model is the basis for the definition of advertising strategy. Having defined strategy and discussed the theory behind strategy formation, the procedures for ascertaining knowledge of consumers' "ways of thinking" or cognitive structures necessary for strategy development will now be discussed. Several such schemes have been developed (Young and Feigin, 1975; Howard, 1977, Gutman, 1982; Gutman and Reynolds, 1979; Olson and Reynolds, in press). The scheme developed here is based on the work of Gutman (1982) and Olson and Reynolds (in press). It includes the following levels for categorizing the contents of consumers' cognitive structures.

Level of Abstraction

Abstract	Terminal Values
	Instrumental Values
	Psycho-Social Consequences
	Functional Consequences
	Abstract Attributes
Concrete	Concrete Attributes

Attributes have been divided into concrete and abstract levels because it is necessary to distinguish between aspects that are literally part of a service (a smiling face) and those that are attributed to a service because of those attributes (friendly). At the consequence level, a distinction has been made between functional and psycho-social consequences to separate those consequences accruing directly to the consumer from the service (i.e., styled hair from visiting a hair stylist -- for men, what used to be called a barbershop) and consequences accruing to the consumer from having "styled hair" (i.e., romance, promotion, etc.). And, at the values level, instrumental values (i.e., self confidence) have been distinguished from terminal values (i.e., success).

Identifying the Content and Organization of Cognitive Structure

The procedure for gathering data to reveal consumers' cognitive structures is to give respondents simple tasks involving the competitive service class. Subjects are required to verbalize the salient concepts or distinctions they use to differentiate among these types of providers. However, it is not these elements by themselves that are of primary importance (for this would be like typical qualitative research). Rather, it is the linkages among these and other elements in consumers' cognitive structure that leads to developing an understanding of the total perceptual framework.

To identify the full set of linkages connecting means to ends, consumers are given a laddering task (Gutman and Reynolds, 1979; Reynolds, 1982). Laddering consists of a series of directed probes based on mentioned distinctions the individual has with respect to the competitive service class. The purpose of the laddering is to force the consumer up the "ladder of abstraction" -- i.e., to uncover the structural aspects of consumer knowledge as modeled by the means-end chain.

The first step in analyzing the large number of laddering responses is to conduct a thorough content analysis of all the elicited concepts. Then each thought/response from each subject is assigned a category code. All laddering responses are now expressed in a set of standard concepts.

What remains is to identify the linkages between the concepts, the arcs of the network model. We begin by constructing a square matrix in which the rows and columns are denoted by the concept codes developed in the content analysis. The unit of analysis is an "adjacent" pair of concepts -- a linked pair of responses from the laddering task. That is, whenever the row concept was the probe stimulus that elicited the column concept, an entry is made into that cell. Thus the total entries in any cell of the matrix correspond to the number of times (across all subjects) that particular concept (row) directly elicited the other concept (column). It is from these data that the overall structure map of means-end relations relating to the service category usage is determined (Olson and Reynolds, in press).

THE RELATION BETWEEN IMAGE AND ADVERTISING STRATEGY

In thinking about the application of these procedures to the services area, the concept of image will be helpful. After all, it is an image that an advertising strategy seeks to create, firm up, or maintain. Image can be most usefully defined as a network of memory linkages associating a discriminating attribute to a desirable consequence which, in turn, satisfies a higher level value. The only way image can become a reality is when products or services are related to self at the values level. And, it is only at the values level that products or services can be directly compared to self. That is, the product or service has to be given certain attributes which by a process of association evoke a positively valenced meaningful relation with respect to self.

In effect, what has been argued here is that image management is the relating of a product to self in a desired way. The strength of image being the strength of the connections. The quality of image being the degree to which the relevant higher order value is tapped. This, in essence, is what advertising strategy is all about. The remaining question, then, is whether this concept of image management applies equally well to strategy development with respect to services as it does to products.[1] To fully consider this question, we must first turn to a discussion of how services are classified.

CLASSIFICATIONS OF SERVICES

Many authors have contributed to the literature in defining services and their relation to products (Bateson, 1977; Judd, 1968; Shostack, 1978; Blois, 1974). The key criteria for defining services as opposed to products include intangibility, inseparability, and variability (Kotler, 1980, p.624). Intangibility suggests that it is difficult to inspect services before they are bought. Inseparability suggests that production and consumption occur simultaneously and that the source (be it a machine or a person) is necessarily present for the service to be rendered. And, variability suggests that the "who" and the "when" associated with a service are important -- that there is far less standardization with respect to services than there is for products.

Another aspect of intangibility comes from another part of its definition which means "incapability of forming a mental image." To the extent that this holds true for services, means that advertising strategy development based on image management as defined here is doomed to failure. However, there are all sorts of services, just as there are all sorts of products. Indeed, Levitt (1972, p. 41) has argued that "there is no such thing as service industries. There are only industries whose service components are greater or less than those of other industries. Everybody is in service." Such a viewpoint demands that we classify services as to the extent of their "service component."

Other major classifications of service are useful here, such as whether the service is equipment based or people based; and, whether or not the client's presence is necessary for the production of the service. It is the authors' contention that where the client's presence is necessary and the service is more people-based, a dynamic interactive situation is created such that it is most difficult to create a strong image leading to a viable advertising strategy.

The more control the service provider has over the situation, the more capable they are of creating a strong image. This, of course, allows for more standardization as well. But, this begs the question of how you get that image position in the first place -- most likely, such an image has to be created outside of the advertising arena, although it can be maintained and nurtured by advertising. Vidal Sassoon is a good example of this; the publicity he attained as a hair stylist carried over into the development of a company with the attendant efforts at image management.

The task of creating an appropriate "aura" is critical in such cases as it allows for maximum consumer anticipation. Thus, the role of advertising strategy development under conditions where the consumer is directly involved with, and participates in the production of the service which is personally administered, is to create optimal conditions for favorable perceptions to occur. Perhaps the service of "being psychoanalyzed" is the purest example of this circumstance. "Faith" or belief in one's analyst is critical to successful completition of therapy -- but, could a good advertising strategy be developed for an analyst? The problems in conceiving of such a strategy

make the point rather well. And, have you seen much good legal advertising lately (although much of the work is done without the client being present)? Again, it is possible, but difficult.

From the means-end theory perspective, the focus should be on key outcomes the service provides and the values driving these outcomes. Nuances will come from identifying behavior patterns (attributes) in the service provider that will trigger these desired outcomes.

At the opposite extreme, where the client's presence is not necessary, and the service depends heavily on equipment, image creation should not present any different problems than those (which are a lot) for a product. An example here is one-hour film developing services. All one has to do is to look in the window to see how the machine dominates the operator. Variability is reduced to a minimum, regardless of who actually performs the service.

Of course, there are many types of services that lie in between these two extremes. Banks are a good example of a service that has strong people components and has taken on strong equipment components with the onset of electronic banking. Electronic banking leads to standardization across occasions, but also leads to homogeneity among competitors, thus making it more difficult to create differentiable images. Airlines are another industry that lie between these two extremes. They, unlike banks, have a heavy equipment orientation, but have stressed their personnel as an approach to differentiation.

Perhaps one might add one more aspect of advertising strategy development that can uniquely distinguish services marketing from product marketing. The "product" doesn't care what you say about it -- the people providing the service may well care, and as a result, become an important part of the audience for the advertising. They have to conform to the image created by the advertising. As such they may be critical links in developing the executional framework for services advertising. This also relates to the issue of creating proper anticipations on the part of potential users of the service. The usage situation may be even more important in services marketing that in product marketing because situation is a more important component of consumption than for products. In effect, the consumption situation may impact "product design" for services as the situation contributes importantly to the dynamics of the services delivery environment.

EXAMPLE OF THE APPLICATION OF MEANS-END CHAIN ANALYSIS TO IMAGE DEVELOPMENT IN SERVICES MARKETING

The procedures for studying the content and organization of cognitive structure were discussed in an earlier section of this paper. To make matters more concrete, an example of a hierarchical structure map has been generated (without the benefit of actual data from consumers). It is more idfficult than one might think, to anticipate what such a map might look like -- consumers, as many of us have found, have more degrees of subtlety than some give them credit for. Airlines have been chosen as the service category for our example as they have strong equipment and people components. The first step in presenting the data is to present the "contents" of cognitive structure as would be uncovered in the research procedures. The element shown in Table 1 would come from content analyzing the responses obtained in the laddering procedure.

As can be seen in Table 1, the concrete attribute level includes such service elements as Advanced Seat Reservations, Ground Service, and On-Time Performance. Product components such as Aircraft Type, Aircraft Interior, Fares and Food Quality are also represented here. At the abstract attribute level are elements such as More Space, No

---

[1]The authors have applied this framework in several proprietary studies, including snack foods, convenience restaurants, soft drinks, hair products, and alcoholic beverages.

Distractions, and Dependability which are implied by more concrete attributes.

At the consequence level are functional consequences such as Saving Time, Tension Reduction, Able to Plan, and Can Do More which result from elements at the attribute level. Also at the consequence level are psycho-social consequences accruing to the person from the functional benefits he or she receives -- Personal Status, Ability To Cope, and Being In-Control. At the instrumental values level are Accomplishment and Safety; and, at the terminal values level are Self Esteem and Security.

The hierarchical structure map in Figure 1 shows the relations among the elements listed in Table 1. One way to examine such a map is to trace the "routes" from the bottom of the map to the top. As can be seen there are a number of ways of moving from the attribute level to the consequence level, and then to the values level. Advanced Seat Reservation, Aircraft Type and First Class Cabin all lead to More Space, which in turn, leads to Physical Comfort. Physical Comfort is an important node (also reached through No Distractions) leading to Status, Getting More Done, and Reducing Tension. These consequences are the gateways to higher order consequences and values level considerations.

Reduce Tension, itself, is also an important node in the hierarchical structure map. Save Time and Dependable lead into it; and, it represents a crossover point for the lower level attributes of Ground Service and On-Time Performance to reach up to the values of Accomplishment and Self Esteem. On the right side of the map, the functional benefits of Able to Plan and Prudent lead eventually to Security. On the far right side of the map, Food Quality leads to Enjoyment, but not to any higher order values. This has been done to demonstrate that preferences do not always tie in to higher values (on the other hand, actual data might have uncovered a link between Food Quality and Accomplishment/Self Esteem).

The box in Figure 1 contains the element, Personal Interaction, which was not listed in Table 1. This has been done in an effort to demonstrate a nuance which might represent something respondents did not explicitly say, but which was implicit in much of what they did say. It suggests that Personal Interaction is a key factor in translating Physical Comfort into a Relaxing Environment leading to feelings of being In-Control and eventually to Security. The suggestion here is that the flier gives up control when he or she makes a commitment to fly. These feelings of being locked in an artificial environment can be dealt with through the medium of personal interaction.

Strategic Direction

The opportunities for strategic direction afforded by the hierarchical structure map stem from the manner in which the map is constructed. The map represents the dominant connections between the key content elements across consumers. Creating an image positioning, then, is accomplished by tapping into higher level values. Having identified the central pathways already in existence, a strategy reinforcing the connected content elements can be specified, thereby making the strategy construct (the total pathway) maximally concordant. Using the Olson and Reynolds (in press) framework, strategies can be constructed by following what are determined to be the key pathways. It must be remembered, however, that the value to be tapped into must be important to whatever consumer group is the target. Thus, by making the links "tight," the strength of associations leading to a value becomes possible. By selecting the appropriate value (and pathway), the image positioning becomes a reality.

It must be noted, however, that prior to development of

strategic direction, a competitive advertising review must be undertaken using the same framework. This will avoid simply replicating an already entrenched position.

SUMMARY

This paper has extended use of a means-end interpretation of advertising strategy development to services. The nature of services as compared to products has been discussed, providing a basis for incorporating the unique aspects of services into the image development process. Further, research will more intensively examine differences among types of services with respect to image creation and strategy development. Using image creation and advertising strategy development as criteria for classifying services should provide a more realistic assessment of how (or whether) they differ from products. Such knowledge should be of use to service marketers in an environment which will become increasingly competitive as more and more disposable income is spent on services.

REFERENCES

Bateson, John (1977), "Do We Need Service Marketing," Marketing Consumer Services: New Insights, Report 77-115, Boston: Marketing Science Institute.

Blois, K.J. (1974), "The Marketing of Services: An Approach," European Journal of Marketing, 8 (Summer), 137-149.

Gutman, Jonathan (1982), "A Means-End Chain Model Based on Consumer Categorization Processes," Journal of Marketing, 46 (Spring), 60-72.

_____, and Thomas J. Reynolds (1979), "An Investigation of the Levels of Cognitive Abstraction Utilized by Consumers in Product Differentiation," in Attitude Research Under the Sun, John Eighmey, ed., Chicago: American Marketing Association, 128-150.

Howard, John A. (1977), Consumer Behavior: Application and Theory, New York: McGraw-Hill Book Company.

Judd, Robert (1968), "Similarities or Differences in Product and Service Retailing," Journal of Retailing, 43 (Winter), 1-9.

Kotler, Philip (1980), Principles of Marketing, Englewood Cliffs, N.J.: Prentice-Hall, Inc.

Levitt, Theodore (1972), "Production Line Approach to Service," Harvard Business Review, September-October, 41-52.

Olson, J.C. and Thomas J. Reynolds (in press), "Understanding Consumers' Cognitive Structures: Implications for Advertising Strategy," in Advertising and Consumer Psychology, Larry Percy and Arch Woodside, eds., Lexington Books.

Reynolds, Thomas J. (1982), "Advertising is Image Management," Keynote Address at The American Academy of Advertising Meeting, Lincoln, Nebraska.

Shostack, Lynn G. (1978), "The Service Marketing Frontier," in Annual Review of Marketing, Gerald Zaltman and Thomas V. Bonoma, eds., Pittsburgh: Graduate School of Business, University of Pittsburgh, and the American Marketing Association.

Young, Shirley and Barbara Feigin (1975), "Using the Benefit Chain for Improved Strategy Formulation," Journal of Marketing, 39 (July), 72-74.

TABLE 1. ELEMENTS OF COGNITIVE STRUCTURE FOR HYPOTHETICAL
          AIRLINES EXAMPLE

TERMINAL VALUES

    SELF ESTEEM
    SECURITY

INSTRUMENTAL VALUES

    ACCOMPLISHMENT
    SAFETY

PSYCHO-SOCIAL CONSEQUENCES

    PERSONAL STATUS
    ABLE TO COPE (WITH KIDS, WITH THE DAY)
    IN-CONTROL

FUNCTIONAL CONSEQUENCES

    RELAX (READ, SLEEP)
    REDUCE TENSION (FEEL AT EASE)
    GET MORE DONE
    ABLE TO PLAN
    PRUDENT (DON'T WASTE MONEY)
    LESS FATIGUE
    ENJOYMENT

ABSTRACT ATTRIBUTES

    MORE SPACE
    NO DISTRACTIONS (FROM KIDS, NON-BUSINESS TRAVELERS)
    DEPENDABLE
    BETTER VALUE
    RELAXING ENVIRONMENT
    PHYSICAL COMFORT

CONCRETE ATTRIBUTES

    ADVANCED SEAT RESERVATIONS
    AIRCRAFT TYPE (WIDE BODY, ETC)
    FIRST CLASS CABIN
    AIRCRAFT INTERIOR (COLOR, DESIGN, CLEANLINESS)
    GROUND SERVICE (EFFICIENT BAGGAGE CLAIM, TICKETING)
    ON-TIME PERFORMANCE
    FARES (DEALS, DISCOUNTS)
    FOOD (QUALITY, CHOICE)

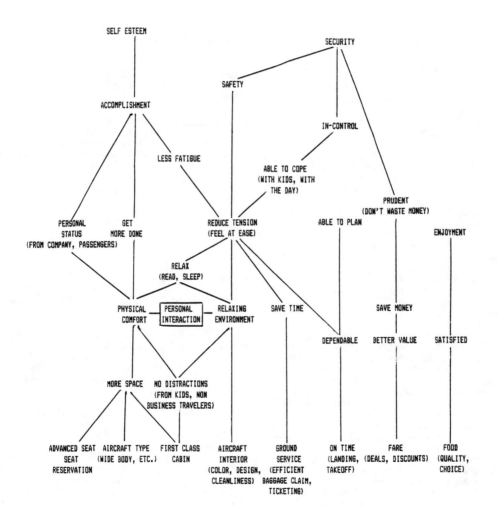

FIGURE 1. HIERARCHICAL STRUCTURE MAP FOR HYPOTHETICAL AIRLINE STUDY

THE DRAMATURGY OF SERVICES EXCHANGE: AN ANALYTICAL FRAMEWORK FOR SERVICES MARKETING

Stephen J. Grove, Oklahoma State University
Raymond P. Fisk, Oklahoma State University

deals with personal selling

ABSTRACT

This paper reviews some of the ways in which environmental and interpersonal characteristics may influence the consumer's perception of the services marketing exchange. This is followed by a discussion of a potentially useful framework for analyzing a service exchange offered by the sociological literature, termed "dramaturgy." Finally, some implications that dramaturgy may have for services marketing are examined and conclusions are presented.

INTRODUCTION

Ever since Kotler and Levy (1969) first suggested "broadening" the scope of marketing, the discipline has expanded its horizons beyond the confines of traditional economic transactions. Following the lead of Kotler (1972) and Bagozzi (1975), marketing has found new applications for the exchange framework, such as social and nonprofit marketing. In addition, traditional concepts have been re-examined from different perspectives. One outcome of such an endeavor has been the recognition that goods and services may represent different product categories. While controversy abounds over the dichotomization of products into goods and services, one cannot ignore the growing attention given to services marketing.

Whether services and goods are indeed distinct categories seems to be an issue not easily resolved. Many writers (Berry 1981; Eigler and Langeard 1977; Bessom and Jackson 1975; Shostack 1977; Bateson 1979) have gone to great lengths to demonstrate the qualitative difference between goods and services, while others (Wycham et al 1975; Enis and Roering 1981; Lovelock 1981) have noted that their similarities outweigh their uniqueness. It may well be that the distinction between goods and services is mainly one of emphasis. In this light, services and services marketing can be characterized as "more" intangible than goods and "more" likely to require simultaneous production and consumption (Berry 1981).

Another emphasis pertinent to services marketing which is recognized even by some who argue for a reconsolidation of the two product categories is that environmental and interpersonal influences are "more" critical in services evaluation (Bessom and Jackson 1975; Shostack 1977; Bateson 1979; Berry 1981; Lovelock 1981). Services and goods may be similar to the extent that they both offer the consumer a bundle of benefits (Enis and Roering 1981), yet marketing strategies associated with each may be different due to the greater degree of intangibility and simultaneity of production and consumption among services, as cited above. These aspects of services suggest that a keener awareness of the social and physical context of the marketing exchange is necessary in order to ensure consumer satisfaction (Berry 1981; Lovelock 1981). By understanding the symbolic meaning consumers attach to characteristics of each, strategies may be developed to create a more favorable impression of the service.

THE SOCIAL AND PHYSICAL CONTEXT OF SERVICE EXCHANGES

No marketing exchange occurs in a vacuum. Each time a transaction takes place--whether it is for profit or nonprofit, or involves goods or services--the interpersonal and environmental setting offer some measure of influence. Certainly, as Belk (1975) recognizes, these aspects of the exchange situation have the capacity to create favorable or unfavorable impressions. In the absence of a tangible product upon which to base one's evaluation of the exchange--such as in services marketing--the social and physical contexts increase in importance (Berry 1980, 1981; Lovelock 1979; Shostack 1979). The social interaction that facilitates the exchange and the environmental conditions within which it occurs are often employed by the consumer as cues to the quality of the service rendered. In the words of Bessom and Jackson (1975), "the appearance of the establishment and its personnel are often the only tangible aspects of a service." (p. 81). Based upon this observation, services marketers would do well to "tangiblize" their product through enhancing these aspects of the exchange (Bessom and Jackson 1975; Shostack 1977; Berry 1981). Specific ways in which this may be accomplished are discussed below.

The Social Setting

Aspects of the social setting which may be particularly influential with respect to the consumer's evaluation of a service include the appearance and demeanor of those involved in facilitating the exchange. From the consumer's perspective, those assisting in the production of the service may represent the service itself. However, as Berry (1981) notes, services may vary in the degree of personal contact they afford to the consumer. In high contact services such as airlines or banks, the interpersonal influences are of particular concern, while in low contact services such as public utility companies they may not be of such great relevance. Nevertheless, since services are generally consumed and not possessed, the performance of those providing the service offers some clue as to the quality of the product.

Under high personal contact situations, those taking part in the provision of the service (and consequentially the service itself) may be evaluated in terms of their technical and customer-related skills, personalities, attitudes toward their work, consistency of quality performance, and appearance (Berry 1981; Bessom and Jackson 1975; Lovelock 1981). Right or wrong, all of these offer the consumer some tangible evidence of a basically intangible product. The unfriendly bank teller, the inarticulate mechanic, the disenchanted waitress, and the slovenly-attired merchant create a negative image which influences one's satisfaction with the service. However, the services marketer who understands the potential impact of these interpersonal influences can utilize this knowledge to create a favorable impression of the service. This may be accomplished by involving in the production of the service those who are adequately trained, possess strong interpersonal skills, enjoy their work, and are well-groomed.

Certainly, other aspects of the social setting may impact upon the consumer's evaluation of the service. Social conditions such as crowding, presence of others not directly involved in the exchange, and demographic characteristics (age, sex, race, etc.) of those providing the service, among others, may influence the consumer's assessments. These, however, seem to be less critical as general determinants of consumer's satisfaction with services than those cited above.

The Physical Setting

Also important as a factor influencing consumer satisfaction with a services exchange is the physical setting within which it occurs (Bessom and Jackson 1975; Lovelock 1979; Shostack 1977; Bateson 1979). While the physical setting may have an effect upon the exchange of goods as well as services, it is suggested that the setting's symbolic value has greater impact upon the evaluation of a service. This, again, is largely due to the relative absence of tangible product characteristics with which to assess in the exchange of a service.

Kotler (1973) suggests that the physical setting of an exchange may be described in terms of "atmospherics," including visual, aural, olfactory, and tactile perceptions. Noting that the physical environment has the potential to influence one's impression of the service (Shostack 1977), such characteristics as the colors or brightness of the surroundings, the volume and pitch of the sounds employed and/or present at the setting, the scents and freshness of the air, and the temperature prevailing at the time of the exchange may all help to shape a consumer's feelings concerning a service rendered. In addition, the use of space and the style of furnishing, as well as the presence or absence of other "clues," may provide the consumer with tangible indications of the service.

While these aspects of the physical environment may be rather subtle in effect, the implication is that the services marketer may manipulate the physical setting to create a positive perception of the exchange situation and ultimately the service itself. It seems intuitively obvious that the exact manipulations required to accomplish this may vary depending upon the nature of the impression sought. Whatever is attempted, the marketer's chief concern is to satisfy the consumer's expectations. For instance, if the consumer expects a low-cost, no-frills service, the marketer would be encouraged to create such an image through the physical surroundings. However, if the service is to be positioned as a "specialty" product, the atmospherics and other physical cues should reflect the image desired.

In essence, as Shostack (1977, p. 77) notes, service realities appear to be shaped to a large extent by the things that the consumer can comprehend with his five senses. Accepting this and the idea that services are generally "experiential" (Lovelock 1979), it is suggested that management of the physical environment should be one of the service marketer's highest priorities (Shostack 1977).

Viewed together, it becomes apparent that it is difficult to separate service's personnel or environment from the consumer (Bateson 1979), and that both may play a role in influencing the consumer's evaluation of a service. While many suggestions have been offered in the literature with respect to how management might best create a favorable impression in these regards, these suggestions have not been grounded in any particular theory or framework. Within the sociological literature, however, there is an analytical perspective known as "dramaturgy" which addresses these issues.

DRAMATURGY

The dramaturgical perspective in sociology has its roots in the Symbolic Interactionist school of thought. The major premise underlying symbolic interactionism is that man is a symbol user and interacts with others based upon interpretations assigned to different features present at the behavioral setting. Symbolic interactionism is consistent with Bagozzi's thinking (1975) concerning symbolic exchange. Any action or object, including gestures, expressions, properties of the physical environment, language, etc., has the potential to influence one's assessment of the interactional situation, and, ultimately, one's reciprocating behavior. As a "subtheory" of this perspective, dramaturgy cloaks social interaction in a theatrical framework utilizing terms and concepts familiar to a dramatic production. As such, dramaturgy is not a means of explaining behavior, but rather a description of it. The focus of dramaturgy "is not to discover or to impute to human behavior causal kinds of relations. . .the concern is simply to describe the process of human behaving" (Brissett and Edgley 1975, p. 4).

Dramaturgy owes its early origins to the writings of Kenneth Burke (1945, 1950, 1968). In discussing what he termed "Dramatism," Burke (1945) noted that imagery at the end of a behavioral sequence determines how individuals form attitudes toward what they are doing, and that the order and understanding upon which this imagery is based arises in and through communication. He maintained that the process of assigning meaning to actions can be analyzed using five concepts: act - what takes place in thought or deed; scene - the background or situation in which the act occurs; agent - the actor(s) involved; agency - how the act was performed by the agent; and purpose - why the act was performed. One's perception of this pentad of concepts determines one's understanding of the interaction taking place. According to Burke, man continually seeks motives or understanding of behavior by evaluating these components. In other words, the meaning of a behavioral situation is defined in the process of interaction.

Much of the contemporary dramaturgical perspective is based upon the work of Erving Goffman and his book The Presentation of Self in Everyday Life (1959). Using as a framework the metaphor of the theatrical performance, Goffman examines the structure of social interaction that emerges when people are in one another's presence. Of particular importance, according to Goffman (1959, p. 254), is the maintenance of a definition of the behavioral situation which must be able to persist even in the face of a multitude of potential disruptions. The implication generated is that the actor as a symbol user, manipulator, and communicator, strives to create and maintain a definition of reality to which other parties respond. Noting that the meanings assigned to the communications may be partially a function of previous learning, Goffman stresses that their validation must occur during or after the behavior. In this sense, the observer's understanding of the social interaction unfolds as the interaction occurs.

Like Burke, Goffman utilizes a number of terms derived from a theatrical framework to describe the properties of social interaction. Providing much greater detail, these terms and the meanings they convey help to organize and depict the dramaturgical essence of social behavior. Some of the more important concepts employed by Goffman (1959) which may be relevant for the analysis of services marketing include the following:[1]

Performance

Performance is a term given to the total activity of an individual which occurs during a period marked by the individual's continuous presence before a particular set of observers or "audience," and which has some impact upon them (1959, p. 22). A performance may be characterized as sincere, in which case the actor is taken in by his own act, or cynical, wherein the performance is viewed by the actor as only a means to an end.

In order to communicate a believable performance to the audience, the actor may intentionally or unwittingly employ certain expressive equipment collectively termed the front. Included in this collection is the setting, involving a combination of effects offered by the decor, furnishings, and physical layout evident at the performance's location, and the personal front, involving aspects of the actor's personal appearance and manner such as his dress, facial expressions, demographic profile, and personality. When consistent with one another, the personal front and setting combine to create a source of interpretive information for the observer. With this in mind, it is understandable that the actor may seek to conceal or underplay any aspects of the front which might be incompatible with the performance he desires. Certainly, the reality portrayed by the performance is a very sensitive one and can be easily upset by even a minor contradiction.

[1]The following discussion borrows heavily from Goffman's work, The Presentation of Self in Everyday Life.

Performance Teams

Goffman and the dramaturgical perspective recognize that the definition of the situation fostered by an actor is often part of a projection created through cooperation with others. The term "performance team" or simply "team" is given to the set of individuals who cooperate to create a single definition of reality (1959, p. 79). The team may be relative to the performance situation--that is emergent at the scene, itself--or a part of the enduring social structure. Whichever the case, the team members' interactions foster a single impression to which the audience responds.

Involved in this collusion of sorts is a common bond among the members of the team not to undermine or disrupt the performance. In essence, those taking part in the show have a reciprocal agreement to respect one another's dependence upon each other; realizing that their behavior is a performance, it would be easy to shatter its reality by "unmasking" the other actors involved. With this in mind, actors pay crucial respect to each other's rights of familiarity in the quest of a believable performance.

Regions and Region Behavior

The dramaturgical perspective notes that different regions--places bound to some degree by perceptual barriers (Goffman 1959, p. 106)--reflect different behaviors. A front region is where a performance is given and it is open to the audience's inspection. Consequently, behavior in the front region requires attention to standards meeting the audience's approval. A back region (or backstage) is normally beyond the audience's inspection. Here, the performer can drop his "front" and step out of character. Often in the backstage, actors may be found rehearsing their parts or memorizing their scripts, and "teams" may be seen running through their "performance" in order to correct its flaws.

The backstage and front regions are usually kept quite separate due to the risk involved with the audience's possible discovery of behavior contradictory to the actor's performance. Beyond the potential observation of imperfection of performance, there is the possibility that the audience may be exposed to all kinds of improper behavior not found in the front region, such as cursing, slovenly demeanor, and complaining. In order to guard against such a mishap, careful attention is given to keeping the passageway between the two regions closed to the audience.

Aspects of Impression Management

Of key importance to the dramaturgical perspective as noted by Goffman is the issue of impression management. Ultimately, the actors involved in the staging of a performance are concerned with creating a believable show for the audience's approval. To this end, certain "defensive practices" aimed at reducing the probability of an untimely "scene" are expected from the performance teammates. Specifically, dramaturgical loyalty, discipline, and circumspection are called for.

Dramaturgical loyalty refers to the notion that teammates must act as if they have accepted a moral responsibility to sustain definitions associated with their performances (Goffman 1959, p. 212). Basically, this suggests that the actors should avoid disclosing secrets of their performance to the audience or others not intimately involved in the production. Betrayal of this loyalty could have a great impact upon the credibility of the show.

Related to this notion is dramaturgical discipline (1959, p. 216). Here, the observation is that the performers are obliged to remember their parts and to avoid unwittingly committing gestures or mistakes which might destroy the performance. This may involve being able to keep one's

personal problems away from the "front region" and exercising self control in the execution of one's part. In essence, the actors must at all times demonstrate the demeanor and decorum necessary for a successful production.

Another defensive practice noted by Goffman (1959, p. 218) is dramaturgical circumspection. Similar to the strategies noted above, this practice is aimed at creating a favorable impression. The focus of attention in this case is upon the necessity of the performers to determine in advance how best to stage the show. Knowledge of the audience and proper casting of the parts may be of crucial importance in this respect. While all contingencies can never be controlled, a certain amount of circumspection is usually needed for a successful performance.

The above treatment of dramaturgy by no means exhausts all of the concepts available for analyzing social situations. However, those cited above seem to have particular analytical potential for describing the services exchange context. Certainly, other concepts derived from the dramaturgical perspective may also be of value; many additionally pertinent ideas have not been explored in the concern for brevity.

DRAMATURGICAL APPLICATIONS OF THE SERVICES EXCHANGE

Several similarities exist between the services marketing literature and the dramaturgical perspective on behavior. Both are interested in the strategies and actions required to create and maintain a favorable impression before an audience, and both recognize that this may be accomplished through the successful management of "expression given off" by the actors and their physical surroundings (Goffman 1959, p. 2). Reflecting insights similar to those of numerous services marketing scholars, Goffman (1959, p. 77) notes that

. . .performance serves mainly to express the characteristics of the task that is performed and not the characteristics of the performer. Thus one finds that service personnel, whether in profession, bureaucracy, business, or craft, enliven their manner with movements which express proficiency and integrity, but whatever this manner conveys about them, often its major purpose is to establish a favorable definition of their services or product.

Because of the congruence between the interests of services marketing and of dramaturgy, an examination of dramaturgy's applicability to services marketing is warranted.

Perhaps the major contribution which dramaturgy may offer services marketing is a unifying framework for analyzing the exchange situation. While many marketing writers have posited valuable suggestions concerning how to create consumer satisfaction with a services exchange (Berry 1980, 1981; Lovelock 1979; Shostack 1977; Bateson 1979; Eigler and Langeard 1977; Bessom and Jackson 1975), these suggestions have seldom been grounded in any singular perspective or theory. Dramaturgy provides a conceptual foundation complete with a developed vocabulary which has the potential to facilitate understanding and communication about services marketing.[2]

For a long time marketers have realized the importance that consumers assign to symbols present in the exchange of goods and services (Levy 1959). The dramaturgical perspective aptly articulates the processes which operate when the services consumer interacts with the symbolic world. The notion of the "performance" offered by dramaturgy also suggests that the services marketer needs to be attentive to

[2]Lovelock (1981) approached this realization in his treatment of the services marketer as a dramatist. However, his brief discussion does not embrace the notion of dramaturgy of Goffman's work.

the "personal front" (appearance and behavior) of those
representing his firm. In addition, the "setting" (physical surroundings) must be carefully controlled to exude the
proper impression. Ultimately the performance of service
actors is greatly enhanced if they are successful in their
impression management. Figure 1 displays three dramaturgical components of service performance. Each of these
components of the performance has potential symbolic meaning for the consumer, and, consequently, may influence his
satisfaction.

FIGURE 1

DRAMATURGICAL COMPONENTS OF SERVICE PERFORMANCE

In order to ensure a positive evaluation from the services consumer, the dramaturgical perspective suggests that
the "performance teams" (those cooperating to perform the
service) must abide by the conventions of "dramaturgical
loyalty" (keeping secrets related to the service sacred,
"dramaturgical discipline" (learning one's part or providing the service and controlling against mistakes or the
intrusion of personal problems), and "dramaturgical circumspection" (coordinating the roles of those involved with
the service in order to assure a good performance).
Certainly, careful selection of the team members and
delegation of responsibilities among them, as well as a
keen knowledge of the "audience" (those receiving the service) and its background (a concern similar to market
segmentation) can increase the likelihood of consumer
satisfaction. In addition, attention to prohibiting the
consumer from entering the "backstage" (behind the setting
where the service is performed) can help assure a favorable
consumer response.

The relevance of the dramaturgical perspective is
strongly dependent on two essential dimensions of services.
First, the dramaturgical perspective is particularly useful
to those service organizations that serve many people
simultaneously rather than provide individualized service.
Examples of such services would include restaurants,
hotels, professional sports, hospitals, and of course, entertainment. The risks of failure are greater for these
organizations. In essence, a failure to successfully stage
their service will be witnessed by a large number of people
rather than one or two persons. Second, dramaturgy is also
more relevant to services that have a high degree of contact between the service provider and the customer. Examples of such services would include physicians, lawyers,
educators, restaurants, and hotels. For such services, the
amount of direct contact between the customer and the service provider offers an excellent opportunity for dramaturgical analysis. In essence, the more customers and the
more personal contact the service provider seeks to maintain, the greater the usefulness of the dramaturgical perspective.

Figure Two displays a matrix developed with the dimensions of "audience size" (which we have defined as the
number of people being served simultaneously by the service
provider) and "contact" (which we have defined as the ratio
of the amount of front stage time to back stage time).
Among these four cells, dramaturgy is less relevant to services in Cell One, such as car repair, because of small
audience size and limited contact. However, dramaturgy is
very relevant to the services in Cell Four. For simplicity, we will focus on restaurants as a case example of the
usefulness of dramaturgical perspective.

FIGURE 2

DIMENSIONS OF DRAMATURGICAL SIGNIFICANCE

| | | Contact | |
		Low	High
Audience Size	Low	(1) Car Repair / Watch Repair / Shoe Repair	(2) Physician / Barber / Lawyer
	High	(3) Utility / Insurance / Discount Retailer	(4) Airlines / Spectator Sports / Restaurants

Audience Size = Number of people receiving the service
simultaneously.
Contact = Amount of time front stage/amount of time back
stage.

Using a restaurant as a specific example because of
its high contact and large audience size, one finds a
number of possible applications. For instance, dramaturgy
suggests that the performance of the waiters, waitresses,
and other service personnel is contingent upon how well
they, as team members, meet the dramaturgical obligations
of loyalty, discipline, and circumspection. A sour demean-
or caused by a personal problem or the inability to polite-
ly deal with a discourteous patron could influence the
consumer satisfaction with the service in general. Likewise, a lack of coordination among the bus boys, waitresses, cooks, and cashiers resulting in a long wait for the
patron could be ill-perceived. Certainly, undermining a
fellow worker's performance by revealing private information concerning his contribution--for instance, disclosing
the secret ingredients in the cook's masterpiece--could
have a negative effect on the service evaluation (particularly if the ingredient is something unattractive to the
consumer).

Obviously, the staging of the performance in terms of
its setting, and the personal fronts of the workers in the
front region is of great concern in a restaurant. The
"atmospherics" (Kotler 1973), and other "expressive equipment" (Goffman 1959) as well as the manner and appearance
of the service personnel create an impression. Uncleared
tables, dirty silverware, a cold draft, dim lighting, and a
brazen waitress can make even the most superbly prepared
dish taste like yesterday's oatmeal. On the other hand, a
well-appointed dining room supported by neat and efficient
personnel will do much to enhance the patron's satisfaction
with the restaurant's product. However, to reiterate an
earlier observation, satisfaction is ultimately a matter of
realized expectations and if the patron enjoys and expects
an ambiance associated with the former scenario, it is
probable that he would be dissatisfied with the latter.

Dramaturgy further suggests the necessity of keeping
separate the front region from the backstage. In a restaurant this is an especially crucial concern. The misguided
patron who mistakingly stumbles into uncharted reaches of
the restaurant's kitchen while seeking the men's room is
often exposed to all sorts of discomforting spectacles.
Foul language, inappropriate behavior, messy working conditions, and the uncomely vision of his family's meal in its
various stages of preparation often offer the patron an
image contradicting the impression given by the front.
Needless to say, such an experience can have dire consequences for the patron's satisfaction.

However, dramaturgy can also suggest an alternative to keeping the kitchen in the backstage: move it to the front region in full view of the restaurant patrons. This of course means that the kitchen will have to be kept very clean and be run very well. Many customers will be impressed with the appearance of the kitchen area and fascinated by observing the food being prepared. This approach would also have the advantage of eliminating common consumer beliefs about dirty kitchens. This strategy, in fact, has been successfully employed by numerous establishments.

CONCLUSION

Dramaturgy provides a unifying framework for describing and communicating aspects of the services exchange. The restaurant example above illustrates but a few of the concepts and insights offered by the dramaturgical perspective. Of particular interest is the use of dramaturgy as a tool in understanding the contextual dimensions of an exchange setting and how they may influence the observer's perception. Cognizant of this knowledge, services marketers could develop strategies to "tangibilize" their products (Berry 1981).

Arguments have been presented in the services marketing literature indicating the importance of such an endeavor for creating and maintaining consumer satisfaction. In the final analysis, the goal of any organization, especially retail firms, is to demonstrate a "differential advantage" over its competitors. In this respect, attention to the dramaturgical details of exchange may enable the services marketer to deliver consistently high levels of quality leading to positive consumer evaluations (Lovelock 1981). This is of crucial importance in light of the evidence suggesting the powerful impact of "word of mouth" advertising for services marketing (Eigler and Langeard 1977; Johnson 1969; Lovelock 1979; Weinberger and Brown 1977).

However, dramaturgy's potential is not limited to services marketing alone. The scope of the dramaturgical perspective can be extended to include any situation in which the participants are engaged in a "conspiracy of exchange" (Mitchell 1978, p. 106). Particularly relevant extensions may be made into the areas of retail management in general and personal selling. Still, due to the intangible nature and the concurrent production and consumption of the services product, dramaturgy seems to have its greatest potential with services marketing.

REFERENCES

Bagozzi, Richard P. (1975), "Marketing as Exchange," Journal of Marketing, Vol. 39 (October), 32-39.

Bateson, John (1979), "Why We Need Services Marketing," in Conceptual and Theoretical Development in Marketing, O. C. Ferrel, Stephen W. Brown, and Charles W. Lamb, eds., Chicago: AMA, 131-146.

Belk, Russell W. (1975), "Situational Variables and Consumer Behavior," Journal of Consumer Research, Vol. 2, 157-164.

Berry, L. L. (1980), "Services Marketing is Different," Business (May-June), 24-29.

_____ (1981), "Perspectives on the Retailing of Services" in Theory in Retailing: Traditional and Nontraditional Sources, Ronald W. Stampfl and Elizabeth C. Hirschman, eds., Chicago: AMA, 9-20.

Bessom, Richard and Donald Jackson (1975), "Service Retailing: A Strategical Marketing Approach," Journal of Retailing, Vol. 51 (Summer), 75-84.

Brissett, Dennis and Charles Edgely (1975), Life As Theatre: A Dramaturgical Sourcebook, Chicago: Aldine Publishing Co.

Burke, Kenneth (1945), A Grammar of Motives, New York: Prentice-Hall.

_____ (1950), A Rhetoric of Motives, New York: Prentice-Hall.

_____ (1968), "Dramatism," in International Encyclopedia of the Social Sciences, VII, New York: Macmillan, 445-452.

Eigler, Pierre and Eric Langeard (1977), "A New Approach to Service Marketing," Marketing Consumer Services: New Insights, in Eigler et al, eds., Cambridge: Marketing Science Institute, 31-58.

Enis, Ben M. and Kenneth J. Roering (1981), "Services Marketing: Different Products, Similar Strategy," in Marketing of Services, James H. Donnelly, and William R. George, eds., Chicago: AMA, 1-4.

Goffman, Erving (1959), The Presentation of Self in Everyday Life, New York: Doubleday and Co.

Hawkins, Del I., Kenneth A. Coney, and Roger J. Best (1980), Consumer Behavior: Implications for Marketing Strategy, Dallas: Business Publications, Inc.

Johnson, Eugene (1969), "Are Goods and Services Different? An Exercise in Marketing Theory," Unpublished Dissertation, Washington University.

Kotler, Phillip and Sidney J. Levy (1969), "Broadening the Concept of Marketing," Journal of Marketing, Vol. 33 (January), 10-15.

_____ (1972), "A Generic Concept of Marketing," Journal of Marketing, Vol. 36 (April), 46-54.

_____ (1973), "Atmospherics As A Marketing Tool," Journal of Retailing, (Winter), 48-64.

Levy, Sydney J. (1959), "Symbols for Sale," Harvard Business Review, (July-August), 117-124.

Lovelock, Christopher (1979), "Theoretical Contributions from Services and Non-Business Marketing," in Conceptual and Theoretical Development in Marketing, O. C. Ferrell, Stephen W. Brown, and Charles W. Lamb, eds., Chicago: AMA, 147-165.

_____ (1981), "Why Marketing Management Needs to be Different for Services," in Marketing of Services, James H. Donnelly and William R. George, eds., Chicago: AMA, 5-9.

Mitchell, Jack N. (1978), Social Exchange, Dramaturgy, and Ethnomethodology: Toward A Pragmatic Synthesis, New York: Elsiver North Holland, Inc.

Shostack, Lynn G., "Breaking Free From Product Marketing," Journal of Marketing (April), 73-80.

Weinberger, Marc G. and Stephen W. Brown (1977), "A Difference in Information Influences: Services vs. Goods," Journal of the Academy of Marketing Sciences, Vol. 5 (Fall), 390-402.

Wycham, R. G., P. T. Fitzroy, and G. D. Mandry (1975), "Marketing of Services: An Evaluation of Theory," European Journal of Marketing, Vol. 9, 59-67.

THE SELF-SERVICE CUSTOMER - EMPIRICAL FINDINGS

John E.G. Bateson, The London Business School

ABSTRACT

This paper presents empirical findings that suggest that
there is a proportion of the population who find "doing
it for themselves" intrinsically attractive. Across a
number of services there is a group of people who, without reward of any kind, are prepared to work in the
service firm, e.g. to pump their own gas. The data also
suggests that "propensity to participate" in this way may
carry over from one service to another.

INTRODUCTION

One of the biggest problems facing the service sector is
that of productivity. This is a problem at both the
macro and micro levels. At the macro level it has been
argued for a number of years that the productivity of the
developed economies is being depressed by their growing
service content (Fuchs 1968). At the micro level the
heavy labour content of service firms means that even
small improvements in labour productivity can make major
impacts on profitability.

To date, two broad methods of improving productivity
within the service sector have been suggested. Levitt in
his pioneering articles (1972, 1976) has suggested the
application of a "production line approach". This
approach was developed in the manufacturing sector and
involves the substitution of capital for labour and the
deskilling of jobs. He uses McDonalds as an example of
a company that has used hard technology and soft technology, the systems analysis type of approach, to achieve
productivity gains.

Gartner and Riessman (1974) suggested that when thinking
of the service sector it was insufficient to talk only of
labour and capital intensity. They proposed that the
amount of work performed by the customer should be recog-
nised through a measure of "consumer intensity". Their
argument was that consumers were being called upon to increase their participation in the production of the
service they were buying. This same idea was developed
by Lovelock and Young (1978) who provided examples of many
ways in which the customer was being induced to increase
the amount of work they did for the service firm.

The purpose of this research was to investigate this
latter method of improving productivity, but to look at
it from the customers' perspective. In particular, it
was designed to address two questions:

- Is there a proportion of the population who find
  "doing it themselves" in this way intrinsically
  attractive, i.e. is there a group of people who
  would do this "work" for the firm without the
  usual incentives of price or convenience?

- Does that "propensity to participate" carry over
  from one service to another?

METHODOLOGY

The initial phases consisted of exploratory research
which highlighted that consumers' choice between the
different ways of receiving a service was highly influenced by situation specific variables (e.g. What
is the occasion? What time is it? Who is in the

party? etc.). To overcome this, situational scenarios
were developed which were realistic from the standpoint
of the respondents, controlled for a wide range of factors known to affect behaviour (including monetary incentives) and offered respondents a choice between two alternative service delivery systems. Appendix A gives an example.

In total six scenarios were developed:

1. At a service station -- pump your own gas versus
   having an attendant do it for you.

2. At a bank -- using an automatic teller machine
   versus using the services of a human teller.

3. At a quick service restaurant -- getting your own
   food at the counter versus receiving table service
   from a waiter or waitress.

4. At an airport -- carry your own bags onto an aircraft with special storage facilities versus
   checking your bags.

5. At a hotel -- using a self-service food and drink
   dispenser versus obtaining the same food and drink
   from room service.

6. At a travel agent -- purchasing travellers
   cheques from an automatic teller machine versus
   buying them from a clerk.

For each scenario, respondents were asked to indicate on
what percentage of such occasions they would use the more
participative alternative. Thus, the respondents gave an
intention measure.

The survey was conducted by mail and two different questionnaires were used. The first (Questionnaire A)
included scenarios 1, 2 and 3; the second (Questionnaire
B) scenarios 1, 4, 5 and 6. The questionnaires were pre-
tested in a pilot mailing.

The Sample

Questionnaire A was mailed to a stratified random sample
of 1,500 customers of three financial institutions located
in three different regions of the United States. Five
hundred of these customers were known to be users of a new
self-service facility. Questionnaire B was mailed to a
stratified random sample of 1,000 customers of a nationwide financial institution equally divided between users
and non-users of a new self-service facility offered by
that institution.

The overall response rate was 57.5% after deducting mail
returned as undeliverable. The response rate for questionnaire (A) was 52.5% and for questionnaire (B) 67.5%.
The overall differences in response rates between the two
samples reflected subsample-related variables rather than
questionnaire-related variables. The results are consistent with less than up to date mailing lists and known
poorer return procedures for undeliverable mail in certain
cities.

As a general comment, a more than 50% response rate to a
long questionnaire mailed to a nonspecialist audience and
dealing with a general interest (as opposed to highly
specialised) topic is a reasonably good result. Although
some nonresponse bias may be introduced by the failure of

many subjects to respond, it should be emphasised that the research interest was <u>not</u> in identifying and generalising the proportions within the population who might be expected to behave in a particular way.

RESULTS

The responses provided a distribution of intended behaviour for each scenario. Examination of these distributions isolated distinct concentrations of response at the extremes of each scale and a more diffuse distribution between these extremes. For further analysis the distributions were therefore broken into the following groups:

Group	Would Accept the More Participative Alternative
Nonparticipators	in 0% of all occasions
Low Participators	in 1 to 39% of all occasions
Medium Participators	in 40 to 60% of all occasions
High Participators	in 61 to 99% of all occasions
Full Participators	in 100% of all occasions

Figure 1 summarises the size of the resulting groups for each scenario given in the two questionnaires.

A number of points need to be made about the interpretation of Figure 1. Questionnaire A generated a total of 765 responses and B a total of 584 responses. However a screening question appeared before the description of each scenario. Thus, before the gas station scenario was presented, respondents were asked: "Do you ever buy gas?" A negative response to this question resulted in the respondents being asked to skip the scenario and proceed to the next question, since some familiarity with the situation was required for the response to be meaningful.

It was encouraging to find that there was no significant difference between Sample X and Sample Y in the relative size of the groups for the gas station scenario. (This was, of course, the only scenario that was common to both questionnaires.)

Before exploring in more detail these findings, it is important to check the validity of the "intended behaviour measure". Three of the service firms providing mailing lists also indicated individual respondents were users or nonusers of a particular self-service facility, so it is possible to compare actual behaviour (at the time the mailing list was compiled) with stated intentions (as expressed in response to the relevant service scenario question).

The results are shown in Figure 2. For service firms No.1 and No.2, users are concentrated in the groups of maximum or high participators, nonusers are concentrated in the groups of non or low participators. For service firm No.3 the users are concentrated in the medium, high and maximum participation categories, whereas the nonusers are more generally distributed across all the categories. In this case, the service had only recently been established and differed significantly from that portrayed in the scenario. Thus, the nonusers of that service may not yet have made a conscious choice about the self-service option and may indeed have not even heard about it.

The overlaps between actual and intended behaviour is very high. The chi-square tests show that the association between user and nonuser categories on the one hand and participation level on the other are statistically significant. This is all the more striking because the intention measure is based on a highly constrained situation with no incentives such as price for the customer.

The table shows that for each scenario there was a sizeable group who would choose the participative approach on all occasions for a particular service, even though the scenario actually controlled many of the benefits of that approach. Thus, the gas station scenario specified equal prices and waiting lines of equal length; the bank scenario specified a transaction during banking hours; and the food service scenario specified equal prices and lines. Apparently, some people find participation inherently attractive; likewise, nonparticipators find the more participative alternative inherently unattractive.

However, the distributions vary widely across scenarios. For three of the selected services, the group of nonparticipators is much larger than the group of maximum participators. The opposite is true of other services. In every case the number of medium and high participators is quite large, ranging from 34 percent to 55 percent of all respondents. They are not totally enthusiastic about the participative alternative offered to them, but they are not against it either. Their willingness to adopt the participative option may depend on appropriate incentives and a good communications strategy.

FIGURE 1

PERCENTAGE OF SAMPLE FALLING INTO EACH PARTICIPATION LEVEL GROUP FOR EACH SCENARIO

	QUESTIONNAIRE A			QUESTIONNAIRE B			
	Gas Station	Bank	Quick Service Restaurant	Gas Station	Airline	Hotel	Travel Service
Groups:							
Non participator	31%	22%	13%	32%	11%	8%	8%
Low participator	24%	23%	32%	29%	18%	20%	13%
Medium participator	15%	20%	27%	15%	12%	21%	28%
High participator	24%	24%	21%	19%	33%	31%	27%
Full participator	6%	11%	7%	5%	29%	20%	24%
n	659	731	735	533	522	538	439

FIGURE 2

ACTUAL BEHAVIOUR VERSUS INTENDED BEHAVIOUR IN USING A SELF SERVICE FACILITY

Intended Behaviour Participation Level	Actual Behaviour by Customers of:					
	Service Firm No. 1		Service Firm No. 2		Service Firm No. 3	
	Nonuser	User	Nonuser	User	Nonuser	User
Non	32%	3%	29%	5%	15%	3%
Low	42	8	36	10	20	8
Medium	11	18	19	22	32	25
High	13	55	10	38	19	33
Full	2	16	6	25	14	31
	100%	100%	100%	100%	100%	100%
	$x^2 = 93.0$ $p > .0001$		$x^2 = 92.9$ $p > .0001$		$x^2 = 49.4$ $p > .0001$	

Overlap of Participator Groups Across Scenarios

Is a consumer's propensity to act in a participative or nonparticipative manner in one service situation an indication of how that person will behave in other situations? In other words, is participativeness a general personal characteristic or simply a situation-specific one?

In an attempt to answer this question, respondents' membership in different participative groups across scenarios were examined (four for Sample X and three for Sample Y). To maintain a reasonable cell size, full and high participators were collapsed into a single group, termed "participative", while non and low participators were combined in a "nonparticipative" group. If the revised groups are considered independent of each other, we can calculate a statistical probability of overlap based on the groups' proportion within the overall population. We can then go on to develop an "overlap index" of observed incidence of overlap divided by the expected incidence. The box below shows an example of this calculation.

> Consider the overlap between the nonparticipative groups for the airline and travellers cheque scenarios. In the former instance, 30.2 percent of respondents (for whom the necessary data were available) were in the nonparticipative group; the relevant figure for the travellers cheque scenario was 21.1 percent.
>
> If these two groups were statistically independent of one another, we would expect only 6.4 percent (0.302 x 0.211) of all respondents to be in the nonparticipative groups for both scenarios -- in other words, to overlap. But in reality, 9.5 percent of respondents were in the overlap. Thus, the overlap index is 0.095 divided by 0.064, which equals 1.48.

These overlap indices are shown in Figure 3. Note that the number of observations on which this analysis was performed is less than the total sample, since it requires a respondent to have completed all the scenarios. The higher the index, the more the actual size of the overlap exceeds the expected.

For Sample Y, with three scenarios, there are four poten-

tial overlaps -- three two-ways and one three-way. For Sample X, with four scenarios, there are eleven -- six two-ways, four three-ways, and one four-way. Within each category, the overlap indices are organised in descending size.

Despite the situation-specific nature of the scenarios, the overlap index exceeded 1.1 for all but 8 of the 30 overlap calculations. In only one instance did the overlap index fall below 1.0, indicating the overlap was less then expected.

DISCUSSION

In many service firms the idea of getting the customer to do "more work" is one that is very attractive. This is usually approached as a cost saving exercise. It is generally assumed that it will be necessary to offer the consumer some added benefit as "payment" for the work done, in the form, for example, of a price reduction.

This study suggests that for some respondents at least, participating more in the production of the service is intrinsically attractive. For these customers the introduction of such a "do it yourself" option may provide an added benefit and differentiate the service in their mind. For this group it would not be neccesary to cut the price.

Whether it is the same customer who would be participative in all these different kinds of service is less clear. There is an overlap between the different services for both the participator and the nonparticipator groups. The patterns within those different overlaps are inconclusive.

To be useful as a segmentation tool, this approach requires that the participative and nonparticipative groups be identifiable in some way. Other studies based on this data (Bateson and Langeard 1981, Langeard et al. 1981) suggest that this may be possible. Generally, demographic factors do not differentiate between these groups. However, clear discrimination appears possible on some pschographic measures (particularly attitude towards technology) and on a number of 'dimensions' developed within the study. Of particular interest are the dimensions of time and 'control over the situation'.

The concept of a 'participative' consumer is one that is intrinsically very attractive. To make such a concept useful would require additional research. This study needs

52

FIGURE 3

OVERLAP INDEX ACROSS SCENARIOS FOR PARTICIPATIVE AND NONPARTICIPATIVE GROUPS

SAMPLE X (N = 411)

Nonparticipative		Participative	
Gas/Hotel/Airline/Travellers' Cheque	3.42	Gas/Hotel/Airline/Travellers' Cheque	1.59
Hotel/Airline/Travellers' Cheque	2.41	Gas/Airline/Travellers' Cheque	1.39
Gas/Airline/Travellers' Cheque	2.08	Gas/Hotel/Travellers' Cheque	1.37
Gas/Hotel/Travellers' Cheque	1.80	Hotel/Airline/Travellers' Cheque	1.24
Gas/Hotel/Airline	1.69	Gas/Hotel/Airline	1.17
Hotel/Travellers' Cheque	1.48	Gas/Travellers' Cheque	1.23
Airline/Travellers' Cheque	1.46	Airline/Travellers' Cheque	1.12
Hotel/Airline	1.35	Gas/Airline	1.09
Gas/Travellers' Cheque	1.20	Gas/Hotel	1.08
Gas/Hotel	1.18	Hotel/Travellers' Cheque	1.08
Gas/Airline	1.15	Hotel/Airline	1.02

SAMPLE Y (N = 736)

Nonparticipative		Participative	
Gas/Banks/Fast Food	1.23	Gas/Banks/Fast Food	1.64
Gas/Fast Food	1.10	Gas/Fast Food	1.40
Banks/Fast Food	1.07	Banks/Fast Food	1.16
Gas/Banks	1.01	Gas/Banks	0.97

to be replicated using other services. Scale development work might be valuably used to measure 'propensity to participate' directly. Alternatively, the dimensions discussed above could be expanded and measured more carefully.

Lastly, it should be pointed out that because of the stratified nature of the samples used it is not possible to estimate the actual size of the different participator groups and indeed this was never the intention of the study.

APPENDIX A

The Bank Scenario

"It is 10.00 a.m. and you wish to withdraw $50.00 from your cheque account. You have a card which would enable you to use an automatic teller machine or you could go to a human teller with your cheque book. So your choices are:

Either use the automatic teller machine;
or use the human teller.

There are equally short lines of people waiting to use the machine and at the teller window."

REFERENCES

Bateson, J.E.G. and E. Langeard (1981), "Consumers Uses of Common Dimensions in the Appraisal of Services," Advances in Consumer Research, IX, A. Mitchell, ed., Chicago: ACR.

Fuchs, V. (1968), The Service Economy, New York: National Bureau of Economic Research.

Gartner, A. and F. Reissman (1974), The Service Society and the New Consumer Vanguard, New York: Harper and Row.

Langeard, E., J.E.G. Bateson, C.H. Lovelock and P. Eiglier (1981), "Services Marketing: New Insights from Consumers and Managers," Cambridge, M.A.: Marketing Science Institute Monograph No. 81-104.

Levitt, T. (1972), "The Production Line Approach to Services," Harvard Business Review (September-October), 41-52.

_____ (1976), "The Industrialisation of Service," Harvard Business Review (September-October), 63-74.

Lovelock, C.H. and R.A. Young (1977), "Marketing's Potential for Improving Productivity in Service Industries," in Marketing Consumer Services: New Insights, Cambridge, M.A.: Marketing Science Institute Report No. 77-115.

ACKNOWLEDGEMENTS

The author would like to thank the member companies of the Marketing Science Institute without whose support and co-operation this study could not have been undertaken. This paper is based on a much larger study and would not have been possible without the input of my fellow project team members - Professor Pierre Eiglier, Professor Christopher Lovelock and Professor Eric Langeard.

CONSUMERISM IN THE SERVICE SECTOR: SELECTED ISSUES AND OPPORTUNITIES

Ronald Stiff, University of Baltimore
Julie Pollack, University of Baltimore

ABSTRACT

Although consumerism has been hypothesized to be in the
maturity stage of its life cycle for products, it appears
to be in earlier stages of its life cycle for some service
sectors. A typology of service sectors in terms of their
relative degree of customer contact and their economic
concentration reveals several types of service sectors
where consumerism is in its introduction or growth stage.
Selected service-specific consumer issues are defined and
opportunities for new growth areas in services consumerism
are proposed.

INTRODUCTION

Consumerism as a movement has reportedly entered the
maturity stage of its life cycle (Bloom and Greyser 1982).
In this paper it is proposed that while this may be true
with respect to consumer products, this may not be the
case with respect to some consumer services. In reaching
its maturity stage consumerism focused heavily on product
quality and product safety. A possible product line
extension strategy for consumerism is therefore an
increasing focus on consumer issues in the service sector.
Trends in the services' marketplace suggest the likelihood
of this happening.

Services account for an increasing share of the
consumers's income. Expenditures for consumer services
represented forty-four percent of personal income in 1980
(Predicasts 1981). This percentage is forecasted to
increase at least through 1995. At the same time many
services are undergoing deregulation at the federal level.
This paper first discusses the nature of consumerism which
distinguishes between different service sectors and
services from products. Next, trends influencing services
consumerism are reviewed. The paper concludes with an
analysis of methods for resolving consumer issues in the
services sector.

CONSUMERISM IN SERVICES

The Nature of Services and Consumer Issues

Several characteristics of services suggest that consumer
issues in services differ from those for products, and
vary substantially across various service sectors. The
ways in which services are provided, distributed,
evaluated, purchased and consumed affect consumer issues.
For example, many services are provided by a large number
of small competitors as contrasted with consumer products
which are generally produced by a few, large
manufacturers. Many service sectors have low economic
concentration where providers are either individual owners
or franchises. Examples of these include personal and
professional services, automotive repair services, legal
services and beauty shops. For these small organizations
the chief executive officer and complaint handling methods
generally are readily accessible to the consumer. Other
service sectors have higher economic concentration and
greater geographic dispersion of headquarters and service
provision locations. Examples include services such as
passenger transportation, hotels, utilities, insurance
and telecommunications. For these services the chief
executive officer is generally not immediately accessible

to the consumer and the complaint handling methods are
more complex and potentially confusing. On the other
hand, these larger organizations may find a specialized
consumer affairs function to be a cost-effective
competitive offering.

Consumer evaluation of many services is difficult.
Services often are high in credence or belief
characteristics and as intangibles they often cannot be
directly evaluated by the consumer before purchase
(Zeithaml 1981). It is difficult for the consumer to
identify an attorney who can provide an effective will, a
dentist who can provide comfortable dentures or to
determine which island will provide an enjoyable vacation
without actually experiencing these service. For many
services trial use is difficult or impossible. The use of
a will is the ultimate credence good. As a result there
are often greater difficulties in obtaining objective
prepurchase information when purchasing services than when
purchasing products.

The intangible nature of services makes consumer redress
following purchase more complex than for products.
Evaluating acceptable, marginal or unacceptable quality
for a service is often more difficult than for products.
Services are not easily recalled, although service
providers may be restricted from providing services by
removal of their rights to practice in certain service
industries including health care, transportation and the
sale of securities. The redress for poor quality legal
documents, medical care or funerals may be of limited
value to the consumer. Refunds for poor vacations or
educational services accomplish little in returning the
consumer's lost time.

The difficulties in obtaining redress make actions
preventing consumer problems of significant benefit to
consumers of services. In addition to regulations
certifying who is competent to offer services, there is a
strong need for accessible consumer prepurchase
information for those consumer services where equitable
redress is difficult.

While products generally require the potential consumer to
make relatively few fairly explicit decisions which can be
evaluated rather rapidly before product purchase, services
involve many more sellers, sometimes producing the service
with high consumer involvement and sometimes with credence
qualities which are difficult to evaluate in advance of
purchase and can create severe consumer redress problems
if found faulty following purchase. In addition to
differences in services and products there are several
trends influencing service consumerism specifically.

Trends in Services Consumerism

Trends influencing services include "deregulation", the
debate over state versus federal regulation, the
increasing use of cost-benefit analysis to justify
regulations, and the mergers, acquisitions and branching
taking place in some service sectors. Some services have
a history of substantial federal and state regulation that
appears to be in the decline stage at the federal level.
The taste for less government in general may prove to be a
long term trend leading to further deregulation in
many service sectors. This has already taken place in
transportation, household moving, broadcast communications

common carrier communications, and financial institutions.

The professions have been an area of substantial activity. The focus has been on the "deregulation" of marketing activities such as promotional methods and fee setting. Through various court and Federal Trade Commission actions there are now few state or professional limitations on marketing activities in any of these sectors. The Federal Trade Commission has been quite active in proposing prepurchase information and cancellation rights rules in the professional and quasi-professional sectors including vocational schools, health spas, opthalmic goods and services, and funeral services. However, the recent two house veto of the proposed used car rule and the current rule making policy at the FTC based on "solid statistical evidence" produced by sample surveys raises severe questions regarding the use of rule making as a means of consumer protection at the federal level (Mayer 1982). Case law can be an effective method for consumer protection in these sectors when there is a substantial target such as the recent Supreme Court decision favoring the FTC case eliminating the ethical restrictions against advertising by the American Medical Association. The FTC recently has investigated veterinarians, legal services, dental services and real estate practices. Although case law can be effective where the target is concentrated such as industry wide trade or professional associations, rules may be more effective in sectors such as health spas, vocational schools, home improvement contractors and employment agencies where there is the potential for large numbers of cases. The Federal Trade Commission has been banned from regulating the insurance industry and debate continues on their jurisdiction over the professions. There seems little likelihood of a completed rule making action in any of these sectors in the near future.

States traditionally have been the primary regulators of several important service sectors; professional services, real estate brokers, funeral homes, insurance any many banking activities. It seems likely that the states will have the major responsibility for service regulation in the foreseeable future. This will be appropriate for those services where regional or local variations may be in the consumer's interest such as funerals and legal services. However, state regulation of services which are currently or becoming national in scope such as insurance and banking may be of questionable value to the provision of cost-efficient services. The potential for as many as 51 different sets of regulations may increase the cost of providing consumer protection beyond any reasonable benefit.

A third trend influencing service consumerism is the growing emphasis on cost-benefit analysis of regulations. Cost-benefit analysis is conceptually appealing but operationally complex. Strict, objective analysis of regulations is difficult due to the near impossibility of measuring either or both costs and benefits. This is especially difficult in the evaluation of either prepurchase information or the quality of many services, both of which are intangible. For example, how would one measure the cost-benefit to society of requiring prepurchase information disclosures by service providers? Regardless of which group is involved, use of a cost-benefit argument (either pro or con disclosure) is likely to involve lengthy subjective debates. Such debates would be likely to "freeze" current regulations in place and delay regulatory change.

Another trend in several services sectors is the increase in mergers, acquisitions, branching and franchising with resulting impacts on competition. The technologies used in some service sectors are encouraging growth beyond state into regional and national service areas. Real estate agencies, financial services, nursing homes, legal services, and travel agencies are examples of service businesses that are becoming more concentrated and taking advantage of telecommunications technology, national advertising and other economies of scale. In these sectors the opportunity to devote more resources to consumer issues and to be more visible "targets" for consumer groups will increase.

METHODS FOR PREVENTING AND RESOLVING CONSUMER ISSUES

Methods for preventing and resolving consumer issues vary by service sectors. In order to generalize these methods across sectors, it is useful to group services based on their relative economic concentration and their extent of customer contact. Bell (1981) and Berry (1981) distinguish differences in service sectors based on the degree of contact between services personnel and customers when the service is provided. High contact services involve far greater personal contact between buyer and seller in the actual provision of the service than between buyers and sellers in either low contact service or product sectors. In high contact sectors a substantial part of the service is provided, marketed and consumed with direct consumer involvement (Lovelock 1981). The nature of these services exposes many employees to the complaints of consumers and therefore has the potential for more timely complaint handling than for product marketing. However, this assumes that all employees with client contact are proficient in solving or routing complaints and that consumers are willing to complain to service providers. The typical small size of the average service establishment precludes the cost-efficient use of a local full time consumer affairs specialist. As a result all employees with client contact become "consumer affairs specialists", a difficult training task for most services, especially since this employee is likely to be directly or indirectly involved in the provision of the service and may find it difficult to react objectively.

While many sectors include large numbers of small suppliers and have low economic concentration, some service sectors are relatively more concentrated. Providers in these sectors frequently must contend with a variety of state regulations. Additionally, due to their size they can often afford specialized consumer affairs offices. As a result they operate in a substantially different consumerism environment than the low concentration service providers.

Service sectors are grouped on the basis of their relative customer contact and economic concentration in Figure 1 for high contact-low concentration sectors, some services are proposed as "transition" sectors that are currently or potentially evolving into either low contact or high concentration sectors for at least a portion of their service offerings. Legal services, many financial services, nursing homes, health spas, real estate agencies, and travel agencies are branching and becoming more concentrated. Banking services offered through automatic teller machines are producing many low contact banking services. The evolution of these industries is likely to create new consumer issues. The high concentration sectors are divided into "traditionally regulated" and " non-regulated" since different approaches to consumer issues can be expected based on their expected future regulation which appears to be decreasing for many of the regulated concentrated industries.

The major participants involved in preventing consumer injury or obtaining consumer redress include federal, state and local government agencies, the courts, services producer consumer affairs offices, third party resolution organizations such as the Better Business Bureau and trade association groups, consumer groups and independent consumer information and service providers. The intangible nature of services places a premium on prevention rather than redress. Therefore for services a strong services producer consumer affairs activity is likely to be highly desirable approach to consumer issues.

FIGURE 1: SERVICE SECTORS AS A FUNCTION OF THEIR RELATIVE ECONOMIC CONCENTRATION AND EXTENT OF CUSTOMER CONTACT

	High Customer Contact	Low Customer Contact
Low Econ. Conc.	Beauty Shops (6.3) Barber Shops (2.1) Higher Education Vocational Schools Home Improvement Physicians Veterinarians Hospitals Employment Agencies TRANSITION Banking Dental Services Legal Services (2.9) Funeral Services (5.9) Real Estate Agencies Travel Agencies Nursing Homes Health Spas	Automotive Repair (3.0) Coin-Op Laundry
High Econ. Conc.	TRADITIONALLY REGULATED Passenger Trans. Interstate Moving Stock Brokers NON-REGULATED Hotels, Motels (21.0) Photo Studios (25.9) Tax Preparation	TRADITIONALLY REGULATED Utilities Telecommunications Broadcasting Mutual Funds (no Load) Insurance U.S. Postal Service Cable Television State Lotteries NON-REGULATED Auto Leasing (45.9) Auto Parking (46.2) Elec. Tepair (19.8) Movie Theaters (37.7) Home Info. Services

Number in parenthesis refer to 20 firm economic concentration ratios when available from the 1977 Census of Selected Services (U.S. Census Bureau 1979).

High-Contact Low-Concentration Services

These service sectors include small service providers, many operating within a single state. These sectors traditionally have been regulated at the state level largely through licensing or certifying providers of services. The high credence quality of these services makes prevention of consumer issues through entry certification desirable and for those services with regional variations, regulation of entry at the state level is probably more in the consumer's interest than federal regulation of entry.

The majority of these services are personalized and involve the active participation of consumers in the provision of the service. There is little opportunity for standardizing the majority of these services, thus complicating the prepurchase evaluation process for consumers. When dissatisfied, consumers of these services may attribute some of their dissatisfaction to "their own inability to specify or perform their part of the service" and "complain less frequently about (these) services than about products due to their belief that they themselves are partly responsible for their dissatisfaction" (Zeithaml 1981, p. 189). Quelsh and Ash (1981) found only half as many consumers of professional services (18.4%)

were "highly dissatisfied" as compared to food product pruchasers (35.5%). They hypothesize that this may be a result of the consumer's perceptions of deficiencies in his role in the production process or alternatively a result of better quality service provision, less developed consumer expectations (credence qualities), or the consumer's subjective probability of obtaining redress. Of the 59.8 percent of dissatisfied consumers that took an average of 2.2 personal and/or direct actions, the most frequent actions were to quit using the professional (25.9%) and to warn family and friends (25.9%) (Quelsh and Ash 1981, p. 85). Eleven percent of the actions were for a correction of services, a refund or a fee adjustment while twelve percent of the actions involved contact with a third party such a professional society or government agency.

In many of these sectors, especially professional services, there is an active history of self-regulation. These activities have been designed to control the quality of practitioners through entry requirements, to discipline and dismiss poor quality providers, and to control marketing practices. The later, as discussed, has largely been eliminated by the courts. Due to the credence qualities of these services effective self regulation is of substantial value to the consumer. These controls are not as available in the less organized sectors such as real estate, home improvement contractors, travel agencies and vocational schools. The organizations in these sectors are generally too small to have formal consumer affairs activities and consumer complaints must be solved on an informal, direct basis, through the use of third parties such as Better Business Bureau arbitration or a trade association, or through the courts.

Due to the complexities of providing prepurchase information or means of redress, it is likely that there will be extensive growth in actions, taken in these sectors by consumer groups. How these groups will organize is unclear, although Warland, Herrmann and Moore (1982) have identified an activist type who appears to be middle aged, long time residents of their communities and well prepared to lead local consumer movements.

It seems unlikely that the current national groups as they are organized can effectively prevent or resolve services consumer issues that are so varied in content and geography. More focused groups are likely. These may evolved on a regional, service sector or consumer affinity group basis. National groups with local variations using a franchise like organization are also possible. Due to the extensive fragmentation in these service sectors, specific services groups would seem to be of limited effectiveness in recruiting members. Consumers may be reluctant to join a banking or health care consumer group. Leonard (1982), however, proposed that this form of specialization in the consumer movement is possible.

A more likely organizational mechanism are affinity groups of consumers with similar services and possibly product issues such as retired persons. Groups such as the American Association of Retired Persons or a "Senior PAC" can be expected to increase their consumer actions as the service sector expands their demographic group increases in relative size and those with experience as community activists reach retirement age.

There are likely to be changes in the offerings of local consumer services. Consumer cooperatives may choose to offer more services products such as financial services and insurance. There may be increased consumer demand for local services evaluation publications following the model of Consumer Reports, such as the Washington Consumer Checkbook (Krughoff 1981). Cable television will provide the opportunity for both additional advertising by local service businesses and the communication of consumer information with greater local variations than broadcast television.

Finally, these service sectors can benefit from prepurchase information and there may be a growth in the court's definition of the doctrine of "informed consent." As a result of the rise of health care consumerism, viewing the patient as an active consumer of health care, informed consent prior to medical procedures is a rapidly developing body of law (Johnson 1980). Although many informed consent decisions are based on the individuals right to decide what to do to his or her own body, the extension of informed consent to other areas of consumer injury such as changes in an individual's net worth resulting from a lack of material information regarding a financial product purchase may become an area for contention in the courts.

The future of consumer protection in the sectors shown as transitional in Figure 1 is expected to be quite dynamic. These sectors have the potential for either becoming more concentrated such as through bank, funeral home or legal services mergers or branching or of creating services with low customer contact such as automatic teller machines and the use of telephones for electronic banking transactions. These changes will create consumer issues similar to the high economic concentration or low consumer contact sectors yet to be discussed.

Tensions can be expected to arise as the transition service organizations increasingly cross state lines and are faced with a wider variety of regulations. This is already occuring in banking where an office for bank cards is located in a different state than the bank itself to take advantage of more favorable state bank card laws regarding interest rates and annual charges. A national mechanism for unifying the prevention and resolution of consumer issues might be cost-effective for services crossing state lines.

Low Consumer Contact-Low Economic Concentration Sectors

These sectors produce relatively uncomplex consumer issues compared to the high consumer contact sectors. Typically the consumer brings in an automobile or piece of clothing which is improved by the service provider. There is, however, one major consumer issue; unnecessary repairs to working components. The problem of unnecessary automotive repair has parallels with unnecessary services provided by professionals. It is very hard for most consumers to evaluate whether they need an organ transplanted, a complex will or divorce, or their brakes relined. In 1977 there were over 150,000 auto repair establishments. Most of these were owner operated (U.S. Bureau of the Census 1979). The large number and variety of these establishments and the ability to define and detect unnecessary repair makes this issue difficult to solve. Since judgement in repair is required the most promising approach is control of the quality of auto mechanics through certification or through standards established by national repair firms such as Ford and Lincoln-Mercury (Automotive News 1982). This issue may be partially resolved through the evolution of national or regional specialty firms specializing in specific sub areas such as tune-ups, mufflers, brakes and other auto components. These firms may have the economies of scale to develop uniform training of employees and effective quality control practices. These may be used as a competitive advantage directed to the quality oriented consumer.

This area is also promising for local "Consumer Reports" magazines. In larger areas it may be possible to obtain sufficient subscriber support to conduct consumer evaluations of various maintenance organizations. There are, however, substantial methodological issues involved in these surveys (Krughoff 1981).

High Customer Contact-High Concentration Sectors

These sectors are relatively lower in credence qualities, are generally more standardized than personalized services and although involving high customer contact generally require limited active consumer participation in the provision of the service. The major exceptions to this are services provided to high income consumers by stock brokers and tax preparation services, however, for the most part the consumer expects a fairly standardized service. As a result sufficient prepurchase information is generally available to meet consumer needs. Consumer problems for these services typically involve redress for rather specific problems; transportation not arriving on time, luggage lost, stocks not purchased when requested, reservations canceled by the supplier or income taxes not calculated correctly. The large size of most of these firms makes it cost-efficient to establish formal means for redress. Often provision of the service with compensation for out of pocket expenses is the offered solution; a new flight, meals and a hotel room for the night by airlines or a room in another hotel with a free taxi ride by hotels.

For the traditionally regulated sectors the rules for redress have often been very rigid. As passenger transportation, household moving and stock brokers become less regulated, redress provisions can be expected to become a competitive tool. For example, some low price flights are sold with less refund or exchange protection and the consumer must trade-off price for previously regulated protections. In household moving there may be increasing opportunity to trade-off delivery time promises against price. In short deregulation now permits those previously protected consumer rights to become part of the competitive offering of these offerings to consumers, some perhaps in quite innovative forms such as airlines have done in paying consumers to not utilize overbooked flights.

Low Customer Contact-High Economic Contact Sectors

These services are highly standardized and very low in credence qualities; consumers have well developed expectations regarding most of these services. The high degree of automation in procedures and the use of computers and other technologies assures services that are virtually products and produced in a production line fashion (Levitt 1972). Prepurchase information needs are primarily for accurate price-service schedules. While this information is generallky readily available in some instances it presents some problems for consumers. Equivalent life and health insurance rates are a continuing source of confusion and debate. Comparing prices for various fuels for home heating, automobile leasing, home information services, and comparing yields for mutual funds and state lotteries requires relatively complex mathematical comparisons to utilize the information that is currently provided. These comparisons, however, are somewhat similar to product price-quality comparisons. Price-service comparisons for many of these services can be made at the national level and have been for some products such as life insurance costs and mutual fund yields.

Redress for faulty or unsupplied services in these sectors is relatively straight forward. It is fairly easy to establish that the services were not provided; rented autos break down, cable or subscription television does not operate, cars are damaged in parking lots, or movies were cancelled. Redress is generally a refund of price rather than providing the service again. Consumer dissatisfaction for non-regulated sectors and some regulated sectors can also be remedied by switching to another supplier. This solution to consumer problems is not possible for many of the traditionally regulated sectors where there is a monopoly supplier. The forms of consumer redress that will evolve if these sectors are deregulated is unclear. Industry self-regulation may occur if there is enough pressure from consumers and government groups. In summary, the standardization of these services limits consumers problems and makes them fairly well defined. Most of these services are similar to products. Some of the deregulated sectors such as telecommunications may produce greater consumer demand for comparative price information provided by suppliers through comparative advertising or by independent information suppliers such as Consumer Reports.

CONCLUSIONS

Examination of various service sectors suggest that while consumerism for products may be in the maturity stage, for some services sectors consumerism appears to be in the introduction or growth stage. This is found to be the case for many high customer contact sectors and for service sectors that are subject to "deregulation." Several developments in consumerism are expected:

In high customer contact-low economic concentration sectors, especially the professional services sectors, there will be strong consumer demands for prepurchase information. There will be an increasing interest in the content of interpersonal client-supplier communications which may result in a trend toward written records of some parts of these conversations.

Some services supplied by high customer contact-low economic concentration suppliers will evolve into high economic concentration and/or low customer contract services. These serices will require new approaches to consumer protection. They will become somewhat more "product-like" in their forms of prevention and redress of consumer problems. The evolution of formal consumer affairs offices for these transition services is expected.

In low economic concentration sectors there will be a growth in local Consumer Reports like publications providing comparative evaluations of services.

Traditionally regulated high economic concentration service sectors can be expected to use the prevention and effective redress of consumer problems as means of competition where competition exists. There will be an increase in price competition and comparative advertising or prices. Formal means of redress will be developed and advertised.

Traditionally regulated service sectors without competition that are deregulated represent an unknown for consumerism.

REFERENCES

Automotive News (1982), "FPSD Programs Beefing Up Dealer-ship Training Programs," (2-17-82), 20, 44.

Bell, Martin L. (1981), "A Matrix Approach to the Classification of Marketing Goods and Services," in Marketing of Services, James H. Donnelly and William R. George (eds), Chicago: American Marketing Association, 208-212.

Berry, Leonard L. (1981), "Perspectives on the Retailing of Services," in Theory in Retailing: Traditional and Nontraditional Sources, Ronald W. Stampfl and Elizabeth C. Hirschman (eds), Chicago: American Marketing Association, 9-20.

Bloom, Paul and Stephen A Greyser (1981), "The Maturing of Consumerism," Harvard Business Review (November-December), 130-139.

Krughoff, Robert (1981), "Service Evaluation," in Marketing of Services, James H. Donnelly and William R. George (eds), Chicago: American Marketing Association, 242-244.

Johnson, George (1980), "An Overview of Informed Consent: Majority and Minority Rules," in Legal Medicine with Special Reference to Diagnostic Imaging, Robert James (ed), Baltimore: Urban and Schwarzenberg, 281-294.

Leavitt, Theodore (1972), "Production-Line Approach to Service," Harvard Business Review, (September-October), 41+.

Leonard, Rodney E. (1982), "Specialization and the Consumer Movement," in Consumerism and Beyond: Research Perspective on the Futured Social Environment, Paul N. Bloom (ed), Cambridge, Mass.: Marketing Science Institute, 54-55.

Lovelock, Christopher H. (1981), "Why Marketing Management Needs to be Different for Services," in Marketing of Services, James H. Donnelly and William R. George (eds), Chicgo: American Marketing Association, 5-9.

Mayer, Caroline E. (1982), "FTC May Narrow Its Consumer Shield," Washington Post (6-12/82), 2.

Predicasts (1981), Forecasts, Cleveland, Ohio.

U.S. Bureau of the Census (1977), "Projections of the Population of the United States: 1977 to 2050," Current Population Reports, Series P-25, No. 704, Washington, D.C.: U.S. Government Printing Office.

U.S. Bureau of the Census (1979), "1977 Census of Service Industries: Establishment and Firm Size," SC77-S-1, Washington, D.C.: U.S. Government Printing Office.

Warland, Rex H., Robert O. Herrmann, and Dan E. Moore (1982), "Consumer Activism, Community Activism, and the Consumer Movement," in Consumerism and Beyond: Research Perspectives on the Future Social Environment, Paul N. Bloom (ed), Cambridge, Mass.: Marketing Science Institute, 11-15.

Ziethaml, Valarie A. (1981), "How Consumer Evaluation Processes Differ Between Goods and Services," in Marketing of Services, James H. Donnelly and William R. George (eds), Chicgo: American Marketing Association, 186-190

SCRIPT-BASED EVALUATIONS OF SATISFACTION WITH SERVICES

Ruth A. Smith, University of Wisconsin, Madison
Michael J. Houston, University of Wisconsin, Madison, Wisconsin

ABSTRACT

The unique characteristics of services may necessitate that consumers base their satisfaction evaluations of such offerings on expectations which are substantially different than those for physical goods. This paper will propose an evaluation process for services which is based on expectations defined by a cognitive script. The implications of script-based evaluations for service marketers will be identified.

INTRODUCTION

The escalating significance of services in the economy suggests that satisfaction with such offerings is a growing concern for both consumers and businesses. It has been acknowledged that certain unique characteristics of services may necessitate that satisfaction evaluations be based on expectations quite different from those for physical goods (cf. Liechty and Churchill 1979; Zeithaml 1981). However, the precise nature of the expectations which determine satisfaction with services has not been specified in the extant literature.

This paper will describe a process by which satisfaction evaluations of services are made which is based on expectations defined by a cognitive script, a type of mental representation of knowledge. Preliminary to describing the script-based evaluation process, the following discussion will first review the disconfirmation paradigm which models satisfaction evaluations for physical goods. The unique qualities of services which limit the generalizability of this model to the services sector will then be identified. The concept of a cognitive script will then be defined, and a script-based evaluation process described. The paper will conclude with a discussion of the implications of script-based evaluations for services marketers.

THE DISCONFIRMATION PARADIGM

Much of the satisfaction literature in marketing has attempted to identify the process by which consumers make satisfaction evaluations. Typically, it has been assumed that expectations are compared to actual product performance, a process which is modeled by the disconfirmation paradigm. As described by Churchill and Surprenant (1982), the disconfirmation paradigm "holds that satisfaction is related to the size and direction of the disconfirmation experience (and) where disconfirmation is related to the person's initial expectations. More specifically, an individual's expectations are (1) confirmed when a product performs as expected; (2) negatively disconfirmed when the product performs more poorly than expected; and (3) positively disconfirmed when the product performs better than expected" (pp. 1-2). The consumer will experience satisfaction when expectations are confirmed or positively disconfirmed. The disconfirmation paradigm is presented graphically in Figure 1.

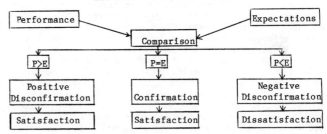

FIGURE 1
THE DISCONFIRMATION PARADIGM

Empirical support for the model has been provided by several investigations in which either expectations or performance have been experimentally manipulated (cf. Cardozo 1965; Olshavsky and Miller 1972; Anderson 1973; Olson and Dover 1976; Trawick and Swan 1980). More recent studies have focused on the structural relationships among expectations, performance and disconfirmation (cf. Oliver 1980a; Churchill and Surprenant 1981). However, these studies exhibit a strong bias towards satisfaction evaluations based on expectations about the performance characteristics of physical goods. The generalizability of these findings to the services sector is somewhat constrained by the characteristics of services which distinguish them from goods.

DISTINCTION OF GOODS AND SERVICES

Several authors have attempted to identify the characteristics of services which set them apart from goods (cf. Rathmell 1974; Eiglier et al. 1977; Shostack 1977; Liechty and Churchill 1979; Zeithaml 1981). While there is some diversity in the qualities mentioned, there is consensus that services are both intangible, and involve an inseparable production and consumption process. Each of these characteristics has some important implications for the expectations which underly satisfaction evaluations for services.

Services are intangible both in that they lack a physical referent and they are dominated by highly abstract qualities which are difficult to grasp mentally. Consequently, a consumer of services may lack a set of product-related expectations upon which to base satisfaction. The absence of such expectations would not pose a barrier to the evaluation process if some other alternative set of expectations were available. The consumer of a physical good, for instance, who lacks product-related expectations due, perhaps, to inexperience, might alternatively base his satisfaction on expectations about the shopping, purchasing, or consumption processes, or on his own abilities as a consumer.

However, in the case of services, the alternative sets of expectations are also unavailable, due to inseparability. That is, since the production and consumption of the service occur simultaneously, expectations about one of these processes cannot be formed independent of the other. Furthermore, since services involve the joint participation of the buyer and seller, one's abilities as a consumer are inextricably linked to the characteristics of the seller. Thus, in the absence of both product-related expectations and any alternative set of expectations, the question arises as to what does constitute the expectations upon which satisfaction evaluations of services are based. This issue can be resolved through the concept of a cognitive script.

COGNITIVE SCRIPTS AND SCRIPT-BASED EVALUATIONS

A cognitive script is a type of schema, or mental representation of knowledge. A schema is a unit of generic knowledge about some stimulus domain which is stored in memory and guides the processing of information about any particular instance of that domain. Schemata of are several types, and may be categorized according to the nature of the stimulus domain which serves as the organizing theme. Thus, an individual may develop schemata for objects or object classes (e.g., appliances); for people or personality types (e.g., extravert); for social or occupational roles (e.g., parent or librarian); or for events (e.g., attending a lecture). The schema will contain a set of expectations about the typical characteristics possessed by any instance of the stimulus domain. Thus, one would expect a librarian to be intelligent, well educated, and bookish. Expectations about the job activities associated with this role and the setting in which the activities would be performed may also exist.

The present discussion is especially concerned with event schemata, or scripts, which represent general knowledge about some commonplace, repetitive event such as going to the dentist or dining in a restaurant. Specifically, a script may be described as "a predetermined, stereotyped sequence of actions that defines a well-known situation" (Schank and Abelson 1977, p. 41). Abbott and Black (1980) extend this definition as follows: "A script for a commonplace event consists of the standard actions, characters and objects involved in the event. Scripts are intended to represent knowledge about events which are so well practiced in everyday life that their performance is stereotyped" (p. 5). Thus, the expectations contained in a script will specify the set of actions which compose the event, the order in which they would normally occur, the actors who would perform the actions, and the setting in which the event would take place.

A growing body of research in cognitive psychology supports both the presence of scripts and their impact on human information processing. While the significance of the script concept to marketing has not been widely acknowledged, the presence of scripts for such marketing-related events as dining in a restaurant and visiting a health professional has been demonstrated (Bower, Black and Turner 1979). Furthermore, there is evidence of a high degree of consistency across individuals in terms of the actions which compose a script-defined event, and the order of their occurrence (Bower et al. 1979; John and Whitney 1982).

As do all schemata, scripts perform several functions which facilitate the efficient processing of information. Of particular concern in the context of services marketing is that scripts provide a basis for evaluating current experience. Taylor and Crocker (1981) describe this evaluation process such that the script-defined expectations act as a normative structure against which a particular event is compared to determine goodness to fit. The evaluation of the event is a function of goodness of fit, so an event would be positively evaluated if it matched the script-defined expectations and negatively evaluated if it did not.

It will be noted that this evaluation process is quite consistent with that modeled by the disconfirmation paradigm. In each case, a set of predetermined expectations is compared to a stimulus, and the resulting evaluation depends on the confirmation or disconfirmation of the expectations. However, the script-based evaluation process

is not constrained to expectations about an object such as a physical good. Rather, the expectations which guide the evaluation may include any aspect of an entire event, including the component actions and their order, the actors, and the setting in which the event takes place. Such script-based evaluations may be quite relevant to services marketing.

SCRIPT-BASED EVALUATIONS OF SERVICES

As previously noted, the expectations underlying satisfaction evaluations of services are troublesome for marketers to identify due to the unique qualities of these offerings. However, a marketing transaction involving a service may be conceptualized as an event, composed of a set of ordered actions, actors and objects. Through repeated involvement in purchasing/producing/consuming a service, the consumer may develop a script for the event which will define his expectations for the offering. Once formed, these expectations will serve as the basis for evaluating subsequent occurrences of the service transaction. The script-based expectations are not reliant solely on the performance attributes of a product, or on those of either the production or consumption process. Rather, the script specifies expectations relative to the transaction as a complete event.

The example of retail banking services provides a vivid illustration of this process. Banking services are highly intangible, with the only physical manifestation being the receipts that accompany a transaction. Furthermore, each transaction is produced and consumed simultaneously and involves the joint participation of the consumer and the bank's representative. Thus, a consumer's feelings of satisfaction following any particular transaction may be only tenuously linked to product-related attributes or the qualities of either the production or consumption process.

It is plausible to suggest, however, that most adults have experienced frequent enough exposure to routine banking transactions that they possess scripts for these situations. Depositing a check in one's account is such an event, and the related script might include the following sequence of actions: (1) enter the bank; (2) go to the customers' desk; (3) fill out a deposit slip and endorse the check; (4) wait in line for a teller; (5) complete the transaction with the teller; (6) leave the bank.

In addition to this action sequence, the script will define expectations relative to the stock characters who participate in the event, and the setting in which it will occur. The actors, in addition to oneself, would include other customers, tellers, security guards, and bank officers. The setting typically would be a large, open space with centrally located desks for customers and tellers' cages around the perimeter. The customers' desks would be stocked with the bank's forms, pens, and a calendar. While variations on these components of the script may occur depending on the particular transaction (e.g., making a deposit at a branch bank or at a drive-up window), the action sequence, actors, and setting described constitute a hypothetical script for a stereotypical event.

According to the script-based evaluation process, any particular deposit transaction would be compared to this script. To the degree the script-defined expectations were met, the experience would be positively evaluated, and the consumer would presumably express satisfaction with the service. Any one of several deviations from the script-defined expectations, involving either an action, an actor, or the objects in the setting, would, hypothetically, reduce satisfaction.

One such deviation, an obstacle, involves the absence of a condition which enables the occurrence of a subsequent action (Schank and Abelson 1977). In the context of the bank example, an obstacle could occur in the third action (fill out a deposit slip) if there were none of these forms at the customers' desk. Lacking the forms, the event could not continue unless the consumer were to engage in some action to provide the missing condition. The delay and inconvenience associated with overcoming the obstacle may result in feelings of anger, frustration, and ultimately, dissatisfaction on the part of the consumer.

A second deviation from script-defined expectations that may lead to dissatisfaction is an error. An error occurs when an action in the script is completed, but the outcome is inconsistent with what was expected (Schank and Abelson 1977). In the context of the bank transaction, an error could occur in action five (complete the transaction with the teller) if the teller incorrectly recorded the amount of the deposit. Although an error may not prevent the continuation of the event in the prescribed manner (the customer may leave the bank without noticing the mistake, for instance), ultimately the deviation will become evident. When this occurs, the consumer will have to take corrective action, and tolerate the associated inconvenience. Thus, the deviation from the script-defined expectations will eventually lead to a decrement in satisfaction.

A final type of deviation from the script-defined expectations may occur if the banking transaction includes a non-central attribute. Some attributes are inappropriate in the context of an event, even if they might be considered desirable independent of the script (Taylor and Crocker 1981). In the bank example, a non-central attribute would be present if the security guards were overly friendly. Given their function, friendly overtures from a security guard could make a customer quite nervous. Thus, even though friendliness would ordinarily be considered a favorable quality, the presence of this attribute in these actors in the banking event would constitute a deviation from the expectations defined by the script. As in the case of the other deviations, the predicted result would be a negative evaluation of the event, and an expression of dissatisfaction.

The previous example serves to illustrate both the process of a script-based evaluation and several sources of deviations from script-defined expectations which may result in dissatisfaction. The nature of these deviations underscores the difference between the relevant expectations in evaluations of goods versus services. None of the deviations described in the examples involved a product-related attribute. Rather, the obstacle involved part of the setting in which the product was produced/consumed; the error occurred in the process of producing the product; and the non-central attribute was present in an employee of the seller/producer of the product. Thus, while it appears to be the case that satisfaction evaluations of both goods and services involve a comparison similar to that modeled by the disconfirmation paradigm, the expectations upon which services are evaluated may be defined by the script for the transaction, while those for goods are tied much more directly to the object purchased in the transaction.

MARKETING IMPLICATIONS OF SCRIPT-BASED EVALUATIONS

The significance of the script-based evaluation process for marketers of services lies in its potential to offer some much needed guidance in designing and implementing marketing strategies for services which will ensure satisfaction. To the degree that consumers possess scripts for service transactions, and that the expectations defined by those scripts provide a basis for evaluating current experience, a full understanding of the nature and function of scripts is prerequisite to successful services marketing.

In particular, scripts will be important to marketing strategists in two situations: first, when a services marketer wishes to ensure the continuing satisfaction of con-

sumers with current offerings; and secondly, when the marketer wishes to introduce modifications or substantial innovations in some mix element. In the first situation, the marketer's success in satisfying consumers will depend on his ability to provide an offering which is a good match to the consumers' script-defined expectations. These expectations may extend well beyond specific attributes of the service per se, and include aspects of the production and consumption processes as well. In addition, expectations may be defined for objects included in the service transaction and the setting in which the service is performed, as well as for the actors who participate in the transaction. A full understanding of all these script-defined expectations is necessary to the effective execution of the marketing task for a service.

In the second situation, when a services marketer wishes to introduce a modification or a major innovation in his offering, he is faced with a more complex task in terms of the script concept. If a consumer possesses a script for the service transaction, even minor modifications may constitute a deviation from the script. Thus, the new offering will be a poor match to the script-defined expectations, and the resulting evaluation will decline as a consequence. The low evaluations will be likely to be accompanied by a reduction in consumer satisfaction and, eventually, lost sales.

To minimize or counteract these undesirable outcomes, it would be in the interests of marketing strategists to understand precisely the nature of the consumer's affective responses to the various script deviations described previously (errors, obstacles and non-central attributes). Should it be the case that the negative impact on evaluations is the same for each type of deviation, then obviously the marketing strategy which is easiest to implement would be indicated for the new service. However, if there is a difference in the impact on satisfaction which accompanies the various deviations, then the interests of both marketers and consumers would be best served if strategies were implemented which avoided those deviations leading to the highest levels of dissatisfaction. Furthermore, an understanding of the relative impact of the various deviations is necessary in order to develop marketing strategies which counteract their negative effect, regardless of magnitude. To the degree that marketers face increasing pressures to be innovative in order to retain a competitive position, the effect on consumer satisfaction of the various script deviations is both an important and timely consideration for services providers.

SUMMARY

This paper has described a process by which consumers may evaluate satisfaction with services which is based on a cognitive script. Specifically, it was suggested that if a service transaction is conceptualized as an event for which a consumer possesses a cognitive script, the expectations defined by that script will serve as a basis for the evaluation process. An understanding of these script-defined expectations will offer the marketer of services a basis for designing and implementing strategies which will ensure consumer satisfaction. The validity of a script-based evaluation process is an empirical question which may provide a direction for future investigations of consumer satisfaction with services.

REFERENCES

Abbott, V. and J. B. Black (1980), "The Representation of Scripts in Memory," (Cognitive Science Technical Report #5), New Haven, CT: Yale University Press.

Anderson, R. E. (1973), "Consumer Dissatisfaction: The Effect of Disconfirmed Expectancy on Perceived Product

Performance," Journal of Marketing Research, 14 (February), 38-44.

Bower, G. H., J. B. Black, and T. J. Turner (1979), "Scripts in Memory for Text," Cognitive Psychology, 11, 177-220.

Cardozo, R. N. (1965), "An Experimental Study of Consumer Effort, Expectation and Satisfaction," Journal of Marketing Research, 2 (August), 244-249.

Churchill, Jr., G. A. and C. Surprenant (1982), "An Investigation into the Determinants of Customer Satisfaction," Working Paper Series, University of Wisconsin-Madison.

Czepiel, J. A., L. J. Rosenberg, and A. Akerele (1975), "Perspectives on Consumer Satisfaction," in 1974 Combined Proceedings, R. Curan, ed., Chicago: American Marketing Association, 119-123.

Eiglier, P. E., E. Langeard, C. H. Lovelock, J. E. G. Bateson, and R. F. Young (1977), Marketing Consumer Services: New Insights, Cambridge, MA: Marketing Science Institute.

John, G. and J. C. Whitney (1982), "An Empirical Investigation of the Serial Structure of Scripts," AMA Educators' Conference Proceedings, Chicago: American Marketing Association, 75-79.

Liechty, M. G. and G. A. Churchill, Jr. (1979), "Conceptual Insights into Consumer Satisfaction with Services," AMA Educators' Conference Proceedings, Chicago: American Marketing Association, 509-515.

Neisser, V. (1976), Cognition and Reality: Principles and Implications of Cognitive Psychology, San Francisco: Freeman.

Oliver, R. L. (1980a), "A Cognitive Model of the Antecedents and Consequences of Satisfaction Decisions," Journal of Marketing Research, 17 (November), 460-469.

_____ (1980b), "Theoretical Bases of Consumer Satisfaction Research: Review, Critique and Future Direction," paper presented at the American Marketing Association Second Special Conference on Marketing Theory.

Olshavsky, R. W. and J. A. Miller (1972), "Consumer Expectations, Product Performance, and Perceived Product Quality," Journal of Marketing Research, 9 (February), 19-21.

Olson, J. C. and P. Dover (1976), "Effects of Expectation Creation and Disconfirmation on Belief Elements of Cognitive Structures," in Advances in Consumer Research, B. Anderson, ed., Vol. 3, Chicago: Association for Consumer Research.

Rathmell, J. M. (1974), Marketing in the Service Sector, Cambridge, MA: Winthrop Publishers.

Schank, R. C. and R. P. Abelson (1977), Scripts, Plans, Goals and Understanding, Hillsdale, NJ: Lawrence Erlbaum Associates.

Shostack, G. L. (1977), "Breaking Free from Product Marketing," Journal of Marketing, 4 (April), 73-80.

Swan, J. E., I. F. Trawick, and M. G. Carroll (1981), "Effect of Participation in Marketing Research and Consumer Attitudes Toward Research and Satisfaction with a Service," Journal of Marketing Research, 18 (August), 356-363.

Taylor, S. E. and J. Crocker (1981), "Schematic Bases of Social Information Processing," in Social Cognition: The Ontario Symposium, E. T. Higgins, C. P. Herman and M. P. Zanna, eds., Hillsdale, NJ: Lawrence Erlbaum Associates.

Trawick, I. F. and J. E. Swan (1980), "Inferred and Perceived Disconfirmation in Consumer Satisfaction," AMA Educators' Conference Proceedings, Chicago: American Marketing Association, 97-101.

Zeithaml, V. A. (1981), "How Consumer Evaluation Processes Differ Between Goods and Services," in Marketing of Services, J. H. Donnelly and W. R. George, eds., Chicago: American Marketing Association, 186-190.

CONSUMER RESEARCH IN THE SERVICE SECTOR

Alan R. Andreasen, University of Illinois

A number of articles in recent years, including those at this conference, have pointed out the unique features one encounters when studying the service sector. Some of these differences are in degree. For example, Stiff and Pollack (1982) point out that service businesses are more often apt to be of small scale and locally owned and as a consequence, service industries often have lower concentration ratios. Of relevance to the consumer behavior researcher is the fact that services also more often involve intangible rather than tangible attributes (Rathwell 1974, Liechty and Churchill 1979). For instance, rental of a motel room does involve tangible factors like the temporary use of a bed, dresser, and a swimming pool plus "permanent" consumption of tangible goods such as food and liquor, soaps and shampoos. However, one also gains access to intangibles such as ambience, location, reservation assistance, and staff friendliness or competence.

Other differences between the product and service sectors of interest to the consumer behavior researcher are differences in kind. For example, the purchase of many services involves both consumption and production on the part of consumers. "Purchase" of an education clearly requires a good deal of production on the part of the student. As students are often told, "the more you put into a course [produce], the more you get out of it [consume]." What is crucial is that in buying such services as a movie, a concert, psychiatric care or home improvement tool rental, the quality of the service can be materially affected by the consumer's own input.

Further, because many services are created in the process of consumption, this means that, by definition, they cannot be pretested in advance of purchase. One typically cannot practice visiting a doctor, getting a television repaired, or staying at an out-of-town hotel.

IMPLICATIONS FOR CONSUMER BEHAVIOR RESEARCH

The differences outlined above raise both interesting research issues for consumer behavior theorists and specific cautions about carrying out any kind of research in this growing area. They also suggest several interesting practical implications. We shall touch briefly on each of these characteristics in turn.

Intangible Attributes

The fact that services involve features that do not have a physical counterpart means, of course, that for such features consumers cannot examine objective measurements of likely performance. As a consequence, they must rely either on the evaluations and recommendations of others—including formal consumer advisory groups—or on their own personal investigations. Where the latter is used, an interesting set of research questions then involves consumers' use of cues as surrogate predictors of performance. Basic questions to be asked are:

1. What cues do consumers in fact use to evaluate service offerings?
2. Do these cues vary significantly across service categories?
3. Do given consumers tend to use the same cues for all services or do the cues vary by service type?

4. Can consumers be segmented on the basis of the types of cues they prefer to use?
5. Do consumer preferences for cues vary with their personality traits, past experience with the service, general confidence as consumers, education, or social class?

While these are questions that have been studied before in the product sector (Urban 1975), their heightened salience in the service sector recommends replications of the product studies to see if important differences appear in this new context.

The importance of intangible features in service purchase decisions also makes it imperative that in any such decisions researchers learn how each consumer perceives the service offering since the nature of that offering is very much in the eye of the consumer, even more so than is the case for products. For this reason also, it may often be desirable in the analysis stage of such studies to use consumer definitions of the service when aggregating responses or otherwise trying to segment services and/or consumers.

Consumers as Producers

If one recognizes that consumers are involved as producers for many services, then to define the service, to predict whether it will be purchased (and from which supplier) and to understand how consumers evaluate the outcome of the transaction, one must study the consumer's role in the process. This would include, where possible, both subjective and objective measurements of this role. As Bateson (1982) points out, consumers vary in their participation in the service production process both out of necessity and out of preference. To continue the education analogy, many schools force students to be active producers of their own education while many schools "spoon feed" their student body. At the other end of the transaction, many students are excited and active learners and would be such at any institution while others would be very passive, even antagonistic to education.

While Bateson (1982) has made an important beginning in cataloguing the extent to which consumers of different services prefer to engage in "production," it is also important to understand how often in practice they carry out their preferences and how often they must play other roles as specified by the service supplier. Finally, it is also important to learn whether and when these two role definers interact. That is, under what circumstance does the consumer choose a service supplier who yields him or her the extent of role participation he or she prefers. Where there is a mismatch, one must ask whether this is really due to low role preference on the part of the consumer, mitigating circumstances or supplier pressure.

Such research could have very important practical as well as theoretical implications. For example, it may be that given service suppliers may be able to segment their offerings to tap new markets. For example, traditional auto or appliance repair outlets might set aside certain spaces or certain times of the week for those who wish to do the repair work themselves. Or, alternatively, they might offer different levels of service assistance from complete hands-off through minimal guidance to complete

63

hands-on intervention, again depending on the consumer's preference for involvement--and possibly his or her trust in the service supplier or reactions to the supplier's schedule of charges. Such a modular approach to service offerings would also seem to be applicable to home repair, home construction, and legal and medical care. In the near term, case studies of any services now offering such modular systems and the different kinds of consumers they serve would prove particularly instructive.

A second area in which considerations of consumer involvement in service production is important is at the evaluation stage of the process. The more that the consumer is an active producer of the service, the more important it becomes to understand his or her perceptions of each party's relative contribution to the outcome. Again, both objective and subjective measures should be taken. For example, although a consumer may clearly have an active role in the process (e.g., education) by objective standards, it may be that he or she for whatever psychological reasons, perceives the success or failure of the outcome to be solely attributable to the supplier. ("I studied hard, but the teacher was terrible, didn't prepare me well..."). Clearly, "locus-of-control" theory would be an important framework for a program of research on this issue.

Lack of Trialability

When the consumer cannot pretest a service, the decision to purchase is probably one of the clearest cases we have of consumer risk-taking. For this reason, the classical models from Bauer (1967) onward should prove useful. However, as has been emphasized in this note, the consumers' perception of the risk and their method of handling it may well depend on their definition of the service situation. Thus, a student's evaluation of various university programs may depend on what he or she perceives the role of a university education in his or her future life. Thus, a student interested in having a "good time" and then going on to graduate school may see the risks in a school choice to be very different from a pre-law student anxious to use a law school degree as the key to a position at a major law firm. Or alternatively a restaurant choice may have very different risk connotations depending on whether one is grabbing a quick bite alone, taking out a first date, or entertaining a business client.

Again, it would seem that a systematic program of research ascertaining consumer risk-reduction strategies as they vary across consumers, services and situations would be extremely valuable from both a practical and theoretical standpoint.

SUMMARY

The present movement toward carving out a special interest area for services within the field of marketing suggests a number of possibilities for expanding our theories about consumer behavior and our ability to provide practical guidance to service suppliers. In particular, the unique role of consumers in service production, the intangible character of many services and the impossibility of trial in many service situations, all require renewed attention to old issues in marketing--i.e., defining the offering, understanding the nature of the risks involved, and identifying the cues consumers use to predict performance. These characteristics also raise one important new issue--understanding how the consumer views his or her own role as it affects the overall evaluation of the outcome of the service. It is hoped that all of these topics will receive the attention their potential contributions to the general field of marketing recommend.

REFERENCES

Bateson, John (1982), "The Self-Service Customer--Empirical Findings" in Proceedings of the 2nd American Marketing Association Services Marketing Conference. Chicago: American Marketing Association.

Bauer, Raymond A. (1967), "Consumer Behavior as Risk Taking" in Donald F. Cox, ed., Risk Taking and Information Handling in Consumer Behavior. Boston: Division of Research, Harvard Business School.

Liechty, M. B. and Gilbert A. Churchill (1979), "Conceptual Insights into Consumer Satisfaction with Services" in Proceedings, American Marketing Association Educators' Conference. Chicago: American Marketing Association, 509-515.

Stiff, Ronald and Julie Pollack (1982), "Consumerism in the Service Sector: Selected Issues and Opportunities" in Proceedings of the 2nd American Marketing Association Services Marketing Conference. Chicago: American Marketing Association.

Rathwell, John M. (1974), Marketing in the Service Sector. Cambridge, MA: Winthrop Publishers.

PERSONAL SELLING OF SERVICES

William R. George, Villanova University, Villanova
J. Patrick Kelly, Brigham Young University, Provo
Claudia E. Marshall, The Chase Manhattan Bank, N.A., New York City

ABSTRACT

Marketing management strategies for services require different perspectives and approaches than for goods. The unique characteristics of services and the particular problems that service marketers experience necessitate these differences. One strategic area of concern for the services marketer is the tailoring of each component of the promotion mix. Usually personal selling is the predominant component of this mix. Based on empirical data collected by the authors, seven guidelines for the personal selling of services are presented.

INTRODUCTION

Five characteristics of services have a major impact on the development of services marketing strategies. Simultaneous production and consumption may provide the greatest challenge for the services marketer since this entails both a direct organization/consumer interface and the consumer's participation in production (Gronroos 1980; Eiglier and Langeard 1977). In addition to traditional marketing considerations, this simultaneity necessitates interactive marketing which includes both buyer-seller and buyer-producer interactions. The service consumer must interact with the physical/technical resources, with the contact personnel, and with other consumers. The other important characteristics of services are intangibility, the importance of the producer, perishability, and nonstandardization.

Another set of factors that impact on the personal selling function of services as compared to goods is the sequential differences and the interrelationships between production, marketing, and consumption. A good is first produced, then sold, and lastly consumed. In contrast, a service is first sold and then produced and consumed simultaneously. This means that there is only a tangential relationship between producer, seller, and consumer with goods transactions, while there is a considerable overlap between the three in the selling, producing, and consuming of services.

Based on these characteristics of services and the differences in sequential and interrelationship factors of production, marketing, and consumption of services, it is our contention that personal selling usually dominates the promotion mix of services marketing strategies. Booms and Bitner (1981) suggest several unique marketing problems of service firms: quality control, customer/firm interface, and fragmented marketing base. These problems also reinforce the role of personal selling in services marketing. Brundage and Marshall (1980) note that the service fit is a function of consumer need to service capability with the overlapping of these two defining the selling, producing, and consuming that occur. A sales approach emphasizes the increase of consumer usage of existing service capability, while a marketing approach focuses on extending service capability. In both cases, it is again clear that personal selling will dominate the services promotion mix.

Because of this great importance of the personal selling function in services marketing, we have collected empirical data on the differences between the selling of goods and services as perceived by sales representatives from both goods and services firms. From that data we have derived the following personal selling of services model. This model was then validated by comparing it to an actual marketing program of a major bank. The bank program chosen was their International Institutional business, where the role of the primary sales force is termed "relationship management." Each of the seven guidelines of the model was reviewed and tested against a part of this program which had been actually implemented in the International Institutional business. An outline of the model and applications for each of the guidelines follows.

MODEL AND APPLICATIONS

1. Orchestrate service purchase encounter.

   a. input: to solicit buyer needs and expectations; to assess knowledge of evaluative criteria.

   b. processing: (application of skills = technical; presentation issues = selling)
      to apply technical expertise;
      to recognize the representative as surrogate for the service;
      to manage the impressions of the buyer-seller and buyer-producer interactions;
      to elicit positive customer participation.

   c. output: to generate a pleasant, satisfying service purchase experience long term.

Applications

   a. Coordination of customer sales over time through the Relationship Manager.

   b. Management of quality service delivery and positioning for cross-selling of services.

   c. Integration of non-sales marketing support activities -- internal sales and product customer training.

2. Facilitate quality assessment

   to establish reasonable levels of expected performance;
   to use established expectations as basis for judging quality after purchase.

Applications

   a. Set customer expectations for standard servicing and exception handling. Example: The Regional Service Center.

3. Tangibilize the service:

>   to teach what the buyer should look for --
>   evaluative criteria;
>   to educate the buyer on comparing alternative
>   services -- comparative analysis;
>   to teach the buyer about the uniqueness of the
>   service -- differential advantage(s).

Applications

a. Relationship Manager Training is key. Role of product knowledge: customer needs and competitive distinctions.

b. Use visual aids in the selling process - e.g., videotape, slides, and films.

4. Emphasize organizational image:

>   to assess customer's awareness level of the
>   generic service, the firm, and the representative;
>   to communicate relevant image attributes of the
>   service, the firm, and the representative.

Applications

a. Research emphasizes relationship-based buying by customers (versus commodity-based buying).

b. Advertising and marketing support materials reinforce overall bank image and individual service capabilities.

5. Utilize references external to the organization

>   to encourage satisfied customers to become
>   involved in the communication process -- manage
>   word-of-mouth "advertising";
>   to develop and manage favorable publicity.

Applications

a. Importance of "word-of-mouth" reinforces use of customer sales seminars.

b. Public relations support aids marketing programs.

6. Recognize great importance of all public contact personnel.

>   to sensitize all personnel of their direct role
>   in the customer satisfaction process;
>   to minimize the total number of people
>   interacting with each specific customer.

Applications

a. Multiple customer contact points need coordination -- e.g., Relationship Manager, customer service assistants, technical sales reps., operations personnel, and senior management.

7. Recognize customer involvement during the service design process to generate customer specifications by asking questions, showing examples, etc.

Applications

a. Expand capability of Relationship Manager as gatherer of competitive intelligence.

Conclusion

A model of seven guidelines for the personal selling of services was derived from empirical data and then validated by comparison with an established bank marketing program.

A CASE HISTORY

Note: The three cases which follow were designed to provide a mechanism of discussion for participants of the workshop.

The A.J. Hogle Company is a medium-sized stock brokerage firm located in a major midwestern city. Jim Nielsen had been the manager of the 11-man brokerage company for the past three years. Although the firm was profitable, Jim was concerned about expanding the customer base of A.J. Hogle. Increased competition from a new E.F. Hutton office and a shift of some existing customers away from full service brokerages to discounters had Jim concerned about his firm's future growth. In an attempt to explore new market opportunities, Jim came across a study conducted in early 1982 by an independent research company.

This study was conducted on public attitudes toward investing. This report concluded that the vast majority of brokerage firms had penetrated several market segments quite deeply. These included experienced older investors, experienced realists, and conservative upscale clients. The study suggested that clients and prospects have different financial goals, attitudes, and opinions about investment opportunities, expectations about performance of investments, willingness to take risks, and knowledge about investments.

Two segments were identified as having excellent potential. These were first, the affluent blue-collar segment comprising 14.8 million households. This is the largest and most affluent segment of people who have never owned securities. In this segment, most are employed full time, largely as skilled craftspeople and labor supervisors. Fewer than 20 percent attended college and 85 percent are young, married, and have children.

The second segment consists of both single and married working women. Women constitute more than half of all American millionaires, and more than half of adult stockholders. The study also indicated 36 percent of women who play an active role in their financial affairs do not enjoy making these decisions. Those who do not participate in financial affairs feel they lack the education to make proper judgments, are afraid of losing money, and do not know whom to trust.

Four significant barriers in the marketing of securities to these two segments were identified. One, many in these groups must be reached in their homes for they are otherwise inaccessible. Two, brokers have consistently used language and other interpersonal cues to show their lack of interest, especially in the blue collar segment. Three, potential customers fear investments and are ignorant of opportunities. Four, account executives do not feel comfortable dealing with these prospects.

Jim called a meeting of the other 11 male brokers in his office and a unanimous decision was made to become more aggressive in pursuing both of these market segments. When additional training was suggested to deal with this new approach, each of the brokers expressed confidence they knew all there was to know about selling securities and that additional training would not be necessary. One of the brokers expressed a view typical of the others when he said, "All we need is to be pointed in the right direction. We can take it from there."

After a two-month effort, Jim was not pleased with the process most of his account representatives were achieving in reaching the blue collar or working women segments. He decided to question some and listen to others' conversations to evaluate how they handled their sales presentations. Here are briefly some of the promotional tactics and actual conversations of those brokers. Can you identify where improvements might be made in personal selling efforts?

Case #1

Roger Clarke had been a broker with A.J. Hogle for just over six months. Prior to joining the brokerage firm, he had sold waterless cookware door to door using the referral system. He was convinced that using referrals and contacting prospects in their homes was a great way to reach the working women segment he had been told to pursue. After the last few unsuccessful attempts to sell a retirement program to the secretaries of a nationwide insurance company, Roger was more than a little discouraged. He had made over ten presentations to these secretaries in groups of between three to six at each meeting. His approach was one of spreading a dark purple velvet cloth on the floor as soon as he entered the home of a prospect and placing a prospectus from the mutual fund he was selling in a golden colored pouch. He began his presentation by removing the fund from the pouch and asking each of the young secretaries if they wanted to be as poor when they retired as their parents were today. Then he would explain the benefits of a no-load mutual fund that operated like an annuity fund. He always asked if there were any questions and because no one ever asked any and he knew he spoke slowly, he was convinced all potential questions were handled in the presentation. To help close the sales, he would pass around the contracts for each girl to sign and indicate if they signed up tonight he had a free plastic rain bonnet for each of them.

Case #2

Bob and Sally Wise were both in their early thirties. Bob was a foreman at a local castings company. They had contacted the A.J. Hogle Company to see what they could do with part of their savings to earn more than the 5-1/4% they were currently earning. They came to the office late one Friday afternoon and asked to see someone. Because Larry Adams was the next broker to receive a walk-in customer, they were directed to his desk by the receptionist. Larry finished discussing his plans for that evening with another broker, and after a brief introduction by the receptionist, Bob and Sally sat down. After Larry noticed Bob's soiled hands, he said, "Well what can we do for you?"

Bob replied that they thought they might be interested in earning more than 5-1/4% on their savings. Larry said, "The A.J. Hogle Company has some excellent investments and the sky is the limit. Don't worry about a thing. I helped another couple just like you earn a lot more than just 5-1/4% on their money. How much money do you have to invest?"

Just then the phone on Larry's desk rang. When Larry finished the call, he turned back to where Bob and Sally were sitting and found them gone.

Case #3

Brent Wilson was a specialist in financial estate planning. He had been with A.J. Hogle for 12 years. He consistently was the sales leader in his office. Most of his clients were successful businessmen and many had been with him for 11 to 12 years. Brent was not happy with the pressure placed on him to sell more to the working women segment, but he decided to give it a try to keep the manager off his back.

Brent's office wall was covered with sales awards he had won over the past 12 years. He was proud of these accomplishments and felt he could be successful in selling his services to anyone. One of his clients who was vice-president of sales at a large printing firm told him about their company president who was very much into the stock market. This vice-president's name was Chris Turner and Brent was shocked to learn the president was a female. Brent was about to ask her to come to his office but decided it might be best to meet her at the printing firm. An appointment was made and Brent began to plan his strategy.

Brent was prompt for his appointment and after shaking hands, they both sat down. Brent began by saying, "I understand you do a lot of trading in the stock market. Because most of my clients speak highly of me and my skills in helping them manage their accounts, I thought I might be of service to you."

Chris came right to the point and asked, "What can you do for me that my current brokers can't do?"

"I have been a broker for 12 years and most of my customers seem very satisfied."

Chris indicated she used a number of different brokers and because she did her own evaluations of the securities she purchased, all she needed a broker for was to transact the order and any of the discount brokers could do that very well and for a lot less money than what Brent's firm charged.

After a few more attempts to convince Chris he was a good broker, she indicated she was busy and asked him to leave.

REFERENCES

Booms, Bernard H. and Mary J. Bitner (1981), "Marketing Strategies and Organization Structures for Service Firms," in Donnelly and George, Services Marketing (Chicago: American Marketing Association).

Brundage, Jane and Claudia Marshall (1980), "Training as a Marketing Management Tool," Training and Development Journal (November).

Eiglier, Pierre, et al. (1977), Marketing Consumer Services: New Insights (Cambridge: Marketing Science Institute).

Gronroos, Christian (1980), "Designing a Long-Range Marketing Strategy for Services," Long Range Planning (April).

STRATEGIC MANAGEMENT OF SERVICE DEVELOPMENT

Eric Langeard, Institut d'Administration des Entreprises, Université Aix-Marseille III
Pierre Eiglier, Institut d'Administration des Entreprises, Université Aix-Marseille III

ABSTRACT

The objective of this paper is to present a framework for
the strategic management of service development. Based on
the success or failure of a sample of European service
firms coping with service development, the paper proposes
a typology of multisite-multiservice choices, presents the
key elements of the new service formula, and introduces
four alternative service development strategies.

INTRODUCTION

Service development is still experienced by many managers
as a predominantly entrepreneurial process when dealing
with the discovery of new services or as an intuitive and
random process when taking care of the innovative redesign
of an existing service.

A more systematic, managerial approach of service development (Shostack 1982) and of strategic management of service
firms (Thomas 1978, Sasser et al. 1978, Carman and Langeard
1980) recently has been the focus of several studies.

The objective of this paper is to present a framework for
the strategic management of service development. It is
based on an investigation of service innovation processes.
At the request of the French National Research Center
for Social Sciences, an inventory of innovative service
firms has been completed. The scope of the study has been
limited to innovative service offerings leaving aside
back-office or purely functional innovations in finance or
personnel management. A total of 43 public or private
European firms has been surveyed ; most of them manage a
multi-site service operations ; they belong to a large diversity of service industries dealing with consumer and
business services (airlines, lodging, banking, restaurants,
institutional food, computer software, maintenance, security, insurance and retailing). The methodology included
the selection of a specific service by the research team
and the firm, the interviews of managers having played a
key role in the service development process, the communication of internal written documents, and the assessment of
the evolution of that service over time by top management
representatives.

Based on the success or failure of a well diversified
sample of service firms coping with service development,
. part one proposes a typology of multisite - multiservice
choices
. part two presents the fur key elements of what has been
called: the new service formula
. part three introduces four alternative service development strategies.

A Typology of Multisite - Multiservice Choices

This typology is relying upon the prior research of Sasser
and all (1978). Looking at the service firm life cycle,
they explored the breadth of service and geographic market
decisions and the evolution of their relationship over
time. In a previous article, Carman and Langeard (1980)
argued that "profitable growth service strategies are more
related to multisite development than to multiservice development". The research findings help to identify three
broad categories of scenarios located on the multisite -
multiservice grid (Figure 1).

FIGURE I: MULTISITE - MULTISERVICE GRID

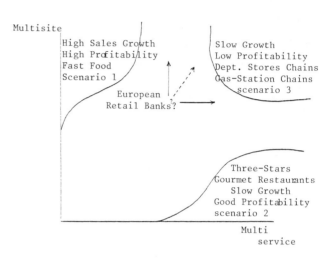

a) Scenario 1: A Multisite Network with a Narrow Line of
Services.

For the last twenty years the fast food industry has sus-
tained a spectacular growth through the development of
restaurant chains delivering a limited menu: hamburgers or
chicken or pizzas or croissants. A narrow line of services
limits the complexity of the delivery system and facilitates quality controls and new outlets development. When the
market is expanding rapidly, aggressive firms after having
simplified their service offering duplicate their delivery
system as fast as they can. Such a marketing strategy
favoring multi-units over multi-services brings a high
rate of sales growth and of profitability.

Standardization and specialization are two main characteristics of scenario 1. They create a working environment
that lacks flexibility, and any adjustement of the service
offering is a difficult task.

b) Scenario 2: A Large Number of Core Services Offered
Through a Few Sites.

Many service firms have made such a choice. The owners
have usually a very good knowledge of their local markets
and they are able to make an appropriate selection of
consumer segments, carefully watching the development of
new needs and rapidly serving them. The rate of sales
growth is usually limited by the narrow geographic boundaries of the market and depends on the ability of adding
new services. The percentage of local market share is high
and the profitability is good or very good although the
level of managerial complexity related to the rather small
size of these organizations is quite substantial. Such is
the case of a fully independent local department store.

A few large or medium-size firms have made the explicit
choice of scenario 2 by limiting their network to a small
number of units. The managerial complexity of each unit
derives from the objective of being excellent: the best

68

service performance. High quality becomes a marketing tool for expanding their geographic market. This is the case of amusement parks such as Disney World and gourmet restaurants with international visibility. For example, a gourmet restaurant is offering the following core services to several market segments: business lunch, gourmet week-end, "nouvelle cuisine" seminars, the mail-order business of selling high-quality wine and food products, the publishing of sophisticated cookbooks.

c) Scenario 3: A Multisite - Multiservice Organization.

This scenario is usually followed by service firms which belong to a mature industry. At an early stage, they may have started with secanrio 1. When their network has reached market saturation, they have slowly slipped away from scenario 1 by adding more and more services: gas service station chains.

Another category of firms are found within scenario 3. They have a long history behind them and they have never made an explicit and voluntary choice between a multisite and a multiservice development. Such is the case of European department store chains.

They are in great danger of suffering from slow sales growth combined with uncontrollable costs increase. Their sales growth is slowing down because on the best market opportunities they are competing with the highly specialized firms of scenario 1. Costs are difficult to control because their network is usually made of heterogeneous units which have attempted to fit the needs of local markets. Therefore comparisons are meaningless.

Some experts have wondered if European retail banks with huge network of branches will fall in the trap of scenario 3 or cut down their offering and simplify their delivery system.

It is very difficult to manage efficiently many services and many units at the same time and this is why scenario 3 is a trap. Every service firm has to face a choice between two opportunities for growth: scenarios 1 and 2. In both cases it is necessary to develop new services and the investigation of many failures strongly supports the need for a well-thought service development framework.

THE "NEW SERVICE" FORMULA

For an existing service firm, the introduction of a new service has far-reaching consequences. It has an impact on the logistics, on the way contact personnel works, on consumer behavior when interacting with the service organization. It may explain why innovative new services seem to be related to new service organizations.

Based on many observations across service industries, it appears that the lack of success of a new service offering is related to the managerial unability of handling a set of four key decisions and of preserving coherence and cohesiveness among them. The four decisions deal with the service concept, the market segment, the organization-client interface and the service image.

a) A Unique Service Concept

The service concept has to be clearly defined. At what consumer benefit, the service firm is aiming? Which service attributes express best the consumer benefit? Answering these two questions, the service firm will move in the direction of a well defined service concept. However it is necessary to go one step further: unlike product attributes, service attributes are not only related to the outcome but very much also to the process that is to say the ways and means the service is produced, distributed and consumed. Without an assessment of the respective roles of outcome-

related and process-related attributes a clear definition of the service concept cannot be obtained.

b) One Well-Identified Market Segment

The market segment has to be identified. The socio-demographic and psychographic characteristics have to take into account dimensions which measure not only the need people have of a specific service but also what kinds of trade-offs in terms of service accessibility they are willing to make (such as time versus money, proximity versus exclusivity, propensity to participate to service performance, etc...). Segmentation is usually given to the service firm as a consequence of operating constraints, network localisation and service atmosphere and ambiance. It is crucial to manage an active segmentation policy and to control over time the coherence of the market segment with the service concept.

The singularity of the service concept aiming at one market segment has to be stressed. It has to be a unique concept compared to all those already implemented by competing service organizations. It is also a streamlined, tailor-made service concept that takes into account the needs of the choosen market segment.

c) A Specialized, Easy to Duplicate Delivery System

The organization-client interface has to be organized in a network. Each unit has at the same time to be easily integrated to its specific geographic and cultural environments and to have a similar operating system than other units. This similarity is necessary for two reasons: speed is often a competitive advantage when building a multi-units service network, and clients know well what role to perform. What kind of participative behavior is expected from clients, is a key dimension of the management of interface and it is strongly related to market segment identification. Complexity is a growing danger accompanying the evolution of large service networks. The control of interface complexity is related to management's capacity and willingness to keep the service concept simple.

d) A Clear, Easy-to-Remember Service Image

The service image has to facilitate a clear communication between the service organization and its potential clients. Due to the double intangibility of services, it is not an easy task to create a good communication about services. A clever use of mass medias with the help of a creative advertising agency is not enough. The whole service organization is building its own image when interacting with clients. Clients themselves are spreading an image when sharing their experience with other people. The service image is a key decision highly dependent on the three other. The lack of singularity of the service concept, the lack of simplicity of the delivery system prevent the diffusion of a significant image. The service image should bring forward the harmony and the fitness of the formula.

e) The Management of the Service Formula: A Three-Stage Process

Thus, each key element has to find its own coherence. However the cohesiveness of the four elements is essential for the building of a profitable and well-accepted service formula. The development of this cohesiveness is a three-stage process (Figure 2).

FIGURE 2
THE SERVICE FORMULA: A COMMON SET OF KEY DECISIONS

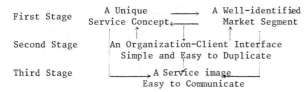

. First stage has to deal with the matching of a simple concept with a market segment primarily identified on the basis of its participative or non participative behavior.

. Second stage has to deal with the design of an organization-client interface which is easy to duplicate and to control.

. Third stage has to deal with the building of an image which is easy to communicate.

This three-stage process is obviously an iterative process. For example, the design of the organization-client interface may not succeed to fit the characteristics of the market segment. In that case the redefinition of the market segment may imply a new formulation of the service concept.

FOUR SERVICE DEVELOPMENT STRATEGIES

The development of new services is happening at all stages of the service firm life cycle. A few entrepreneurs start a new firm with the help of an innovative service. The service formula is applicable at its best and a network strategy is usually adopted. Many existing firms market new services during the growth, maturity or decline phase of their life-cycle. The service formula should be applied. However, many firms make compromises at the expense of policy coherence. They may use one of the two strategies under one brand or under multiple brands. In Figure 3 the four service development strategies are positioned on the multisite-multiservice grid.

a) The Network Strategy (I)

Mostly used by entrepreneurial firms opening a new mass market with an innovative service concept.

The market potential is important and requires a large network.

Imitation being expected, priority is given to the fast spread of new units at premium locations.

Service offering is kept narrow in order:
. to ease the duplication of the servuction which is made of the physical support, the contact personnel's and the client's respective roles as it is implemented in each unit of the network (Langeard et al. 1981);
. to implement a rigorous control of service quality and costs
. to facilitate the communication with the market segment.

The service concept is strong. It has an excellent price-quality ratio. Therefore, it is a key-element of the marketing mix together with the choice of locations: "product" policy and "distribution" policy have a major impact, communication policy and pricing policy are only supporting policies.

The marketing management of each unit is very simple. If a wrong choice of location has been made, an aggressive price and communication mix is not likely to overcome the mistake.

The marketing function within the service organization is

unsophisticated. It relies on the ability of:
. the technical department to improve the physical support of rhe service formula ;
. the operations department to maintain a consumer-oriented quality control of significant attributes ;
. the training department to upgrade the communication skills of the contact-personnel.

The life expectancy of this strategy is rather short - ten to fifteen years. When one reach market saturation, this strategy has to be abandonned.

The identifiable characteristics of this strategy are :
. a narrow offering backed up with a strong service concept
. a cookie-cutter type of a servuction
. a single brand with a simple image

Examples:
. Courte-Paille - Restaurant Industry - France
. La Quinta - Hotel Industry - U.S.A.

b) The Service Cluster Strategy (II)

Mostly used by firms opening a new professional market or a consumer - high quality market ;

Priority is given to choice and quality, as a consequence the network is small or highly selective to ease quality control and capacity management ;

Service offering is rather complex. It requires a flexible handling of the service situation. Many different services are offered. Their common denominator is a characteristic of exclusive, original quality which contributes to strengthen the global image ;

The strength of the service concept is a high level of quality performance which creates a strong customer loyalty.

Service image is critical to keep minimal the size of the network. One is reaching and attracting far-away potential consumers instead of implementing an intensive network.

"Product" Policy and Communication Policy are the two key-elements of the marketing mix.

Pricing policy is important because profitability is more related to the respective net margin of a large number of services than to total revenues. The choice of a location is not a complex decision and it is a marketing factor of secondary importance.

Image building requires time. Therefore, priority is not given to a high rate of business development but to the management of quality evidence.

The servuction system is as complex as the service offering. If many services are delivered from the same place, a polyvalent use of human resources should not be obtained at the expense of professional skills. When services are physically dispersed, it raises the problem of maintaining a coherent system in the eye of the customers.

Marketing is not as critical as operations management.

The marketing function is located at the top management level and it has two main tasks:
. Internal marketing, that is to say explaining to all categories of personnel the service philosophy of the firm and obtaining a commitment on how to work with clients :
. Service offering optimization, managing changes, matching evolving clients' needs with available resources.

Life expectancy of this strategy is high: twenty years and many more.

The identifiable characteristics are:
. A multiple offering backed up with a high quality image
. A diversified servuction taking place in a few locations
. A single brand with a sophisticated image.

Examples:
Four Seasons - Hôtel Industry - U.S.A.
FNAC - Distribution of Leisure Products - France

c) The Diversified Network and Service Strategy under one Brand (Strategy III)

Mostly used by service firms having inherited a heterogeneous network offering many different services. This strategy is implemented in order to clarify the offering and to control the heterogeneity of the network.

Overall, this strategy is complex. It combines brand visibility and network effect with micro-opportunities related to local markets.

Each network unit is generally a sizable piece of investment with a large operating budget supporting the delivery of several core services.

For the implementation of this strategy an audit of each unit is required. Common characteristics are identified and homogeneous groupings of units are organized. Original units are kept separate, closed down or sold.

Marketing priorities are made for each group of units.

The service concept has to be strong at the local (or group) level. It may be strong at the brand level if one succeds in elaborating a service philosophy which is adaptable to a wide diversity of market situations.

Several marketing mix are managed throughout the network. "Product" Policy and Communication Policy are predominantly local and they are the key elements of the mix. The Pricing Policy is attempting to limit incoherent and cumbersome price differences. The distribution policy is not critical. At best it maintains a limited impact of the network effect.

An overall brand communication is often used with an institutional appeal at a global level and as a network reminder at the local level or accompanying the promotion of a specific service.

The marketing function is sophisticated. There is a need for a high level of cooperation between marketing managers at the Headquarters and operating field managers.

This strategy has a life expectancy which is difficult to predict. On one hand, it is not sensitive to market saturation, on the other hand it could be easily hurt by a drastic change of competitive service offerings.

The identifiable characteristics of this strategy are:
. a diversified offering adjusted to local market conditions
. an adaptative servuction taking place in a large number of locations
. a single brand with a broad image.

Example:
. American Express   Travel and Financial Industry - U.S.A.

d) The Diversified Network and Service Strategy with Multiple Brands (Strategy IV)

Mostly used by service firms minimizing voluntarily the marketing advantages of the network effect.

each network unit has its own servuction which is not derived from a general model, - a model that does not exist.

Market segments may be different from one unit to another, which, very often, have distinctive brand names.

The local unit manager is planning the marketing mix. "Product" Policy and location are the key elements of the mix. The communication policy is promoting a specific unit with all its offerings or a specific service delivered at a specific place. The pricing policy is taylored at the local level and no attempt is made to organize a global price structure.

A global communication policy may exist. In that case, an "umbrella" brand name is added to local brands. Its content promotes the diversity of the network as its differentiated appeal.

The marketing function takes place in the field. Headquarters marketing experts have little direct action. Their main role is to maintain a high level of internal marketing within and between units.

The multisite heterogeneity is costly even if outside of marketing some positive synergy exists throughout the network (purchasing, training, accounting).

The life expectancy of this strategy depends on the capacity of each unit to maintain an above average contribution to profitability.

The identifiable characteristics of this strategy are:
. a multiple offering
. a diversified servuction taking place in a large network
. a multiple brand policy

Example :
. Grand Metropolitan Hotels - Hotel Industry - U.K.
The group manages a European network of first class hotels, under their own brand names such as Lotti, Meurice, etc...
. Trust House Forte - Hotel and Restaurant Industry - U.K.
The group manages many different units under their own brand names and the THF umbrella.
. Relais & Châteaux - Hotel and Restaurant Industry - France. A European consortium of independent first class hotels or restaurants sharing a luxury appeal that is implemented in many different ways, under individual brand names and the Relais et Châteaux umbrella.

CONCLUSION: DYNAMIC RELATIONSHIPS AMONG
THE FOUR SERVICE DEVELOPMENT STRATEGIES

These four strategies are not used indifferently by any kind of service firms. In our analysis of each of them we have associated them with several environmental and managerial characteristics. A final remark should be made about possible shifts from one strategy to another. The arrows on Figure 3 are visualizing these possible shifts. Strategy I is usually associated with the birth of a new service firm or of a highly visible, fully autonomous division of an existing firm. Therefore, a service firm could implement one strategy I, or develop a portfolio of several strategies I, or shift from strategy IV to a portfolio of strategies I (Arrow I). Strategy II is often a lifetime strategy for a service firm. Sometimes diversification brings so much marketing complexity that a shift to strategy IV is needed (Arrow 2). Strategies III and IV are always implemented by existing service firms, very much in the maturity phase of their life cycle. They are useful strategies for firms trying to escape from quadrant 3 of the multisite-multiservice grid (Arrows 3 and 4). The shift from strategy I to strategy III coincides usually with market saturation and it should be implemented as an explicit strategic move (Arrow 5). Moving from strategy III to strategy IV is a defensive adaptation to an excessive level of marketing complexity (Arrow 6).

FIGURE 3
FOUR SERVICE DEVELOPMENT STRATEGIES
ON THE MULTISITE-MULTISERVICE GRID.

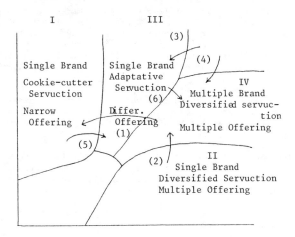

REFERENCES

Carman James M., Eric Langeard (1980), "Growth Strategies
for Service Firms," in Strategic Management Journal,
vol. 1, 7-22.

Langeard Eric, John E. Bateson, Christopher H. Lovelock and
Pierre Eiglier (1981), "Services Marketing: New Insights
from Consumers and Managers," in Marketing Science Institute, n° 81-104, August, Boston, p. 13.

Sasser W. Earl, R. Paul Olsen, D. Daryl Wyckoff (1978),
in Management of Service Operations, Allyn and Bacon,
Boston.

Shohstack G. Lynn (1982), "How to Design a Service," in
European Journal of Marketing, n° 1, 49-63.

Thomas Dan R.E. (1978), "Strategy is Different in Service
Businesses," in Harvard Business Review, July-August,
158-165.

NEW SERVICE DEVELOPMENT: THE CABLE TV CONNECTION

Richard K. Robinson, Marquette University

ABSTRACT

Within the developing literature on service marketing
little attention has been paid to the complex process of
new service development. This paper examines the development process for an innovation in cable television --
the business services network. Applications of product
planning and service marketing concepts in the business-
service development stages completed to date are discussed.

INTRODUCTION

While the past decade has reflected steadily increasing
academic interest in marketing theory and strategy for
services, new service development has remained largely
an uncharted territory. Two service marketing texts
characterized the situation in the mid-1970s by noting
that new service development was "at a very elementary
stage" (Rathmell 1974) and that it fell far short of being a well-developed art (Hise 1977). Unfortunately, the
state of the art has not changed appreciably in terms of
the extent of the literature available on the topic today. Why has research into new service development been
so slow to develop? Recent conceptual articles on services suggest some reasons. In underscoring the complexity of the subject, Shostack (1977) observes that the
successful development of a new service is so difficult
that "it makes new-product development look like child's
play." From a management perspective, Lovelock (1981)
points out that decisions in new product development have
traditionally been excluded from marketing's domain in
the service sector. Finally, since the entire process of
creating services involves concepts, Thomas (1978) notes
that it is difficult to do test marketing or other types
of market research on new services.

This paper examines the process of new service development in a complex arena -- creating new business services
in cable television. It indicates the ways in which
principles of product planning and marketing research have
been employed in the development process. At the same
time, it considers how certain concepts from the service
marketing literature are reflected in the progress to
date and how they may come into play in further development efforts.

CABLE TELEVISION DEVELOPMENT

The dramatic growth of cable television is reflected in
two key statistics: (1) homes passed by cable total 50
percent of all U.S. households, and (2) cable penetration
has reached 30 percent (Grillo 1982). The significance
of the latter statistic is that this is the point, according to analysts, at which cable TV becomes viable, both
as a source of advertising revenue and as a vehicle for
new programming ideas. While much of the attention to
date has been on the use of cable TV in advertising, a
variety of other promising marketing applications have
been recognized, such as its role in new product research
(Bushman and Robinson 1981). As a result of recent advances in cable and satellite technology, however, the
focus of industry observers is shifting from the consumer
market to a new frontier -- business telecommunications.
A major battle, involving a growing array of communications firms, is taking shape, and the stakes are high. A

Charles River Associates' report commissioned by IBM in
1979 predicted that total telecommunications volume will
increase 700 percent between 1977 and 1990 (Whitcraft
1981). Cable television will compete as a data transmission medium by virtue of its broadband capacity.

The advantage of cable as a business communications medium is that it can rapidly transmit large quantities of
information simultaneously. It has been described as "an
ideal purveyor for intra-city data communications"
(Barnett 1982). Coupled with a high-speed satellite link,
urban cable TV systems become a vital element in inter-
city data communications as well. A recent experiment,
for example, blended a variety of technologies, including
satellite, cable TV, advanced user equipment and digital
techniques, in the transmission of business data between
Lower Manhattan and downtown San Francisco (Barnett 1982).
Among the goals accomplished, the experiment provided an
end-to-end communication link which tested user applications of teleconferencing, electronic mail, and high-
speed transfer with users transmitting information in
their own environments.

The prime vehicle for the provision of such business services by cable television in the urban market is the institutional network. Institutional networks have become
a key system design feature promised by the various cable
companies as they vie for the franchises being awarded
by the larger cities across the country. The purpose behind the development of institutional networks is to provide a new communication capability to institutions and
organizations within the community which have the need to
exchange information. Institutions desiring the services
of such a network would be connected through the use of
an addressable tap, which would provide central control
of the network. Messages could travel in two or more
directions; responses could be made directly and immediately. The different parts of the system could thus interact with each other. For example, police and fire departments, libraries, hospitals, and court buildings
could be interconnected to enhance efficient communications.

The business services network is essentially an extension
of the institutional network concept, involving a system
dedicated specifically to the communication needs of area
businesses and manufacturing facilities. Firms desiring
this multi-directional, interactive communication capability would be connected by means of addressable taps
and converters which would assure centralized maintenance
monitoring and protect against unauthorized access. The
broadband capacity of such a cable network would accommo-
date electronic mail, facsimile, computer-to-computer
data transfer, and a variety of other interactions. Further, the system would include audio-only and audio-visual
teleconferencing, as well as the distribution of pre-
recorded audio-visual programming.

Inter-city data transmission, traditionally 20 percent of
business communications costs (Whitcraft 1981), would be
accomplished by means of satellite links between business
networks. Suppose a tool and dye company in Chicago, for
example, has an assignment from a company in Dallas, Texas, and the Chicago company must quickly submit 100 pages
of drawings for client approval. Telecopying would be
too time-consuming. Overnight shipping precludes immediate response and might delay an inflexible production
schedule. But if both companies are linked via satellite,

the graphic material can easily be sent in full-color. Moreover, a business network at either end allows the company's main office to share the picture with subsidiary facilities. This brief scenario illustrated the expanded business communication capabilities which lie ahead. Satellite Business Systems, for example, plans to offer a wideband business communications system using cable TV systems rather than telephone loops for local distribution in 32 cities by late 1986 (Levy 1981).

SERVICE DEVELOPMENT PROCESS

The concept of a special business network has only recently appeared as an innovation in cable system design. With so little precedent and few guidelines for design, it represents a challenging case of new service development. The recently completed design of a cable network to provide business services to firms in a large midwestern city provides an excellent opportunity to analyze the new service development process. The analysis is intended to reveal how certain product planning guidelines and service marketing concepts have been applied in the development process to date.

In providing conceptual guidelines for service development, Shostack (1981) indicates that the first step toward service design is to develop a blueprint of the service entity's main elements. The blueprinting process is facilitated by conducting marketing research to identify these elements. This is all the more important when the entity includes a bundle of different services as is the case with a cable network for business. In the cable network design the process of identifying the service elements entailed a two-pronged marketing research effort. Thorough secondary research was pursued before moving to more costly, time-consuming primary research. The secondary research focused on cable television technology and the market trends for business services. This provided a broader perspective on the role of telecommunications in the office of the future, including developments in office automation, as well as specific details on service forecasts, such as a projected demand for teleconferencing services of over $500 million by 1985 ("Teleconferencing" 1982). Moreover, in terms of value engineering (Thomas 1978), i.e., analyzing the service attributes for cost savings, the research confirmed a differential advantage of the cable network over conventional communications not only in increased capacity, but also in potentially lower usage costs.

While secondary research helped define some of the service "realities" (Shostack 1977), in-depth primary research was required to determine the nature of the business services currently being used or desired in the future by firms in the metropolitan area. The cornerstone of preliminary market analysis in cable television research is a process known as ascertainment. Institutional ascertainment, for example, encompasses an assessment of current communication patterns both within and between institutions in the community and an identification of perceived needs of institutional leaders for better communication. In the case of a business network, the focus of the ascertainment shifts from institutions to area firms to determine their communication patterns and needs.

The ascertainment for the business network involved personal interviews with upper-level executives at 35 commercial establishments in the metropolitan area. Included in the process were manufacturing firms, banks, savings and loans, insurance companies, and other service firms. Analysis of the interviews revealed current practices, such as the frequency of meetings, conference calls, and so forth, as well as interest in various applications of broadband communications technology. For example, there was a high concentration of desired or actual use of video for education and in-service training. Teleconferencing

was a commonly expressed need among large manufacturing and retail firms. While electronic funds transfer was of obvious interest to the financial community, a number of general business firms also indicated interest in such a service.

The need for inter-city business communication was expressed by a number of the manufacturing firms and the insurance companies. These businesses voiced interest, moreover, in specific regional and national interconnections. For example, a large manufacturer was eager to use broadband technology to communicate with its other six facilities across the country. The video and data transmission capabilities were desired to eliminate redundancy in paperwork, to improve data base management, and to establish a uniform communications network throughout the corporate system. As a result of the ascertainment effort as well as the secondary research, a blueprint for the business cable network design had taken shape and thus provided a basis for further service development.

Network Concept Testing

The network ascertainment process had identified perceived needs on the part of the firms for a variety of business communication services. It was clear, however, that the range of alternative concepts had to be narrowed to a reasonable number of network services. Further analysis indicated that certain services were more amenable to broadcast cable technology than others and that, of these, some were mentioned more frequently in the perceived need sections of the ascertainments. This process yielded a feasible set of network service concepts. At this point, reference to the service marketing literature provided guidelines for further development. A framework for the concept testing of services (Murphy and Robinson 1981) pointed to the need for field study to obtain the reactions of target customers to new service concepts. At the same time, Shostack's (1977, 1981) work on service blueprinting emphasized that unless service elements are ranked by market importance, no sensible plan can be formulated to represent the service package effectively.

The concept-testing phase of the network development process was designed to expose the network concept to potential business users, to confirm that a market need truly existed, and to obtain specific indications of the market importance of the network's business services. The personal interview method was selected due to the complexity of the service concepts and the nature of the information desired. Shostack (1981) has indicated the value of a segmentation approach in measuring market preferences for services. For the purpose of the concept test the area businesses were divided into five segments: (1) manufacturers, (2) financial services, (3) health care and insurance services, (4) retail firms, and (5) professional/other services. In this way, similarities in communication needs and concept evaluations could be identified and analyzed. The questionnaire for the concept-test interviews included a description of the proposed business network and brief definitions of seven network services, ranging from a news service to teleconferencing. Questions within each of the service areas covered the nature of service needs, such as speed and frequency, current and projected communication costs, and evaluations of the proposed network services. As a means of determining the priorities for the service elements, respondents were asked to rank the seven services in order of importance to their company.

Personal interviews were conducted with executives in charge of communications in 25 major firms in the metropolitan area. Analysis of the responses revealed commonalities of needs for communications services within the segments of firms interviewed. For example, manufacturing firms shared high-priority needs with regard to data base access and management. Reactions to the network service concepts were positive, with a number of the respondents emphasizing a desire to streamline communications functions within their firms. Anticipated use of the services, however, was closely tied to cost-benefit considerations. Rankings of the service concepts across the segments of firms provided a perspective as to the market importance of the services. For example, use of the network for in-service training received a high ranking across segments in contrast to a low ranking for a security service. The concept testing process thus provided not only detailed evaluative information on the network service concepts, but also a reading on service priorities as a basis for subsequent strategy formulation.

Business Analysis

Results of the concept test in the field were combined with additional secondary research data in the development of a preliminary marketing strategy for the business cable network. A particularly critical part of new service development is the process of defining the new service to be offered to the market. Bell (1981) indicates that new service definition at the initial strategy level is the key to establishing a differential advantage in the marketplace. The complexity of service definition for the business network was reduced by employing a tiered service design. Based on the market research and communications volume and distance, each service concept was defined in terms of low, medium, and high tiers or levels of service. Use of the cable network for training, for example, ranged from a low tier of on-demand access by a subscriber to a library of training tapes to a high tier of live, two-way video training. The divisions into a hierarchy of service levels also facilitated the assignment of intended prices to each business service.

The service tiers and price differentials were used in the construction of a demand index for the network's business services. The demand index essentially involved the anticipated usage of each service across various business segments. Underlying the process of determining market penetration were concepts such as "uniqueness of service," i.e., the service is not currently available in a similar form from any other electronic medium. In addition to the demand estimates, staffing requirements for the business network were outlined based on anticiipated service offerings. Lines of responsibility and task profiles were provided in detail. Rounding out the preliminary strategy was a first-year marketing budget for the proposed network.

In keeping with prudent product planning guidelines, the preliminary strategy was subjected to a hardheaded phase of business analysis. Long-run sales and cost projections were developed from the demand index and other data. These involved basic assumptions about construction completion schedules, construction costs, and operating arrangements. Projected results of startup and operations were evaluated to determine the financial attractiveness of the business network venture. Assessments of the viability of the business also included critical reviews of the overhead and other factors dictated by the service-oriented nature of the network. On the basis of the financial analysis, the business-services network proposal was deemed a sound business investment.

IMPLICATIONS FOR FURTHER DEVELOPMENT

While the remaining stages in the development of the business cable network lie ahead, implications can be drawn from the service marketing literature to provide guidelines for further development. Since the business network has emerged from business analysis as a financially viable concept, resources can now be devoted to completing the

actual mix of services to be provided by the network. In contrasting service planning with product planning, Beckwith and Fitzgerald (1981) emphasize the need to plan services with sufficient flexibility to allow for a broad range of final configurations. Market research to date suggests that differing communication needs across businesses will warrant a fairly broad mix of services to be offered by the network. Indeed, the multi-tiered approach to service design employed thus far has reflected this planning consideration.

Interaction with business executives in the development effort to date suggests the need to analyze the service mix more from the customer's point of view. In particular, more explicit benefit statements should be developed for service positioning. Enis and Roering (1981) have called for a shift in focus in strategy formulation from products and services to bundles of benefits being offered to customers. Banks, for example, offer a service mix encompassing a host of benefits appealing to different market segments. This diversity of benefit-bundles dictates the formulation of a corresponding array of marketing strategies to appeal to the target markets. The same will hold true for the cable network. It is up to the network service planners, moreover, to make the benefits of broadband cable technology as opposed to conventional communication clear to the potential customers to speed market adoption of the business services.

The customer adoption process itself will pose some challenges for cable network planners. The application of cable technology to business communication services is creating a flood of new information in trade magazines, which causes a concomitant increase in uncertainty for those readers who wonder what it all means. Research by Eiglier, et.al. (1977) suggests that the intangible, non-standardized nature of services introduces an added degree of perceived risk into the customer evaluation process for service innovations. While the factors of perceived risk and uncertainty about a new product can be analyzed in test marketing, the process if more complicated for a new service. Thomas (1978), in discussing the problems encountered in the market testing of services, highlights the difficulty of predicting what service concepts will be understandable and attractive to the consumer. Apart from any speculation about market testing of the cable network, the service planners face a formidable task of formulating strategies to deal effectively with the uncertainties in the marketplace.

To move successfully toward commercialization of the business cable network, the service developers need to adhere to the tenets of integrated marketing strategy. A prime requisite for such strategy formulation is a thorough understanding of the market. Further interaction with potential customers for the network's business services may lead to service engineering modifications (Shostack 1981), i.e., prudent changes in the service entities before expensive formal market introduction. The end result of the final research should be a complete service/market segmentation framework. This will provide the basis for total marketing plan development. To avoid the pitfall of piece-meal marketing mix preparation, i.e., separate plans for promotion, pricing, etc., network planners should concentrate on integrating the marketing strategy elements in a comprehensive plan. This will enhance the likelihood of successfully introducing the cable network to the business community.

REFERENCES

Barnett, Toni (1982), "Multichannel Industries Aim At Growing Business Data Markets," Multichannel Technologies Report, (March 1), 17-19.

Beckwith, Neil E. and Thomas Fitzgerald (1981), "Marketing of Services Meeting of Different Needs," in Marketing of Services, James H. Donnelly and William R. George, eds., Chicago: American Marketing Association, 239-241.

Bell, Martin L. (1981), "Tactical Service Marketing and the Process of Remixing," in Marketing of Services, James H. Donnelly and William R. George, eds., Chicago: American Marketing Association, 163-167.

Bushman, Anthony F. and Richard K. Robinson (1981), "Two-Way Television: A Tool for New Product Research," Business Horizons, (July/August), 69-75.

Eiglier, P., E. Langeard, C. H. Lovelock, J. E. C. Bateson and R. F. Young (1977), Marketing Consumer Services: New Insights, Cambridge, MA: Marketing Science Institute.

Enis, Ben M. and Kenneth J. Roering (1981), "Services Marketing: Different Products, Similar Strategy," in Marketing of Services, J. H. Donnelly and W. R. George, eds., Chicago: American Marketing Association, 1-4.

Grillo, Jean B. (1982), "Divided Attention," Cablevision Plus, (February 1), 17-19.

Hise, Richard T. (1977), Product/Service Strategy, New York: Petrocelli Charter.

Levy, Alan M. (1981), "ABS Will Offer Data Via Cable in 32 Cities," Multichannel News, (December 7), 1.

Lovelock, Christopher H. (1981), "Why Marketing Management Needs to be Different for Services," in Marketing of Services, J. H. Donnelly and W. R. George, eds., Chicago: American Marketing Association, 5-9.

Murphy, Patrick M. and Richard K. Robinson (1981), "Concept Testing for Services," in Marketing of Services, J. H. Donnelly and W. R. George, eds., Chicago: American Marketing Association, 217-220.

Rathmell, John M. (1974), Marketing in the Service Sector, Cambridge, MA: Winthrop Publishers.

Shostack, G. Lynn (1977), "Breaking Free From Product Marketing," Journal of Marketing, (April), 73-80.

_____ (1981), "How to Design a Service," in Marketing of Services, J. H. Donnelly and W. R. George, eds., Chicago: American Marketing Association, 221-229.

"Teleconferencing Reaching a Pivotal Stage in Development," (1982), Communication News, (February), 46-48.

Thomas, Dan R. E. (1978), "Strategy is Different in Service Businesses," Harvard Business Review, (July-August), 158-165.

Whitcraft, Virginia (1981), "The New York-San Francisco Satellite Connection," Office Product News, (October), 18-19, 38-39.

THEORETICAL FOUNDATIONS FOR SERVICES MARKETING STRATEGY

Donald F. Dixon, Temple University
Michael F. Smith, Temple University

ABSTRACT

Conventional concepts of services and service characteristics do not provide a significant foundation for marketing theory. Service must be conceptualized from the perspective of the household, the organization from which final demand emanates. In this context, marketing is identified with service, as the total contribution to the household processes which ultimately generate satisfaction.

INTRODUCTION

Although it is a commonplace that the service marketing literature emerged "some 15 years ago," (Lovelock 1980, p. 72) an understanding that marketing is concerned with both material goods and services, as well as many relevant concepts, are deeply rooted in the general marketing literature. Alderson, who perceives the output of marketing as "a bundle of utilities," notes explicitly that this output is the result of a "progressive differentiation of products and services," which continues up to the point of consumer acquisition. (1957, p. 69) This process of fitting economic output to more completely meet the needs of specific consumers is accomplished by means of "shaping" and "sorting", undertaken by successive organizations.

Alderson's approach is consistent with a long tradition in both marketing and economic theory. Adam Smith distinguishes between material goods and services, "which perish in the very instant of their performance." (1776, p. 639) As a result of this characteristic, the productive effort devoted to services "does not fix or realize itself in any permanent subject, or vendible commodity, which endures." (1776, p. 315) This view of services remained unchanged for many years. A standard economics text of the early 1900's defines a good as "anything that is capable of satisfying a human want," and then explains that goods are commonly divided into material things and personal services. Moreover, it is noted that there are special characteristics of services; they "are so perishable that they must be used with the direct cooperation of some other human being...The service of a musician, for example, is personal and must be used the moment it is rendered." (Ely 1920, pp. 105-107)

Service marketing was widely recognized in early marketing textbooks. Breyer's Commodity Marketing includes electric service and telephone service among the sixteen commodities which are treated. (1931) Pyle (1931) and Converse (1936) both have chapters on "Selling Service" and others also deal with the topic. (Killough 1933; Barker and Anshen 1939) These authors devote considerable attention to the characteristics of services which distinguish them from material goods. One list of characteristics (Barker and Anshen 1939) includes perishability, impossibility of storage, difficulty of standardization, inability of customers to make quality-price comparisons, a lack of intermediaries in the channel, and the necessity for the buyer to depend upon the integrity of the seller. (1939, p. 173)

When services marketing was rediscovered in the 1960's, writers emphasized the characteristics of services as a means of identification, and developed lists of such characteristics similar to those found in early marketing textbooks. (Judd 1964, Rathmell 1966, Bessom 1975, Sasser 1976 Lovelock 1979, 1980) In recent years a single characteristic of service has been emphasized; George asserts that "intangibility captures the essence of most services"

(1977, p. 86), and Bateson (1979, p. 139) bases his entire emphasis upon this characteristic. Judd offers a definition of service based upon intangibility; services are involved in a market transaction "where the object of the market transaction is other than ... a material commodity." (1964, p. 59)

But a definition based upon the characteristics of the very thing which is to be identified is tautological at best. It is logically impossible to determine the characteristics of something which has not been identified, and then utilize these characteristics to identify the object of study. If something has been examined, so that its characteristics can be determined, then there must be at least an implicit definition of the object before the process begins. (Blois 1981, p. 1611)

Another problem is that the lists of characteristics typically are developed from the seller's perspective. Lovelock, for example, specifically considers the significance of characteristics for service marketers, and objects to an "arbitrary approach" which "ignores the managerial perspective." (1980, p. 73) It is difficult to accept the view that only the seller's concerns are of interest to a discipline which is purported to take the consumer's perspective as central.

A related difficulty is that some of the bases upon which services are distinguished are production-oriented. (Wyckham, Fitzroy and Mandy 1975, p. 60) Although it is intuitively obvious that a service is "intangible" from a technical production standpoint, it is not clear that customers necessarily perceive "tangibility" as an important aspect of a material good. Certainly the promotional efforts undertaken by sellers of beauty products seem to be based upon a belief that "intangibles" are being sold. And although mass-produced goods are standardized, in the terms of technical specifications, the predilection of customers to consider identical material goods to be different (as in the case of aspirin, for example) suggests a wide divergence between the perceptions of customers and production "facts." It would seem that the place to begin an analysis of services is with customer perceptions, rather than those of the producer.

Rathmell shifts the focus of the discussion to the consumer by asking "Does the utility for the consumer lie in the physical characteristics of the product, or in the nature of the action or performance?" Utilizing this distinction, he suggests a "goods-services continuum with pure goods at one extreme and pure services at the other." (1966, p. 33) Unfortunately, this notion presents a logical difficulty if we consider the types of utilities usually discussed in the marketing literature. If one extreme of the continuum is a "pure good" this must refer to form utility. Thus the other extreme must consist of some jumble of the "non form" utilities: time, place, and possession. This, of course, is inconsistent with typical concepts of services which include the repair and maintenance of material goods, which must involve form utility. Therefore, there is some question as to whether or not the distinction implied in the continuum between goods and services is very useful if one focuses on the utility the consumer derives from an offering.

This paper introduces a view of services from the customer's viewpoint, which not only distinguishes between material goods and services, but indicates the relationship between these and the forgotten element of the trinity - information.

THE FRAMEWORK

The original AMA definition of services - "Activities, benefits, or satisfactions, which are offered for sale, or are provided in connection with the sale of goods," (Alexander 1960, p. 21) provides the basis for the argument developed below. There are three different elements in this definition: (1) a precondition for the identification of services relevant to marketing ("offered for sale"), and two aspects of the operation of marketing systems, (2) inputs ("activities") and (3) outputs ("benefits, or satisfaction"). This section will deal with the precondition, and the following sections with inputs and outputs.

Some services cannot be transferred from one person to another, and these cannot in any circumstance be offered for sale; no one can eat or sleep for another, nor can one student study for another. Neither can one person provide good health to another, since health is the result of many aspects of a person's behavior in a particular environment. A physician can only provide one of the ingredients of good health; the final result depends upon the patient. Moreover, although some services can be performed by one person for another, they may not result in market transactions, because individuals choose to provide these services for themselves; examples offered in connection with the AMA definition, such as amusements, hotel service, electrical service, and transportation, can be generated for oneself or within a household, rather than being purchased in the market.

The essential point is that the study of marketing involves market exchanges, and thus services relevant to the discipline must have the potential of exchange in the market. If we focus upon this potential exchange, or transaction, we have not only a precondition, but also a starting point for the analysis.

What is offered for sale in the market is something which has the power to help people satisfy their requirements, or certain types of "bundles of utilities" which customers anticipate will result in "benefits, or satisfactions," It will be shown below that the "activities" referred to in the AMA definition of services represents one of the inputs required to achieve the output of "benefits, or satisfactions."

ACTIVITIES - THE BEHAVIORAL INPUT

One element of the AMA definition, "activities," refers to action, or behavior, as distinguished from material. The definition of service has long been linked to behavior. Palgrave's Dictionary (1894, III:381) defines a service as "an action performed by a person or body of persons for the benefit of another person or body of persons." In the Encyclopedia of the Social Sciences, service is defined as "any act of an individual in so far as it contributes to the realization of the ends of other individuals." (Parsons 1934, XII:672) Service is also defined as an "act in the Dictionary of Social Science. (Zadrozny 1959, p. 301) Rathmell recognizes this, noting that an "implicit distinction" of the greatest importance is that "a good is a thing and a service is an act. The former is an object, an article, a device, or a material ... whereas the latter is a deed, a performance, or an effort ..." (1966, p. 33) Yet the implications of this distinction generally have not been developed in the services marketing literature.

Human behavior represents an input; the power to bring about a result. Satisfaction is the result or output of human behavior when that behavior is combined with other productive factors in a process which generates satisfaction. One of these other productive factors is material. This view of the productive process, linking behavior and material, is rooted in classical economics, and was accepted by one of the earliest American marketing writers. Shaw states that the essential element common to all business activities is "the application of motion to material." (1915, p. 51) In this context, one nineteenth century economist, defined production as "The creation of utilities by the application of man's mental and physical powers to the physical universe, which furnishes materials and forces." (Ely 1889, p. 144) In contemporary terms, production is a process which modifies elements of the environment; it applies an input (behavior) to create an output (satisfaction).

Because of the micromarketing thrust of the services literature, attention has been focused upon inputs alone; output, the very purpose of productive activity, has been ignored. Perhaps the most extreme instance of this approach is found in the notion of the "industrialization of services." Service is performed "out there in the field" while manufacturing occurs "here in the factory." (Levitt 1972, p. 42) As a consequence of this perspective, it is concluded that service must be thought of as "manufacturing in the field." (1972, p. 52)

Such production-oriented perspectives and the use of the material good as the point of departure in the service marketing literature, leads to a logical dilemma. When a material good is purchased, it embodies input behavior, purchased in the factor market by the manufacturer, and utilized to transform material. The behavioral input is not considered as "service" in the marketing literature, because the productive process has occurred "in the factory." On the other hand, once a material good has been acquired by a household, and behavior is purchased to modify, maintain, or repair that material good, this behavior becomes "service." But what is the significance of the location of the productive process to the customer? In both cases the resulting material good, and the utility derived from that good, are the same.

The logical inconsistency here was pointed out nearly a century and a half ago. Senior argues that "the distinctions that have been attempted to be drawn ... between commodities and services, rest on differences existing not in the things themselves, ... but in the modes in which they attract our attention." In the case of a material good, attention is focused upon the result of the productive process. In the case of a service, "our attention is principally called not to the thing altered, but to the act of occasioning that alteration." (Senior 1836, p. 51) That is, in the case of the acquisition of a material good, we tend to think of the output, while the repair of that material good is thought of in terms of input - the purchase of the behavior required to alter the material good.

Logical consistency requires that analysis focus upon either input or output in any specific investigation. In the present paper, service is perceived as an input to the household. From the consumer's viewpoint; "the mere performance of some activity is not enough if the consumer unit is not affected in some way." (Hill 1977, p. 318) Hence, service associated with a material good is defined as the modification of material which results in a change which more closely approximates a person's requirements. Such changes may take the form of physical transformation, or transportation.

Improvement may mean some physical transformation - such as modification or repair, which may be carried out in the same manner in the factory as "in the field." Conventionally, this has been classified as service rather than manufacturing because the ownership of the good is now vested in the ultimate user. The idea of a goods-service continuum does not apply here, since there is no technical distinction between the "improvement" prior to, or after, the acquisition of the good by the ultimate user. Moreover, this service lacks some "distinguishing characteristics," such as perishability, or the necessity for the user to be present when the service is performed. Moreover, one of the arguments concerning services is that they "disappear" if not utilized; but this is true of any behavior whether the context is the transformation of material in a factory, or in a customer's home.

Physical movement in space is another type of modification to material. Here again, the goods-services continuum is inapplicable since material cannot be viewed as an extreme form of movement in space, nor can space be perceived as an extreme form of material. And again, there is nothing perishable in the modification; there is no a priori reason why a material good, once moved, cannot remain in its new location idefinitely. Moreover, there is no need for either the owner or user of the material to be present during the movement.

But not all service is associated with material; service may also be associated with people. Indeed, what is important in service applied to material is not the change in attributes of the material, but the significance of that change for the customer. Ultimately, the meaning of an improvement of a material good is an increase in the capacity of that good to contribute to the process by which customers gain satisfaction. Thus, what is required in a consideration of services is a shift in emphasis. Production ought to be viewed as human behavior which utilizes material and other resources to obtain satisfaction, rather than a process of modifying material.

One step towards such a shift in focus is suggested by Alderson, who notes that the purchase of a material good in which the production process has been carried further toward the ultimate adaptation to the customer's requirements has the result of "cutting down on the amount of labor required from the user." (1957, p. 264) That is, the acquisition of such a good represents the substitution of work done in a manufacturing plant for work carried out in the household. Similarly, the purchase of maintenance service, after a material good has been acquired, represents a substitute for the household performance of the maintenance task. Hence, the household has two alternatives for altering the assortment of household work: (1) acquire behavior embedded in a material good during the manufacturing process, or (2) acquire behavior which becomes embedded in the material good after the purchase of the good. In either case there is a service to the user, because the user need not engage in the behavior necessary to achieve the particular modification of the material good.

The same approach may be taken when we focus not on service associated with material goods, but service associated with people. Just as there is behavior necessary to repair and maintain material goods, there is behavior necessary to repair and maintain people. With respect to a person's physical state, there are several types of change which may be effected - transportation to a new location, or alteration in appearance, for example.

Many of the service characteristics which are inapplicable in the case of service associated with material goods are applicable here. Just as material must be present for service to be performed in connection with a material good, so service performed in connection with a person requires that the person be present. That is, the productive process involves a joint contribution of the customer's behavior, and the behavior of another person, which is purchased in the market. Individuals cannot jointly contribute behavior to a productive process unless they work together at the same time, whether this process has as its output a material good or something else.

In addition to improvements in a person's physical state, there are improvements in a person's mental state, which influence the quality of behavior. This quality, in turn, depends upon the information available. First, the skill of an actor is derived from information which has become internalized, from a program of education or training, for example. Second, the direction, or control, of the behavior depends upon current information. The household may choose to purchase the behavior of others in the market because the quality of that behavior is greater, and hence the productive process is more efficient than if it were carried out within the household itself. Alternatively, the household may gather information in an effort to improve the quality of the behavior which it contributes to productive processes. This information may be acquired in the market as a "service" which is not inherently perishable in that it may be stored, modified, and retrieved at will.

Since satisfaction, the output of behavior, is the result of a series of productive processes, services must be related to the various stages of the production process. This is the purpose of the following section.

BENEFITS, SATISFACTION - THE OUTPUT COMPONENT

The second element in the AMA definition of services - "benefit, satisfaction," is crucial to an understanding of service as an element in a production process. Since the purpose of production is the satisfaction of human requirements, then behavior acquired in the market which contributes to the process by which people gain satisfaction can be identified as a marketed service. The essence of service is something which happens, some change which is brought about.

Satisfaction is the result of consumption, in which a person combines behavior, material, and information in a satisfaction-generating process. The behavior can be joint, in that the behavior of another person is also required to act as a factor of production. Such behavior may be purchased in the market, as in the case of a recital, in which the behavior of a musician performing is combined with that of the consumer listening. The musician's behavior alone is not sufficient; part of the satisfaction derived from the consumption process arises from the amenities provided by the setting within which the behavior occurs. Some of the behavior required to produce the setting for the performance is joint, as in the case of ushers and concessionaires. Other behavior, such as maintenance, need not be joint.

Of course behavior need not be purchased directly; one may purchase a recording of a concert, so that the musician's behavior is embedded in a material good. Yet listening to music in one's home requires additional behavior to provide the setting, just as in the case of a concert hall. The process of generating the amenities requires a process (household production) which utilizes behavior, material, and information as inputs. This behavior may be provided by household members, or it may be purchased in the market, in the form of catering services, for example.

Finally, the acquisition of goods and services in the market requires an additional process - going into the market. Household members may engage in this behavior, or they may employ someone to perform the task. Typically, however, the process involves joint behavior. The household may choose to purchase various amounts of assistance, by patronizing retail outlets ranging from full service to self-service. Moreover, as in the case of other household processes, information may be chosen as an input to substitute for behavior. And of course, some information is available without purchase, in the form of advertising.

Satisfaction thus is the ultimate output of a series of household processes, which involve the acquisition of material goods, behavior, and information in the market, and the transformation of these inputs to adapt them for use in the consumption process. Each of these household processes represents the behavior of an individual in a different role, such as buying, home-making, and consumption, and each requires a production function with differing inputs. And, in each case, additional behavior may be obtained in the market to combine with behavior contributed by household members.

But all marketing offerings represent substitutes for household behavior, whether the offering is purchased directly, is embodied in material goods, or is in the form of information.

THEORETICAL IMPLICATIONS OF THE "CUSTOMER PERSPECTIVE"

The singular characteristic of service lies in its implication for the customer; service is "the action of serving, helping or benefiting; conduct leading to the welfare or advantage of another." (Oxford English Dictionary 1933 IX, p. 517) This characteristic appears not only in an ordinary dictionary definition, but also in the AMA definition, and other sources quoted previously. Any analytical use of the term ought therefore to recognize this point.

The benefit or advantage to the household provided by marketing activity concerns the opportunity for the household to acquire in the market an assortment of inputs which is required to meet its objectives. Ultimately the provision of the appropriate assortment represents service, irrespective of the particular composition of that assortment. The household chooses an assortment of material, and information, all of which have undergone Alderson's "progressive differentiation" to the extent required, and then adds household behavior to complete the process of differentiation. It is as meaningless to evoke a goods-services continuum as it is to define marketing so as to exclude any adjustment of form utility.

Marketing provides nothing but service to customers. The productive factors utilized by the household - material, behavior, and information are both substitutes and complements. Moreover these factors may be provided at various stages of the economic process, from raw material production to household consumption. Thus, there is no analytical basis for distinguishing one factor from another, except from the individual household's perspective.

By focusing upon such issues as the "service delivery system," the services marketing literature has explored only one aspect of the total productive process, and omitted consideration of the organization from which the ultimate support of the marketing system is derived: the household. A new focus is needed if the concepts emerging from the renewed interest in services marketing is to represent a contribution to general marketing theory.

IMPLICATIONS FOR MARKETING STRATEGY

The conclusion reached above leads to a new approach to two fundamental strategic issues: the segment to which marketing effort is directed, and the nature of the "offering" presented to a segment.

The three household processes discussed above suggest bases for segmentation with respect to consumer products:

1. Acquisition: providing assistance to purchasers, in all aspects of the work undertaken to obtain the goods and services required by the organization.

2. Preparation: providing assistance in carrying out the internal production processes undertaken by organizations. In the household, this means providing the setting for the consumption process.

3. Consumption: assisting the household consumer in the ultimate process of gaining satisfaction from inputs derived from the above processes.

The relevant categories of inputs provided to assist in each of the processes are determined by the particular production functions utilized by the organization, and the assortments of inputs in the organizational inventory. Thus, different assortments of behavior, matter-energy, and information are required for each process. In some instances inputs may be offered as substitutes for inputs provided by the organization itself; in other cases, inputs may be complementary to organizational inputs.

The "total offering" of the seller thus includes both the assortment of household processes toward which the offering is directed, and the particular inputs provided in connection with each process. It is postulated that the customer considers the benefits of this "total offering" in the context of the organizational objectives and the nature of the production functions which have been chosen.

In brief, the seller must decide on the assortment of acquisition, preparation, and consumption services to be offered, and also the assortment of inputs provided for each of these processes. Another question is whether to offer a single, undifferentiated assortment or a variety of assortments. In the latter instance, is each assortment to be priced as a unit, or is each element to be priced separately? On what basis, if any, will the customer be able to bargain for special assortments?

A simple example will illustrate the argument: the acquisition of a personal computer to replace purchased entertainment services with in-house capabilities. With respect to the consumption process, the offering must reflect the requirement that the consumer obtain the knowledge of potential applications and the skill to utilize the operating system and softwear. The extent to which particular inputs are provided depends in part on the consumer's inventory of skill and knowledge. For a sophisticated user the offering may include a minimum of information and it may be supplied in the form of manuals. At the opposite extreme, the novice will require a great deal of information and perhaps personal demonstrations.

To gain satisfaction, the consumer must have an operating system in place. Equipment must be assembled and tested, together with the appropriate softwear. Again, a knowledgable user may perform these activities so that the offering need only consist of a minimum amount of information. In some instances, the offering may include a "kit" rather than assembled equipment, and the user may write the necessary softwear. Alternatively, for a novice, the seller's offering may be an assembled and tested system which requires little more than turning on a switch.

Finally, the appropriate goods and services must be acquired. If the purchaser is highly skilled, the seller's offering may be little more than information as to availability and price, together with an address to which to send an order. But the unsophisticated purchaser may require personal assistance in the choice of both hardware and softwear. Other characteristics of the purchaser may require an offering which includes delivery and credit arrangements.

Consequently, the "service" offered may vary from a minimum of information and unassembled components to a good deal of personal attention with respect to all three processes. The important thing is that the nature of this service must be tailored to the specific set of customer requirements. Since the nature of these requirements may be such that material goods are both substitutes for, and complements of, both behavior and information, any distinction between "goods" and "services" seems to be irrelevant from the customer's perspective.

REFERENCES

Alderson, Wroe (1957), Marketing Behavior and Executive Action, Englewood Cliffs, New Jersey: Richard D. Irwin.

Alexander, R.S. (1960), Marketing Definitions, Chicago: American Marketing Association.

Barker, C.W. and M. Anshen (1939), Modern Marketing; New York: McGraw-Hill Book Company, Inc.

Bateson, John E.G. (1979), "Why We Need Service Marketing," in F.C. Ferrell, S.W. Brown, C.W. Lamb; Conceptual and Theoretical Developments in Marketing, Chicago: American Marketing Association, 131-146.

Bessom, Richard M. and Avid W. Jackson (1975), "Service Retailing - A Strategic Marketing Approach," Journal of Retailing, 5 (Summer), 75-84.

Blois, K.J. (1981), "How Do Consumers Distinguish Between Products and Services?" in Hanne Hativig Larsen and Soren Heede, Proceedings of the European Academy for Advanced Research in Marketing, 1606-1632.

Breyer, R.F. (1931, Commodity Marketing, New York: McGraw-Hill Book Company, Inc.

Chase, Richard B. (1978), "Where Does the Customer Fit in A Service Operation?" Harvard Business Review, 56 (November-December) 137-142.

Converse, P.D. (1936), Essentials of Distribution, New York: Prentice-Hall, Inc.

Davis, Duane L., Joseph P. Guiltinan, and Wesley H. Jones (1979), "Service Characteristics, Consumer Search, and the Classification of Retail Services," Journal of Retailing, 55 (Fall), 3-23.

Ely, Richard T. (1889), An Introduction to Political Economy, New York: Chautauqua Press.

George, William, R. (1977), "The Retailing of Service - A Challenging Future," Journal of Retailing, 53 (Fall), 85-107.

Hill, T.P. (1977), "On Goods and Services," Review of Income and Wealth, 23 (December) 315-338.

Judd, Robert C. (1964), "The Case for Redefining Services," Journal of Marketing, 28 (January), 58-59.

Killough, H.B. (1933), The Economics of Marketing, New York: Harper & Brothers

Levitt, Theodore (1972), "Production-Line Approach to Services," Harvard Business Review, 50 (September-October) 41-52.

Lovelock, Christopher H. (1979), "Theoretical Contributions from Services and Nonbusiness Marketing," in O.C. Ferrell, S.W. Brown, and C.W. Lamb, Conceptual and

Theoretical Developments in Marketing, Chicago: American Marketing Association, 147-165.

_____ (1980), "Towards A Classification of Services," in Charles W. Lamb and Patrick M. Dunne, Theoretical Developments in Marketing, Chicago: American Marketing Association.

Palgrave, R.H. (1894), Dictionary of Political Economy, London: Macmillan and Co.

Parsons, T. (1934), "Service," Encyclopedia of Social Science, New York: The Macmillan Company

Pyle, J.F. (1931), Marketing Principles, New York: McGraw-Hill Book Company.

Rathmell, John M. (1966), "What is Meant by Services?" Journal of Marketing, 30 (October), 32-36.

Regan, William J. (1963), "The Service Revolution," Journal of Marketing, 27 (July), 57-62.

Sasser, W. Earl (1976), "Match Supply and Demand in Service Industries," Harvard Business Review, 54 (November-December) 133-141.

Senior, W.N. (1836), An Outline of the Science of Political Economy, London: W. Clowes and Sons.

Shaw, Arch W. (1915), Some Problems of Market Distribution, Cambridge: Harvard University Press.

Shostack, Lynn G. (1977), "Breaking Free from Product Marketing," Journal of Marketing, 41 (April), 73-80.

Smith, Adam (1776), An Inquiry into the Nature and Causes of the Wealth of Nations, reprinted (1937), New York: Modern Library.

Syckham, R.G., P.T. Fitzroy and G.D. Mandry (1975), "Marketing of Services," European Journal of Marketing (9,1), 59-67.

Zadrozny, John T. (1959), Dictionary of Social Science, Washington, D.C.: Public Affairs Press.

STRATEGIC MARKETING - RE-DIRECTING A SERVICE MARKETING COMPANY

Archie McGill, American Telephone and Telegraph, Basking Ridge

ABSTRACT

Service marketing requires a corporate strategy which is
completely customer-focused, and thus an organizational
structure with trained, motivated people who can anticipate and respond to individual customer needs -- quickly
and totally -- by designing and providing tailor-made
lines of services/systems which meet those needs, not
only today but tomorrow as well.

First, congratulations to the AMA for recognizing the
increasing importance of Service Marketing. As a task
force established by the AMA acknowledged, relatively
little exists as a complete body of theory or collected
knowledge on Service Marketing, compared to the abundance
of information, experience and history dealing with the
marketing of goods.

Such a body of knowledge is badly needed, services --
both in terms of production and consumption -- now
dominate the American economy.

A couple of statistics developed by the AMA's task force
show this clearly:

-- At least two-thirds of the private, non-
governmental labor force in the United
States is now engaged in supplying services, as opposed to products.

-- Out of every dollar that consumers spend
today, nearly 50% goes for services. And
that figure does not include vast amounts
spent for business and industrial services
-- spending for business services has, by
all indications, increased even more rapidly than for consumer services.

Indeed, the marketing of services is the wave of the
future.

But this change from a product-dominated economy to a
service-dominated one presents us in the Marketing
profession with a challenge: we have much to learn
about how to market services.

We all know much about selling boxes -- selling services
is another thing.

Compared to selling products, many aspects of marketing
services are different -- market planning and analysis,
service planning and development, creating channels of
distribution, pricing, promotion. In all of these we
are still going up the learning curve.

I assure you: we in the telephone business have had to
learn how, and we are still learning.

Although we've always considered the telephone business
a service industry, for most of a century we sold our
services as if we were selling boxes. By saying that, I
don't mean to denigrate our past. We had a very good
reason for selling our services as if they were things.

Up until the 1960's the goal of public policy and of the
telephone industry was the achievement of universal

service -- quality telephone service readily available
to everyone at a price everyone could afford. To achieve
this, we priced basic service -- one line and one
telephone -- below cost. To cover the loss, we marketed
services, and sold them at prices above cost -- the long
distance call.

And for most of a hundred years, this strategy of selling
telephone service as it it were boxes worked well: The
American public enjoyed the best telephone service in
the world.

But a series of fundamental changes, which began in the
early 1960's, carried through the 1970's altered this.

First of all, the goal of universal service was achieved
in the early 1960's.

On top of this came new technology, new markets, new
customer needs and expectations, a new public attitude
and new rulings in courts and regulation. The technology - much of it developed by us in the Bell System -
blurred the distinction between telecommunications and
computer-like services. The exploding information
markets and new customer needs and expectations are an
outgrowth of this new technology. The new public attitudes called for less government regulation and more
competition within our industry. And finally a series
of court rulings and regulatory decisions over the last
two decades reflecting these new attitudes - opened
telecommunications to competition.

All of this change -- new technology, expanding (indeed,
global) markets, new customer needs and expectations,
and competition -- caused us in the Bell System to take
a hard look at ourselves. As a reslut, we have redefined
our role as a business.

We no longer see ourselves as just the providers of
universal telephone service. We believe our past as an
admirable one, but it's just that -- the past. It is
not our future.

We believe that our future lies in providing solutions
to communications problems in the emerging world of
information movement and management: information age
solutions for business, for the home.

We are no longer selling boxes. We are providing total,
problem-solving services.

This redefinition of our basic role as a business has
brought about profound change to every aspect of our
company. And marketing is no exception.

From a marketeer's point of view, perhaps the most basic
change is our approach to the marketplace.

For decades, technology was in the driver's seat in the
Bell System. Technology determined what we offered our
customers and when. That is no longer the case.

Today, the cornerstone of our planning is the customer.
At every level of our organization, we are increasingly
customer-focused.

What drives us these days -- as it must drive any company that expects to flourish in the coming years -- is the conviction that we must focus our efforts toward satisfying the needs and expectations of customers -- individually, one by one.

This means providing customers with what they want, and more importantly need. It also means measuring ourselves by their standards of customer satisfaction, not just by our own measurements.

And this means that, in meeting our customers' needs and expectations, we must provide them with total service -- total solutions to their problems -- quickly, completely, and uniquely.

We are convinced that if we are to succeed in the days and years ahead, we must not only know what our customers need, we must anticipate that need. We believe we should be in partnership with our customers to help them achieve -- in a timely manner -- their business objectives and goals by providing them with information-management solutions, tools that help them solve their problems and allow them to operate more effectively, more efficiently, more productively.

That's all well and good, I know. Redefining ones role and taking a new look at the marketplace is one thing. But doing it -- turning a one-hundred-year-old company around 180 degrees, from serving all customers alike to serving each one of them individually -- is quite another thing.

How do you do it?

First let me acknowledge that we still have a lot to learn about redirecting a marketing strategy based on service rather than products. But we have learned a lot in recent years. So I'd like to share a few specifics.

For one thing, we have segmented our markets. Instead of trying to be all things to all people -- treating all customers the same way -- we have dedicated our people to specific industries.

We now have account people who handle the chemical industry, aero-space, banking, government, hospitals, and so on. We have more and more specialists and support teams analyzing individual industries, understanding what are the financial drivers -- key expectations -- critical success determinates -- identifying problems, providing solutions. In short, these are people charged with knowing/feeling their industry and anticipating the needs of that industry.

This approach is working. We've seen customer satisfaction increase, and we'se seen our revenues increase, too.

We've also linked up closer with our research and development people.

As a result, they are developing and designing systems and services that are both responsive and timely in the marketplace.

This closer association and participation with our R and D people has put more emphasis on quicker response time and less on economies of scale.

We also have advanced the notion of producing adaptable and flexible products, systems and services rather than taking a rigid once-and-for-all approach to the marketplace.

As you know, the complexity of our customers products and services, as well as their inability to forecast

changing conditions -- particularly the timing of those changes -- forces vendors to offer more flexible services. Thus, by giving customers systems they can program themselves, by giving them products they can adapt to their own individual requirements, we are giving them something even more responsive to their needs.

So we are emphasizing the development of "evolvable" systems, that can grow as the needs of the customer dictate. Systems that are upgradeable, flexible, and bear a modular architecture that can anticipate and serve customer needs for years. We are wholeheartedly committed to developing information age applications, that not only meet customers' needs but also are easy to use, can be reconfigured by customers and adapted to future needs. We're trying to be sure that our software today will work easily in systems tomorrow, and we're making them "user-friendly," so they won't need specially trained people to make them operate. Customers are telling us to make it simple. So we are.

In June, AT&T formed American Bell to meet a Federal Communications Commission requirement -- one of the regulatory decisions I referred to earlier -- for a fully separated subsidiary to provide detariffed telecommunications services. In July, American Bell began operation by offering Advanced Information Systems/Net 1000 -- Net 1000 for short.

For years, we have been transmitting data on a telecommunications network that was designed for voice communications. The result has been the proliferation of incompatible data terminal equipment.

Net 1000 will change all that. I am convinced that Net 1000 will do for data communications what the switchboard did for voice communications. Just as voice communications has become universal, so will data communications; not only universal, but increasingly faster, more accurate, more flexible.

Net 1000 is an enhanced, shared distributed communications processing service. It provides nationwide accessibility, storage, programming capability, transmission, and network management among data terminals and most data processing systems which would normally be incompatible.

Net 1000 offers an easy way to modify existing systems to meet changing business needs. It provides a basis upon which to build increasingly responsive systems and private subnetworks. New customers' needs can be met by a single, flexible and integrated communications processing service.

This new service epitomizes our approach to systems management. It allows virtually any computer and terminal to communicate with any other, regardless of make of design. It offers a variety of functions and features, for the small user as well as the large. It allows customers to grow -- at their own speed -- and evolve into new applications. It translates and makes data networking as simple as a voice call on the long distance network.

Obviously, this new service is one which we are very excited about. It exemplifies our strategic commitment to total service -- to learning and anticipating our customers' needs and fulfilling those needs.

There are others as well.

We are offering systems which allow customers to better manage their energy consumption, their billing cycles, their credit card operations, their financial matters, their time.

Last July we announced plans for Picturephone Meeting Service -- a two-way teleconferencing system with full-motion video, voice and data transmission.

We're getting ready to introduce advanced mobile phone service, which uses cellular radio technology to allow you to call from your car and maybe even someday -- a la Dick Tracy -- from your wrist watch. Cellular systems are a vast improvement over present mobile phone systems, which have limited capacity but often unlimited room for static interference.

Developing systems and services, however, is only part of the service marketing story, of course. The people part is just as important.

The success of any organization is predicated on its people. Believing this, we began a series of projects in recent years aimed at making all employees marketing-minded.

I won't burden you with a detailed account of our campaigns -- suffice it to say that marketplace considerations are on the agenda of virtually every AT&T executive these days. I couldn't have said that a few years ago.

You might be interested, though, in the effort we made -- and continue to make -- to increase the professionalism within our marketing/sales organizations.

We're establishing training schools around the country to help focus our marketing policies and practices and to ensure that our people are given a chance to be exposed to a nationwide approach to the marketplace.

In Denver, for instance, we have a national sales school, a place where our poeple are given a chance to think big, accept change and to become even more aware of the evolving marketplace. They're exposed to innovative sales methods; they're brought up to date on new technologies; they're taught how to identify customer needs faster and -- just as importantly -- they're shown ways to provide solutions faster than ever before.

These schools provide a growth experience for our people. The courses challenge people's energy, flexibility and abilities to learn.

We also have implemented a compensation plan based on results. This program rewards top performers, risk-takers, people who deliver, people who solve customers' problems.

Changes in organizational structure, were vitally important in redirecting the focus of our people.

And we have formed an organizational structure for our new subsidiary, American Bell, that embodies a line-of-business concept bringing all the components of the development cycle together:
-- need identification
-- development
-- financial
-- marketing
-- service requirements

This concept will be directed to responding to customer needs -- quickly -- at the lowest cost in a dynamic and competitive marketplace. It will do so by pushing decision-making and accountability to the lowest possible levels within our organization.

My organization, the Advanced Information Systems division -- or AIS -- of American Bell, will be responsible for marketing information management systems for business customers. It will have 5 lines of business initially: large systems, intermediate systems, general systems, general products, and network services.

Each line of business will be directed to its specific customers. As I told my people when we announced this new organization:

> "AIS exists to serve customer needs. The line-of-business approach permits a clear assignment of responsibility and accountability and of the resources required to assure that customer needs drive our technologies, our products and services, practices, policies -- everything we do."

In short, our new organization is intended to shorten the time between the identification of our customers' needs and our meeting those needs. We are pushing authority and accountability to the lowest levels possible. That's where a lot of the action is, and that's where much of the responsibility should be. To me, that just makes good marketing sense.

But there's even more to the service marketing story than marketplace considerations, service and product development, sales training and organizational structure.

No less important -- perhaps most important -- is attitude.

A McKinsey and Company report, done by Tom Peters, has noted that there are certain common traits among all outstanding corporations. Boldness is one. Clearly stated objectives, simplicity in goals and the willingness to take risks are others.

But the one that struck me the most was a trait known as "Try it. Do it. Fix it."

That approach means little is gained by stepping up to home plate with a bat on your shoulder and then watching a hundred pitches go by before you swing at the perfect one. It means pick out a good one and swing. And if you foul it off, pick out another and have another crack at it!

The approach of trying it, doing it and then fixing it is founded in a bias toward action. It says that the biggest mistake an organization can make is the failure to act upon a good -- but not perfect -- opportunity.

None of us in today's business environment can put off taking action until the answer becomes obvious. In this highly competitive world, delay is seldom in your favor -- particularly when your customers know it's time to act.

In redirecting the Bell System's efforts, this is the attitude we have tried to instill in our people and the corporation as a whole: "Try it. Do it. Fix it (ready-fire-aim)." We believe that, if we can create -- and maintain -- an activist attitude within our organization, it won't take long before our customers perceive it and view us as a vanguard corporation -- a leader in its field -- a company people can count on.

Another trait we're trying to build into our organization is excellence.

Excellence -- it's the extra effort you put forth even when others might not notice. It's the last try at a competitive case that doesn't look like it can be turned around -- it's an attitude of never quitting, of never giving up, of determining for yourself that you will succeed.

A winning attitude. It's like enthusiasm -- it's contagious. Your attitude controls your actions. You can
take a person with a reasonable amount of ability and a
tremendous attitude -- a will to win -- and that person
time and time again will become a champion.

How does the willing attitude get started? You put
somebody in a group who can really get things done --
who does things that seem to be beyond the possible.
Then the others around him or her have someone to
emulate, someone to keep up with. And they begin to do
things they didn't believe they could do -- because a
winning attitude is contagious.

To sum up then, what are the components of a service
marketing strategy?

    --   The first is determining your customer's
          problems and needs, knowing your customers
          inside and out.

    --   Next is an organizational structure, staffed
          with skilled and motivated people, that can
          respond to those needs quickly, totally and
          individually -- an organization and people
          driven by the desire to serve the customer.

    --   And finally, a line of services/systems which
          meet the needs of each individual customer, not
          only for today but for tomorrow as well.

The world of service marketing is a rapidly growing
one. It is a world that promises to be exciting,
challenging and filled with opportunity.

There is a lot about it we have yet to learn. But this
much we do know: marketing strategies which will meet
the challenges and enjoy the opportunities of this new
world will have to be based on meeting the total needs
of the customer.

It is a world in which the customer has all the votes
and thus must be the focus of each person, every
action -- the exciting, challenging, stimulating world
of fulfilling customers needs.

WHY ADVERTISING A SERVICE IS DIFFERENT

Sidney H. Firestone, Young & Rubicam, New York

ABSTRACT

A major difference between marketing consumer products
and marketing consumer services is the degree of interaction between the consumer and personnel or equipment
of the marketer. Because of the interaction, services
advertising is a surrogate of the marketer. Thus, the
advertising has five specific roles to play.

BACKGROUND

Thank you for your introduction, and good morning.

It's great to be here in Palm Beach in November, especially coming from New York. If you've checked the
weather report this morning, there's a difference of
approximately -- degrees between the two places.

For the next hour or so I'll be talking about and showing examples of "Why Advertising a Service is Different
From Advertising Consumer Products."

Before we go any further, however, I'd like to set the
parameters for what we mean by a service.

A service, for the sake of this morning's presentation,
is not a personalized service offered by an individual
entrepreneur such as a doctor, lawyer, mechanic, car-
penter or dry cleaner.

Rather, it is a general service marketed to large groups
of consumers by the same company, such as a public utility, rent-a-car organization, financial services company
or vacation resort.

From a marketing and advertising planning point of view,
the large service organizations operate in a manner
similar to consumer products companies.

They both prepare formal marketing plans in which short-
term and long range corporate objectives are spelled
out.

The objectives are generally indicated in concrete,
measurable terms -- either sales increases of X percent,
share increases of Y percent, penetration changes of Z
percent, or a desired change in selected consumer attitudes. In any case, objectives should be specific
enough so that it is possible to measure whether they
have been reached at the end of the time period in
question.

The marketing plans of both kinds of companies spell out
the strategies to be employed to reach the specified
goals.

In addition, the marketing plans of both kinds of companies identify the primary source of incremental
volume -- or, to put it another way, the key market
segment to be affected in order for the company to reach
its goals.

And when both kinds of companies go from marketing
objectives and strategies into the preparation of their
advertising programs, they address -- or should
address -- the same set of questions:

. The competitive frame of reference, or with what
   services or products do we compete?

   Do we narrowly compete with very similar services
   or products offered by other companies or do we

more broadly compete with somewhat different products or services offered by other companies which
help meet the consumer need.

To put it more concretely -- does Coca Cola primarily compete with other cola drinks, such as
Pepsi and RC; or with all carbonated soft drinks,
such as the other colas as well as 7-Up, Orange
Crush, and root beer; or with all thirst quenchers,
such as all of the carbonated soft drinks, as well
as juices, coffee and tea.

And from a services company point of view, does
Hertz Rent-A-Car compete primarily with Avis and
National, or should its competitive frame encompass
the other rent-a-car companies, as well as Amtrak,
Greyhound, and American Airlines.

. In addition to the competitive frame of reference,
   both kinds of companies resolve the question of who
   is the most viable target audience, and what advertising message should be directed to that target.

Specific answers to each of these questions -- source of
volume, competitive frame of reference, target audience,
and message are key to the development of any advertising effort -- for consumer products or services.

We have stated that the preparation of marketing and
advertising programs are similar for consumer products
as well as services. Both prepare marketing objectives,
marketing strategies to reach the objectives, select
target audiences which comprise the greatest potential
sources of incremental volume, and both tailor their
advertising campaigns to achieve the greatest levera-
geability.

Thus, why is advertising a service different? Why are
we devoting a good deal of this Conference's time to
that question?

To help answer that, let's spend a few minutes talking
about how marketing a service differs from marketing a
product.

A major difference between marketing consumer products
and marketing consumer services is the degree of
interaction or contact that occurs -- between the consumer and either personnel or equipment of the marketer.

For consumer products, interaction levels can vary considerably, from practically no interaction to high
levels of interaction, depending upon product characteristics.

For services marketers interaction levels are relatively
high, they vary only by degree depending on the services
in question, and they are important in satisfying consumers.

Let's look at a few examples.

In the rent-a-car business, consumers interact with the
Hertz or Avis or National reservations clerks, sales
people, and courtesy bus drivers repeatedly, as cars are
rented on different occasions. This certainly holds for
the heavy business traveler.

For the phone company, consumers have repeated contact
with the phones and other equipment, telephone operators, business office people and installers. In addition, consumer contact will grow as more and more

services become available with the reorganization of the Bell System.

With Merrill Lynch, and other brokerage firms, the investors have continuing contact with their brokers, as well as with various specialists that are employed by the brokerage firms, who are available on a consultative basis to clients of the brokerage firms.

And for a vacation spot, such as Jamaica, there is repeated contact of visitors with various kinds of service personnel, ranging from tourist advisors to hotel clerks and restauranteurs, as well as the residents of the vacation area.

Thus, interaction levels for these distinctly different kinds of services are relatively high.

The interaction is so intense with consumers, that consumers is not the right word to use here. They are not just consumers, they are your customers.

Given the centrality of customer interaction for services, what is the role of services advertising? How can it help manage the relationship between companies who offer services, and their customers.

We view the role of services advertising as that of a surrogate of the marketer. It should implicitly answer many of the key questions that customers would ask of representatives of the marketer. If they could ask questions, what would they want to know, what would they want to feel?

In fact, it is a form of interaction.

To be an effective surrogate, what must the advertising do? We feel that it has five roles to play, which can be identified as follows:

... to create the company's world in the mind of the customer

... to build the appropriate personality for the company

... to identify the company with the customer

... to positively influence company personnel in terms of how they deal with customers

... to help open the door for sales representatives

Let's briefly discuss each of these roles individually.

THE COMPANY WORLD

As a frame of reference, services advertising should describe the world in which the company operates. It should indicate the scope of the company's activities, and what makes that company's services special.

The company's values can be communicated to the customer, and helps develop favorable expectations and attitudes among customers towards the service offered.

Two examples of services' company worlds would be Hertz advertising with O.J. Simpson and the Merrill Lynch A Breed Apart campaign.

The Hertz advertising suggests what Hertz is all about and indicates the usage of the product at airports primarily and the company's expectations that customers will receive quick, trouble free service with a minimum of hassle.

The Merrill Lynch advertising indicates the values that Merrill Lynch can bring to a customer in terms of research, and financial advice, leading to achievement of financial goals.

CORPORATE PERSONALITY

When you think of Services on a simple one to one level, such as a barber or hairdresser, a rapport is established between the customer and the entrepeneur. Two personalities are relating to and interacting with each other.

How do we capture this rapport in the impersonal world of mass marketing of services by large corporations?

Thus, a second major role of services advertising is to build the appropriate personality for the company. By corporate personality we mean the sum total of a customer's experiences with and attitudes towards a company based upon personal contact with the company's representatives, services and equipment, as well as advertising and other marketing efforts. It is the overall gestalt of the company.

Appropriate corporate personality development is especially important for services marketers because of the Surrogate nature of services advertising. The advertising is very often the first and most frequently encountered service company representative to whom the customer is exposed. Over time it helps shape the customers ideas and expectations about the company and its services.

Building the proper personality should be a long-term effort for any services marketer's advertising. The company personality should not change over time, but rather should be reinforced. Eventually the customer should look upon the company as someone with whom he's been familiar over a long time period, whom he trusts, and for whom he or she has the greatest regard.

When the personality is right, and emotionally on target, the customer empathizes with the company and, will feel more favorable towards it. As a result, the services offered will be more readily received, and more fully appreciated.

IDENTIFICATION OF THE COMPANY WITH THE CUSTOMER

It's also important that customers strongly identify with the service company. The company should project an image of itself and the services it offers that appeals to, and is consonant with the needs, values, lifestyles and attitudes of its primary market target. The greater the degree of positive identification, and the greater the relevance of the company to the customer, the greater the likelihood of using that company's services.

We feel that the personal identification of the customer with the company is especially important for a service marketer. The Service Company is much more likely to be dealt with as a self-contained entity in its own right, while many consumer products manufacturers are far less likely to be considered in that light.

TWO AUDIENCES

An important characteristic, and point of differentiation of service advertising, is that it very often speaks to two separate audiences.

The first of these two audiences are the customers. And we've discussed the roles of services advertising to them -- the company world, the corporate personality, and relevance and identification.

In addition to the customers it attempts to influence to purchase or continue using the service, advertising also attempts to positively influence corporate personnel and others who have public contact, of the service Company.

If corporate personnel feel that the Company's advertising does not adequately represent them, or reflect their views, or if they do not fully understand the advertising objectives, they will give only lukewarm support, or no support at all, to the marketing effort. A well thought out program can be rendered ineffective.

DOOR OPENER

And finally, the role of some services advertising is to lead the way for the company, and help open the door for its sales representatives. Thus when a sales representative calls upon a prospect, there is a favorable backdrop toward the company, which will cause the prospect to listen to what the sales representative has to offer. Without that favorable perception, there is a greater probability that the door will be closed on the sales representative before he has an opportunity to make his or her offer.

EXAMPLES

Now I'd like to show examples of advertising for three of our Services Clients -- Merrill Lynch, AT&T and the Jamaica Tourist Bureau.

Y&R became the advertising agency for Merrill Lynch at the beginning of 1979.

Prior to developing any advertising, we reviewed a great deal of information from the following sources:

- Secondary data -- New York Stock Exchange and the Business Press;

- Merrill Lynch Research files;

- Meetings with Merrill Lynch executives; and

- Primary research studies which we conducted among Merrill Lynch's key target groups, retail investors, corporate financial officers for its investment banking activities, and institutional portfolio managers.

Analysis of the data indicated a negative reaction on the part of investors to the then current state of the industry. There was:

- Lack of confidence (primarily in Equities);

- Dissatisfaction with investment achievements, and a desire for assistance;

- Reduced confidence in brokerage Account Executives; and

- General confusion towards brokerage firms and their services.

In addition to these general industry problems, Merrill Lynch was not perceived as any better than competition in terms of services, research, attention to investment objectives of customers, portfolio management, nor offering personalized service so that the customer feels the company is working for him. In fact, the company was very strong in each of these areas, though not so regarded.

Merrill Lynch was well rated in terms of its network of national offices, and offering a range of financial services.

Thus, the objective of the advertising campaign which Y&R developed was to convince individual and professional investors of Merrill Lynch realities -- that the quality of advice, superior products and services available from Merrill Lynch will enhance their chances of reaching their personal or professional financial goals.

The "A Breed Apart" campaign resulted.

By the way, in 1981, the International Broadcasters Association selected the campaign from among 5,000 from more than 50 countries as the most effective TV campaign in the world.

This campaign follows the precepts we discussed earlier.

The symbolism and personality are evident. The corporate values as represented by the Bull, the manner with which it operates to meet customer needs and expectations and to fulfill customer goals is effectively communicated. It creates an emotional bond in a rational world.

In order to assure ourselves that we were talking to our target audience in their terms, we very effectively drew upon Values and Life Styles (VALS) data. It's no surprise that the target audience for the campaign were high income, high asset, well educated, professional and managerial people -- or the VALS Achiever Group.

Undoubtedly, the Achiever-type target would have been chosen whether or not VALS data existed.

However, the VALS information gave us a deeper, richer understanding of the Achiever target. We learned that they tend to look upon themselves as rugged individualists, self-confident, aggressive, risk-takers, success-oriented leaders, who make up their own minds. These facts enabled Y&R to develop Merrill Lynch advertising that speaks to Achievers in their terms; and positions the Firm in that manner.

A recent national tracking study among the target audience has indicated the success of the program. Awareness and especially, attitudes toward Merrill Lynch have increased substantially vis-a-vis competitive brokerage firms.

And, separate internal programs have been developed jointly by the Merrill Lynch Advertising Department and Y&R, whereby the 8,000 or so stock brokers and other employees in the far flung Merrill Lynch network have been kept apprised of the advertising program.

Video-tape cassettes, and kits of print advertising are distributed to field personnel periodically to indicate how the campaign supports their prospecting and selling efforts.

Field personnel support has been outstanding.

Merrill Lynch is having a record year.

THE AT&T CASE

Let's talk about the customers for a moment. What do they think of the phone company? They love it. Indeed, many think of it as their lifeline.

However, as most of you know, the Company is undergoing substantial changes. Changes in organization and ways of operating can be unsettling to customers. Especially when people like the current offering.

What would this kind of company want to do for its customers? They would want to reassure them that the corporation wants to lend a helping hand during the transition period.

Thus, working with AT&T, the campaign was developed by Y&R to:

. Convey to AT&T's customers the corporation's genuine concern about them, and AT&T's desire to help them understand and adjust to changes in how the telephone company operates;

. Establish AT&T as an important and credible source of information about the transition; and

. To encourage a dialogue and interaction between AT&T customer service representatives and its customers, that responds to customer information needs and concerns as they change over time.

Given these objectives, Y&R developed the "Let's Talk" campaign.

We feel that this campaign portrays AT&T's corporate personality as that of a concerned organization really interested in the welfare of its customers. The array of company representatives in the commercial are similar to the kinds of people that AT&T deals with. And symbolically, customers know what to expect from the company.

Additionally, the customer campaign has been complemented by an internal informational campaign directed to AT&T employees. The objectives of that campaign are:

. to convey to its employees AT&T's posture of genuine concern about the well-being of the customers they serve;

. to help support AT&T's credibility with its employees as a source of reliable, candid information about the transition; and

. to help AT&T's employees understand the changes in the operation of the telephone company, and how these changes will affect them.

Both AT&T and Y&R management agree that the "Let's Talk" advertising we saw a few moments ago, also very effectively addresses the corporation's employees -- in terms of its concern about customer well-being, and as a credible source of information.

The effectiveness of this program has been indicated by tracking relevant customer attitudes in test markets.

JAMAICA TOURIST BUREAU

And finally, let's examine the advertising strategy for the Jamaica Tourist Bureau.

Jamaica had always beckoned as a place in the sun. However, the decade of the 70's had been difficult both economically and politically. Because of the unsettled atmosphere, tourism slowed.

However, with a recent change in government, and with priorities placed on economic development, the opportunity for Jamaica to regain its tourist position emerged.

How do you tell this to customers -- to tourists. One way is for the people of the island to speak for themselves -- to say to vacationers (as well as travel agents) that once again they can enjoy wonderful, unique Jamaica vacations, because of its natural beauty, friendly people and diverse and rich cultural history.

Thus, the "Come Back To Jamaica" campaign was developed.

We had to walk a delicate bridge between acknowledging the problem and promising a great vacation. We did it with the people in the advertising.

We feel that this campaign is a prime example of warmly and empathetically communicating consumer expectations of relaxation, sheer physical beauty of the Island, and a friendly, open environment on the part of all with whom vacationers will interact. It's the Island personality.

In addition to talking directly to potential vacationers, the campaign was also aimed at travel agents, and reassures them that they will not make a mistake by recommending Jamaica to their clients.

The results for Jamaica have been gratifying. Visitors to Jamaica have been increasing in number, and the Island's share of total Caribbean vacationers has gone up.

In addition, customer and travel agent tracking studies have indicated improvement in attitudes towards Jamaica among both these market segments.

SUMMARY

In summary, then, we at Y&R feel that Services Advertising is a highly specialized activity in many respects.

Due to its surrogate nature, and quasi-interactive role with the market target, great care must be taken to consider its different objectives:

. Create the company world in the customer's mind, with the desired customer expectations;

. Build the appropriate corporate personality;

. Identify the company with the customer;

. Speak to dual audiences -- corporate personnel and agents as well as customers;

. and, in some cases, help open doors for company representatives.

We feel, however, that development of the appropriate corporate personality is by far the key, over-riding objective.

Successful inclusion of these factors in Services Advertising, however, will result in effective campaigns like Merrill Lynch, AT&T, and Jamaica Tourist Bureau.

Thank you.

DEVELOPING AND IMPLEMENTING A QUALITY STRATEGY FOR A SERVICE BUSINESS - A CASE STUDY

Frank Rothman, General Electric Company

ABSTRACT

This case is about General Electric's Major Appliance Product Service Business. All data are non-confidential and
non-proprietary. Calendar dates cited are approximate.

INTRODUCTION

From 1978-1980, TV advertising was used in an experiment
aimed at increasing sales, shares, and profits of the out-
of-warranty, in-home repair calls segment of this Business.
During this time, TV advertising, at the spending levels
tested, caused increases in awareness and preference, but
failed to generate sufficient revenues to cover advertising
costs. Analyses conducted between 1980-82 revealed that
service quality had two dimensions: readiness to serve
(RTS), and performance quality (QOS). From surveys that
indicated customers' RTS/QOS expectations, performance
standards were established. Based on these findings a
simulation model was developed and refined. This tool
allows both headquarters and local area business managers
to optimize service quality RTS and performance quality QOS
that meet customer expectations. Several different zone
managers used the model in their markets to upgrade short-
term total quality performance and this resulted in increased margin contribution. Product Service is currently
installing the RTS/QOS model in most U.S. geographical
zones and is training local managers in its use to improve
service quality and profitability.

BACKGROUND

In 1978, objectives set for the Service operation of the
Major Appliance Business Group were to increase total
sales, share, and profits of current activities and to
investigate venture opportunities.
A new marketing team led these thrusts.
Business reviews provided the following facts:

Environment	Environment
Our Service Business:	Business Segments:
Covers 80% of the U.S.	Retail/Wholesale:
Services our brands only	In-warranty calls
Has several thousand	Out-of-warranty calls
technicians	Service contract calls
Competition:	Parts (at retail for
Outnumbers us in	do-it-yourselfers
technicians 25 to 1	and at tholesale
Is local independents,	for commercial firms)
and servicing dealers	
Sears is only national competitor	

After finalizing strategies for handling in-warranty calls,
service contracts, and parts, the remaining need was to
make o/w calls, consisting of labor and parts, more
profitable.

Further investigation indicated that out out-of-warranty
segment had low general public awareness (40%); high
seasonality, with demand tilted toward hot weather months;
limited potential, since a sale occurs only when a product
fails; an historical and current share of 8-10% of all
out-of-warranty calls for our brands; customers satisfied
with out performance and that of competitors; known reasons
for selecting a particular servicer; and acceptable customer and prospect definitions.

Two more items, 1)revenues per o/w call were increasing
faster than both imflation and the o/w call load rate and,
2) out-of-warranty calls in a geographic area plateau
about 5 years after startup, indicating that total out-of-

warranty call load increases stem from opening new
offices, and not from increased penetration in existing
areas.

ACCESS SCREEN

Was this business experiencing a "funnel effect"
because substantial parts of P/L responsibility were
placed in the Operations function instead of Marketing?
If so, managing for short-term profit optimization had
occurred. One consequence would be a screen that blocked
potential incoming business by limiting RTS phone line
and call-taker capacity and, perhaps technician availability

After lenghty discussions, the team decided to use advertising to force open the RTS portion of the funnel. How?
By proving that heavy advertising expenditures could
persuade more customers to call us. And if calls did
increase, it was felt that local managers would respond
by expanding RTS.

YEAR 1 TEST

An experiment to determine if advertising could be used
to increase out-of-warranty call profitability in four
typical, average share and average performance markets
was designed and implemented.

Positioning research was omitted. Marketing decided to
use broadcast instead of print. Two TV commercials and
one radio commercial were pre-tested. The winning
commercial and the single radio commercial were run
after making slight modificaitons. One market received
radio alone, another TV only, while a third was given
radio and TV. Each of these three markets had a weight
of about 400 GRP's per month. The fourth area had a
TV schedule of 800 GRP's per month.

Constraints limited the initial experiment to a 6-week
peak demand period starting early in June and ending in
min-July.

Assurances were gicen that sufficient phone lines, call-
takers, schedulers, trucs, parts and technicians would
be available to handle anticipated call load increases in
each market.

Criteria for judging success were (specified) increases
in unaided and total awareness and preference for our
service. Payback of advertising costs was not an issue.

The winning media market was no surprise.

The extra-spending (800 GRP) TV area, called D, had the
most before-after absolute increases in unaided and total
awareness and preference measurements. In the other areas,
each with 400 GRP's, radio was second, TV was third and
radio and TV combined was last. This suggests that
service businesses with limited advertising budgets should
not divide resources between media, because desired
impacts may be diluted.

In D, when TV time costs were subtracted from expected
plus increased o/w revenues, a program break-even point is
almost reached. But now for some excitement: parts and
service contract revenues also were up when these plusses
were added to o/w gains, margin contributions over and
above TV time costs result.

A decision was made to continue TV advertising in D in

the 4th Quarter at the 800 GRP monthly spending level. At year end, D awareness, preference, and call-load levels were about equal to those achieved in the initial 6-week period. In other words, no gain.

Overall, in 1978, all financial business performance goals were met or exceeded. In D, the continuing test area, advertising was helping the business obtain increases in awareness and preference, even through serious questions were emerging about the ability of advertising to raise o/w call-load profits.

YEAR 2 PROGRAM

The marketing manager and his team decided to continue advertising and D, and to expand the program to include five new markets with shares below the national average. All markets receive the original TV commercial. The weitht is about 800 GRP's per month, advertising starts in the second quarter.

Be mid-year, the D market had satisfactory upswings in awareness and preference; calls were up slightly. In the five new markets, awareness, preference, and call-load were flat compared to July, Year 1 benchmarks.

Concerns mount. The marketing manager wants to know why the D market behaves differently from the other five markets. Payback bacomes an issue,

Shortly thereafter, the program changes. One below average share market continued to receive TV advertising but the four other were dropped. A completely new area, one with an average share was added. In these three markets, TV continued as the main media vehicle, with minor exceptions. All markets receive the original commercial and 400 GRP's per month—down from 800 GRP's. Concurrently, four studies were commissioned. They were:

1. A telephone blitz one Monday morning that deluged the system with incoming calls. This tested local zone RTS capability to answer their phones within a stated number of rings. Interestingly, almost half the incoming calls rang "busy."

2. A customer satisfaction data review. Customers rated our performance very high and would use us again if a need occurred. But these ratings were one-sided because non-customers were not included in our satisfaction ratings. Potential customers who could not break through RTS access screens, if asked, probably would have rated our RTS unsatisfactory.

3. An update of customer and prospect subsriptions and definitions. Although characteristics of our appliance owners and our service customers were well documented, prospect clarity and analysis could be improved. Moreover, repeat usage data were unclear and indefinite.

4. A clarification of service quality concepts. There was a need for an improved understanding of readiness-to-serve and quality of service interactions and impact on local area performance.

In D, at the end of year 2, awareness and preference slanted upward significantly and o/w calls were up slightly. In the above average share market,

the market that was added to the program in mid-year, TV advertising increased awareness, preference and o/w calls somewhat; the below average share market that was continued had a minor uptick in awareness and preference, but no gain in o/w calls.

In all three markets, added revenues from increased o/w calls were not enough to recover TV media costs. Additionally, combined revenue increases from parts, service contracts and o/w calls fail to recover TV time costs.

For the second consecutive year, however, total sales and profits for the service Business meet or exceed goals.

The Service Business marketing team wins promotion to new positions. A new group replaced them and questioned the viability of the o/w TV advertising strategy.

THE CUSTOMER FRANCHISE

As the new team familiarized themselves with the prior two years work, more customer dynamics data becomes available. For example, in a typical year, about 2/3 of all customers requiring paid for o/w repairs were repeat customers of a previously used servicer. That is, 2/3 of the available annual potential use a vendor with whom they have had past experience. Only 1/3 of any servicer business book is new...new because customers have never required any repair on their current inventory, or are part of the "unhappieds" shopping around or are recent movers. Another analysis shows that some households requiring multiple repairs share their business among several suppliers.

These customer data tend to support an earlier situation statement indicating that customers with repair experience are satisfied generally with supplier service quality performance. This suggests one reason why customers will pay somewhat more for required repairs; they want to avoid the uncertainties surrounding the search for a new service source.

The 2/3 - 1/3 customer franchise split also indicates that any o/w strategy should include customer retention programs that provide for outstanding quality of service (i.e. lose less, keep more). Another strategic implication appears in those issues underlying the division of multiple repairs in the same houshold (i.e. get more of the available, gain share).

At this junction, silent questions were raised about the role and importance of RTS and QOS, the reasons for area by area variations in market share, and the desireability of continuing TV advertising.

For purposes of this discussion, service quality elements include:

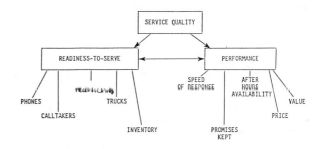

The program focus shifted. The new objectives were to determine if TV advertising severely reduced to about 200 GRP's per month) could increase call-load when an adequate RTS phone and call-taker capacity was present in two different types of market, 1) an area relatively new to the system, undergoing fast o/w growth, with an above national average share, and 2) a mature market, experiencing only average o/w gains, with an average market share.

Advertising tracking research expanded from awareness, preference and call load measurements to include intensive study of customer and prospect attitudes and behavior.

Advertising tracking research expanded from awareness, preference and call load measurements to include intensive study of customer and prospect attitudes and behavior.

YEAR 3 FINDINGS

The two new markets have results similar to earlier outcomes. TV advertising helps to increase awareness, preference and o/w calls. In the newer, fast growth market, some of the advertising costs are recovered. In the mature, average growth market, practically none of the advertising costs are recaptured.

At this time, it was concluded that, is the short term, TV advertising increased awareness and preference but did not produce profits.

Further analysis of the third year program findings indicated that RTS phone and call-taker capacity was the key to achieving whatever gains were experienced in the high growth area. In other words, sufficient RTS capacity to handle incoming demand assisted in achieving above average market, RTS helped to hold share and was required to maintain performance quality.

At least one inference can be made about differential market performance. Markets behave differently because local management RTS/QOS practices overall have serious consequences on customers behavior. This led to a desire to obtain better in-depth understanding of how all aspects of RTS/QOS decisions effect customers and potential customers.

Recommendations to stop o/w advertising and to study the impact of service quality decisions on profit were accepted.

SERVICE QUALITY EFFECTS

In Year 3, questions were raised about whether providing a very high degree of customer service quality over and above "normal" levels produced additional revenues, share, profits, growth, customer loyalty, and so on. Unbiased evidence was sought.

Analyses of Data* verified PIMS conclusions and generalizations about the importance of product quality: namely, that superior product quality results in higher profitability (ROI); in other words, companies with high quality product portfolios have high corporate profits.

Inspection of the instruction forms used in preparing PIMS product quality ratings that PIMS views the product and any accompanying services as a combined entity, wherever such services influence purchase decisions. This suggests another interpretation of PIMS findings about the quality and profitability: high product quality and high service quality lead to high profitability...when auxiliary services have an important influence on customers' purchase decisions.

The following RTS/QOS resource allocation hypotheses were developed:

- "Balancing available resources against customer RTS/QOS expectations and requirements should result in share, performance, and profit increases."

- "If balancing RTS/QOS provides useful concepts for studying the impact of service quality decisions, then is should be possible to build a theroetical foundation for constructing a quantitative model of this marketplace, and to validate the theory.

*From publications describing the impact of strategic planning of profit performance published by The Strategic Planning Institute, Cambridge, Massachusetts.

Balancing starts with selecting one of three basic RTS strategies - overserving, underserving, or balancing RTS with customer requirements. Before choosing a direction, the consequenses of each RTS strategy should be understood:

1. Overserving the market. If RTS is more than market requirements, performance quality (QOS) will be superior. Share will increase in the short and long term. Short run profits will be reduced (or even show a loss), but long haul profit will probably increase. Overserving probably is an unpopular option in a near-term profit pressure situation.

2. Underserving the market. If RTS is below market requirements, performance quality (QOS) will be inferior. Share may or may not decline in the short term, but will suffer long range. Short term profits will be maintained or even increased even though long term profitability probably will decrease. This may be a popular strategy now.

3. Balancing RTS with customer requirements. If RTS meets customer's needs, they can access the system and flow through it when they want. Performance quality (QOS) will equal expectations. Share will grow in the short and long term because customers will be satisfied (repeat business will be high, and this will help increase share). In this ideal state, profits will always be optimized.

Is it realistic to model this Business?

We started with the simplified idea that are three discrete functions that must be managed in this (or any) service firm: marketing, operations, and finance.

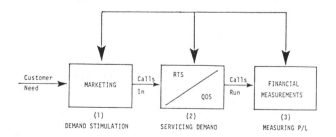

Any comprehensive model that simulates the functional handling of these activities, would start with inputs about customer demand and requirements, would have readiness to serve and quality of service standards that satisfy current and potential customers, and would produce a pro forma P/L.

Our first need was developing the servicing demand part of the total model that was explicit and detailed. The service model outputs would identify the reasons for lost calls at each important decision point and would included these elements:

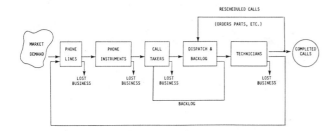

Before implementing modeling, it was assumed that demand could be forecast with reasonable accuracy and that analysis of the outputs from this model would inform operations and other managers about RTS/QOS service levels needed to produce staffing, scheduling and profit optimums.

To determine how RTS/QOS decisions impact on profits, an intensive analysis of o/w results in a peak demand period was conducted.

OPENING BOTH ENDS OF THE FUNNEL PAYS OFF

Eighty-eight markets were divided into two categories: those with o/w call growth and no o/w call growth compared to the same period a year before. One important findings: managers in the o/w growth markets added both call-takers and technicians, increasing capacity and performance capability whereas managers in the no o/w growth markets added only call takers.

It is noted that opening incoming phone capacity alone allowed more than usual in-warranty and service contract calls to enter the system and to be handled faster than required. This happens because customers who pay for services ahead of time, keep calling until their calls are answered. Since our rules are not sophisticated enough to provide for differential scheduling that takes into account customer type call-load mix...in-warranty and service contract customers had their repairs completed earlier than needed. Since technician capacity was not increased, potential o/w customers who counnd not be scheduled at their convenience switched to competitors. Why not? Why should they wait until we are ready to serve them?

But, when both phone capacity and technician availability were increased, a-1 types of incoming customer calls were handled faster and more effectively. Fewer customers were turned away.

Modeling efforts proceeded. About 9 months later, the main part of this work was completed.

TRAINING SOME MANAGERS TO THINK ABOUT CUSTOMERS

How do we influence and persuade a local manager to think about customer needs and the consequences of his RTS/QOS decision on service quality and profits? How do we convince a local manager that RTS/QOS model out-

puts can help him meet his measurements? How do we train a local manager in model uses?

In 1982, three zone managers were persuaded to TV implement the "best" RTS/QOS model service level solution for his area. By fine tuning RTS/QOS in each of these three markets, o/w calls and profits increased within three months.

Since the fourth quarter of 1982, a national progran roll-out has been underway. Local managers are being classroom and field trained to use the RTS/QOS model properly and they have unlimited local access to it.

REVISED PROGRAM APPROACH

If we could redo this program, we would:

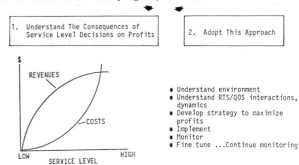

- Understand environment
- Understand RTS/QOS interactions, dynamics
- Develop strategy to maximize profits
- Implement
- Monitor
- Fine tune ...Continue monitoring

LESSONS LEARNED

Some of the more important case conclusions are:

- Service quality in terms of both RTS/QOS must be present before share gain strategies can be sucessful.

- Markets with average or above national average share have the best chance of achieving short-term share increases when promotion is used.

- Below average national share markets may require structural change. Promotion activities will not overcome service deficiencies.

- Local area managers make RTS/QOS decisions that have grave consequences. It is necessary to upgrade their knowledge of RTS/QOS dynamics in order for them to understand how these decisions effect volume-share-profit results.

In a broader context, the findings indicate the need to replicate individual market excellence in any multi-market service business. Success is rewarded for area-by-area achievements which can be obtained by concentrating on local intensive competitive marketing activities.

TECHNO-SERVICES AND DIRECTIONS FOR THE
AMERICAN MARKETING ASSOCIATION IN SERVICES MARKETING

Eugene J. Kelley, The Pennsylvania State University

ABSTRACT

Service producers are in many areas only now emerging
as powerful, sophisticated marketers of their products.
There are three primary reasons: Computerization and
high technology, deregulation and bigness. Taken together, those three factors -- and others as well --
have in recent years created an atmosphere that has bred
the need and the desire for these companies to adopt
highly sophisticated marketing practices. We are in
the opening phases of a "marketing revolution" in
services that is already transforming many of those
industries.

Congratulations to Len Berry, Lynn Shostack and Greg
Upah for putting together a program of excellence
and assembling an outstanding roster of speakers.[1]

Taking a good hard look at who those speakers are
and the companies they represent is quite instructive
about the state of the services industry today and
the potential role for marketing.

I see several major foodservers, an airline, hotel
and motel chains, advertising agencies, several
banks, a travel and credit service company, the
expectant Ma Bell and a number of major universities.
Also interesting -- and instructive -- is the
international representation.

These fine men and women who have already spoken
and whom you will be hearing this afternoon and
tomorrow can offer much better suggestions than I
about ideas for doing your jobs better. Be spring-
boards for new insight and ideas of your own --
in general to be better marketers of services.

So I won't try to cover that ground. What I thought
would be interesting and worthwhile, though, would
be to talk about the socio-economic context in
which this thing called services is growing. About
the changes that are taking place in our business
environment here in the United States, about the
tremendous implications for the growth of marketing
of services and, what directions the AMA is taking
to further that growth and help you increase the
level of your own professionalism and value to your
companies.

There are a number of factors, irreversible forces
of economic life, working in your favor. Working
to push the size of the service economy ever higher
and make its scope ever broader. Reaching into
ever more facets of our business and personal lives.

And there are internal business factors as well that
are increasing the demand for your services as

professional marketers of those services, factors,
which if nurtured properly, will grow at an ever
increasing rate.

There is no doubting the fact that while manufacturing
may have built the American economy, services are now
running it.

At present, services employ more than twice as many
people as do manufacturing and agriculture -- 63.7
million to 30.1 million.

In the last 10 years alone, service industries have
created almost 18 million new jobs, compared with
fewer than 2.5 million created in manufacturing.

In 1981, service industries accounted for fully 64
percent of our gross national produce or more
than 1.9 trillion -- that's trillion -- dollars.

TRENDS IN THE SERVICES ECONOMY

Peering into the future, U.S. News & World Report
for one has predicted the number of services jobs
will grow by 31 percent in this decade alone. By
1990, more than one million new workers will be needed
in banking and finance -- and more than 4 million
in health services -- to name just two.

And, by that year, consumers will be spending more
than 50 percent of their income on service purchases.

This trend toward services has been with us for
quite a while. We did not become a service
economy overnight.

There are some new and some exciting things happening
with great implications for the economy and marketing.

I see two broad trends in the service economy. First,
there are great changes in ways the kinds of
companies represented here operate -- the traditional
powerhouses in the service business -- banking,
transportation, communications, travel and lodging,
credit, advertising. We could add several others
to that list.

But it is clearly evident that all your businesses
have changed -- in some cases drastically -- in
recent years.

But, just as our economy once evolved from agrarian
to industrial and now from industrial to service,
so too our service-based economy is evolving from
one based in personal services to include a myriad
of business services and those involved in managing
resources.

---

[1]It is a pleasure to acknowledge the research
contributions to this paper of Alissa D. Roberts,
Research Assistant, College of Business
Administration, The Pennsylvania State University.

The rather rapid emergence of these totally new and very much different kinds of services has meant they are only now just beginning to come into their own marketingwise.

The growth of these emerging industries along with rapid acceleration in business of the traditional ones means new vistas are now beginning to open for people with your very special kind of expertise.

In fact, I would say there is a "Marketing Revolution" in store for our profession. Whereas much of the marketing action has traditionally been in the manufacturing sector. In the future it will be ever more in services, as it already is in certain highly visible instances.

I want to hold that thought for a moment and look a little deeper into the shift within the services sector -- at these emerging industries.

It used to be that there was a pretty clearcut definition of a service. Some person did something for you that you didn't want to or couldn't do for yourself. It was the corner dry cleaner or shopkeeper. The man who repaired your shoes. Waiters and waitresses at restaurants, hotel people, and cab drivers or railroad engineers. The TV repairman.

Business had its counterparts of people performing services -- but they were typically in support of the main show -- manufacturing. They were clerks and delivery people. Their own repair services.

For the most part service was synonymous with manual. While manufacturing meant machines. Service jobs were low paying and often required few skills. Productivity was difficult to measure because service was labor intensive.

Of course, there were a few other kinds of services that didn't fit the mold -- banks, brokerage houses, wholesale and other "middleman" functions -- and, of course, government and the professions. But in those areas, marketing in a modern sense, was not important or, for the professions, illegal.

But what constitutes a service today? Certainly, all those I just mentioned, some as vastly different than they used to be.

But, as I said, a new kind of service has emerged today with a different face, with new elements. Elements that have many of the markings of a traditional manufacturing industry.

These services are capital intensive. Their workers are highly skilled and highly paid. Efficiencies of scale are attainable and desirable -- meaning productivity can be managed and increased.

Moreover, they require highly sophisticated management systems in order to run efficiently -- including developed marketing structures.

I call these businesses -- Techno-services.

TECHNO-SERVICES

They are the services which offer the latest technology in data processing and communications to their customers -- who find it more efficient to buy the service rather than own the technology.

Computerization and High Technology

You see it in data processing, with a myriad of interconnect services, with cable television, with telecommunciations -- ATT, as well as its new, long distance competitors -- with word processing centers, with mainframe computer centers, with software programmers.

In banking you see the advent of automatic teller machines which are revolutionizing that industry -- opening up new horizons to it -- with much greater operating efficiencies.

Cable television is an excellent example of a Techno-service industry. Cable is really a Techno-utility. It offers a means of connecting the user with a supplier. No different than gas lines connect users with gas companies.

The cable supply, at this time, is mostly entertainment. But soon for most cable users and now for some, it may become more important as a supplier of information, from retailers, creditors, the bank, possibly even the office.

The potential is enormous. And the realization of that potential will depend entirely on the success of the engineers, working with you marketers, in meeting market needs at an affordable cost. Warner's QUBE system is only the most visible example.

One of the many estimates one can read today is that 60 million homes will subscribe to one form or another of cable by 1990. Hundreds of millions of dollars have already been contracted for in cable advertising by some major national advertisers -- most notably Anheuser-Busch, American Home Products, Chrysler, Campbell's, Merrill, Lynch, among others.

Or, perhaps you're one who believes the telephone and computer terminal will be more important than cable. The computer service industry had sales of more than $20 billion last year -- nearly triple that of three years before.

Techno-services are not really new in concept at all. In fact they have been around at least since the days of the railroads which, when you think about it, were really a capital intensive service that provided enormous productivity advances for merchants of the day. Their markets expanded to beyond the horizon for very modest costs.

But when you think about aerospace workers in Washington and California producing rockets and satellites to make your phone calls easier and to keep costs down -- you see in a nutshell the importance of the techno-services to our economy and that a service industry can, despite what some say, produce great wealth.

For every time we hear about the transition in our economy from manufacturing to services, we hear some doomsayer predict that services cannot possibly support economic expansion and the increase in wealth we have all come to expect. They make a quick -- and though I am not an economist I think an incorrect -- correlation between our reduced rate of growth and our switch to services.

I will not go into the counter arguments here except to say that service jobs are not replacing manufacturing jobs, as such. Manufacturing jobs were lost here for a variety of reasons coincidental to the increase in service jobs. In fact, if some manufacturers had been as farsighted in their own marketing as many in the service industries have been, we could have had both. But that is for another forum to explore.

I do not mean to say in stressing techno-services that they are replacing more traditional services. Anyone who has ever looked behind the counter in a McDonald's or Wendy's and seen the lights flashing, buzzers buzzing and the french fries pop up out of the oil by themselves, knows that technology and productivity innovations are not limited to data print-outs and direct dial calls to Australia.

However, technology is really just one of several factors positively affecting the future of marketing in our services sector.

Deregulation

Another primary force is deregulation. Much of the deregulatory activity in the 70s directly affected service industries. Trucking, airlines, communications, finance, securities were all deregulated to one degree or another at federal and state levels in the past decade.

In classic fashion, companies in these industries have given new meaning to the word competition. Airlines, which used to deal only with the government in setting routes and rates -- and then advertised that over which the consumers had little control other than to take it or leave it -- these same airlines are now market driven, designing routes, rates and packages for specific market segments and then advertising their competitive advantages.

Some have failed, while new entries have arisen based on filling unfulfilled needs in the market-place -- or simply with a better idea to fill existing needs.

I have already discussed technological changes in banking and, though still fairly tightly regulated, I think we can all see a point down the road where new opportunities will be opened up for banking as a result of deregulation as well.

In the brokerage business, we have discount houses like Charles Schwab and acquisitions of brokers by such retail oriented companies as American Express and, of course, Sears.

Buy your stocks where you buy your socks? Why not?

Just over a year from now, we will see an enormous change in the Techno-service sector when the largest divestiture in our nation's history occurs.

Suddenly, the largest company in the world will be smaller, but will be able to go into the marketplace and sell everything its Bell Labs unit can develop and Western Electric can produce, thereby solidifying a major Techno-service industry -- data communications. The tele-communications sector of our Techno-service industry will then be changed forever.

Scale and Big Business

The third factor helping to speed the growth of marketing in the service sector is bigness. Many service providers are simply larger than the typical service provider of years past.

Partly, this is a result of deregulation which has allowed for more mergers and acquisitions. It is also due to growth as the demand for these services has skyrocketed.

There are at least two reasons why this has aided the marketing revolution. The first is that bigger companies tend to be more marketing oriented than smaller companies. The second is that the resources are there for doing sophisticated and groundbreaking research, thus developing the potentials even more.

So, we have three factors -- and others as well -- working together to brighten the future of services marketing. We have a burst of technology to expand the reach, expand the potential and expand the need for our services. These are our techno-services.

We have considerable deregulation in place and on the books to provide the incentives for innovation, for expansion, for competition.

And we have a trend toward larger service companies to provide the necessary sophistication and financial resources to make all of the rest possible and to keep the industries moving forward.

It is in that fertile soil that the seed of our Services Marketing Revolution has been planted and begun to grow and in which it will continue.

Now the question becomes, I think, "How do I as a marketer make the most of this situation? How do I maximize this great potential?"

Of course, that is what this conference is all about.

But I would add to this discussion two general rules of thumb for guiding your actions as marketers of services.

One. Know what technology can do for you, whether or not you are involved with a Techno-service.

Two. Understand the strategic potentials and goals of your company, make your marketing plans accordingly, and constantly demonstrate that understanding to your corporate management.

I'd like to elaborate briefly on each.

Technology

Date communications and other advanced technology available, in development or due in the near future, will be to industry what the soybean is to nutrition. It will have nearly unlimited capability to do what we want in the way we want it to perform. hemmed in possibly only by the limits of our imagination.

If you don't believe that all you need do is read the frequent reports out of Silicone Valley on the latest marvels those young, imaginative inventors are cooking up -- this week.

Electronic shopping by credit card -- for everything from securities to vacations -- is already here for some people.

How big is the step from getting a catalogue in the mail, ordering by WATS line and paying by credit card to handling the entire transaction on a TV monitor hooked up to your pushbutton phone. Or over your cable system.

Not a very big step. The roses go to the company that figures out the right combinations of technology guided by you marketers to get there first.

Another example: Recently TravelHost magazine announced plans to put a computer terminal in 500,000 hotel rooms with which you can, using American Express, Visa or MasterCard, check air schedules, write and transmit reports, check your stocks, send and receive messages, even play video-games.

Strategic Marketing

It has unfortunately been a shortcoming within marketing, in my experience that too many marketers see their discipline as somehow isolated from the overall needs of their businesses. And that is a mistake and puts a limit on growth potential.

It is not, afterall, the purpose of a marketing researcher to conduct research studies or of a marketing manager to analyze studies. It is the purpose of a marketing researcher, however, to provide business with vital, timely, accurate information. And it is then the job of the manager to interpret that information for the particular company and make his or her best recommendation for the particular company based on that information.

And nothing is more important to business today, Techno-service, traditional service or manufacturing, than the ability to be a successful strategic planner.

Knowing what your company's strategic plans are... helping to shape those plans...demonstrating your appreciation for the "Big Picture"...and shaping your marketing efforts to help build and improve those plans with the unique contributions marketing can make...by doing those things you will help assure your own rising indispensability to your companies.

You must, in other words, understand and demonstrate that marketing is not an ends but a means to an ends.

And what of the AMA? The AMA is making a start -- and just a start -- at doing more to better serve the needs of our services marketing members and that industry in general.

This has been an excellent conference. I would hope we can make it a regular event.

This coming March AMA will hold a conference on the marketing of health services. It will be our third in St. Louis. But we as an organization need to do more, much more. I hope we are able to speed along our plans to bring new and better services onto line. And I know that sentiment is shared by Elvin Schofield, who becomes the new AMA President in July, 1983.

I ask each and every one of you here to help Len or Lynn or drop me a line with your thoughts on AMA's role in services marketing. We need and want your input.

The AMA Services Marketing Planning Committee

To this end I am announcing the formation of the AMA Services Marketing Planning Committee. I am charging this committee with recommending policy, plans and options to help the AMA become the primary organization in services marketing in the world. The committee members are:

Leonard L. Berry, Chairman
Texas A&M University
Vice President Elect
Professional Development AMA

Kenneth Bernhardt, Vice Chairman
Georgia State University
Atlanta, Georgia

Thomas M. Bloch
President-Tax Operations Division
H&R Block, Inc.
Kansas City, Mo.

Elvin Schofield
Senior Vice Preisdent-Marketing
National Bank of Commerce of
    San Antonio
President Elect of the AMA

G. Lynn Shostack
Senior Vice President
Bankers Trust Company
New York, New York

Gregory D. Upah
Research Account Supervisor
Young & Rubicam
New York, New York

M. Venkatesan
Wright State University
Dayton, Ohio

It is through the work of this committee and your
active participation in AMA activities -- that kind
of networking -- that we will be able to move ahead
that much quicker in this most exciting of professions.

THE MARKETING ASPECTS OF SERVICE QUALITY

Robert C. Lewis, University of Massachusetts, Amherst
Bernard H. Booms, Washington State University, Seattle

Although the concern with product quality is not new the subject is particularly timely. A recent Business Week article (Quality: The U.S. Drives to Catch Up, 1982) points out the effort by goods producing manufacturers to catch up with the high quality standards recognized today in Japanese products. "Doing it right the first time", indicates this article, is being recognized by American industry as promising more benefits to the bottom line than volume increases.

Corporate titles such as quality director, quality vice-president, etc. have become more common in recent years. The emphasis however, in goods producing companies with these positions, is on production. Cost savings are realized by not making mistakes. Further, this assurance enables companies to charge more for their product. Quality control, in those forward looking companies, is executed through statistical measurements.

Services, however, are in a different ballpark. Statistical controls do not have the same application when "mistakes" occur in human interpersonal interactions and intangible product attributes. In fact, in service delivery it often costs no more to do it wrong. To charge more for "doing it right" is incomprehensible when that is the only expectation the consumer anticipates. Unlike manufactured goods, services lack the durability dimension with which quality is often associated. The failure to provide quality in services does, however, cost customers, perhaps more so than in goods producing companies.

Like goods, the quality of services in many instances may have become unbelievable to many consumers to the point that they have lowered expectations at all but the highest prices; in fact, to the point where consumers may not believe it when service firms attempt to market quality.

But market quality we do. Familiar current examples are American Airlines' "Doing what we do best", Marriott's "when Marriott does it, we do it right;" and Holiday Inns' no excuses room guarantee. Thus, aside from the operations aspects, the marketing of services quality presents a real problem even if we accept that service quality exists, i.e. how do we convince the consumer that he/she should buy our service over someone else's because of the quality?

The marketing of services quality presents a number of problems. For purposes of discussion, we suggest the following for openers:

- Quality may be recognized only when it doesn't exist;
- Given the target market, what is the appropriate level of service that represents quality?
- What is the consumer standard of service quality in varying instances?
- What is the optimal services/goods mix?
- How does pure personal service interact with mechanical or non-interpersonal service?
- What is the employee involvement in standard setting?
- How do we measure success or failure?

ISSUES

We see a number of issues that must be considered in any effort at systematic discussion of service quality. First one must be clear about what is being discussed. For any group of 50 people probably 49 different meanings come to mind upon hearing the phrase "service quality." Currently, no consensus definition appears to be in use. In our meaning, quality service delivery is not measured in terms of how grand, or how personalized, or how expensive the service is. These characteristics are all measures of the service level, or service quantity. Service quality is a separate characteristic. Both Westin Hotel and Motel 6 can deliver quality service, but at different levels of service. Service quality is a measure of how well the service level delivered matches customer expectations. Delivering quality service means conforming to customer expectations on a consistent basis.

This notion of quality is more complex than it might first appear and raises several other issues for discussion. Quality, in the terms specified here, is dependent upon customer expectations and customer perceptions of the service experience.

Each of the determinants of quality can be influenced by the customer and the firm. The actual service delivery experience is filtered through the customer's mind and influenced by the actions of the firm. Both the technical and interpersonal aspects of the service assembly process can influence customers' perceptions of the service experience. Thus managing service quality involves managing customer expectations and perceptions as well as the service assembly process. There are marketing aspects in each of these areas.

Once service quality is defined in a broad sense it must be measured. Measurement requires the monitoring and comparing of customer expectations with customer perceptions of the actual service experience.

Measurement is not needed for measurement's sake. The goal of any study of service quality is to assist managers in the management of quality to insure service quality. Measurement is a necessary step toward devising action plans.

Firms can influence both customer expectations and perceptions as well as the reality of the service assembly process. Managers must design plans and implement actions aimed at insuring quality service delivery. What actions can be used need to be studied. Buttons, banners and baloney are not a solution. A real solution requires much more than just urging employees to do better. The task requires an understanding of the determinants of quality, and how the firm and its employees can influence the quality factors.

The second author surveyed marketing vice presidents and operations vice presidents of over 20 national service firms concerning their views on the management of service quality. All those interviewed indicated that service quality was an important challenge faced by their firms. Both marketing vice presidents and operations vice presidents ranked service quality concerns as the number one problem they face. Those surveyed also agreed that there is a need for more conceptual and applied work in managing service quality.

DEFINING SERVICE QUALITY

The American Hotel & Motel Association has commissioned a

"Quest for Quality" program within its membership. The first phase of this program was a field inventory which involved personal interviews with 44 hotel operators "who are, in fact, delivering quality goods and services." Another 350 were surveyed by mail. Collins Hall Associates of Scituate, Massachusetts conducted the research and asked the subjects to define quality.

Respondents agreed that quality is a hard concept to define In fact, 7% of the respondents said they did not know how to define it. In general terms, the other respondents defined quality as follows:

- Best, finest, most - 34%
- Price/value relationship - 20%
- Uniqueness - 14%
- Quality is service - 11%
- Expectation exceeded - 5%

The other 9% defined quality in terms similar to that concluded by Collins Hall Associates as the correct definition:

The consistent delivery of acceptable standards where acceptable standards are defined as the standards which management deems acceptable in light of the target market and which represent the product/service to be made available to the customer.[1]

Following two years of research on the subject of services quality, and preliminary to conducting further research, Michael Nightingale hypothesized more of a consumer perspective in defining quality: quality standards of services are those which both those responsible for policy making and implementation of such services perceive as the key dimensions used by customers in their evaluation of the services.[2]

Both of the above definitions are ones which have been arrived at only after extensive research, evaluation and examination of many definitions by others. The difficulties in defining quality of service are readily apparent.

Quality of service interpretations will always depend on our own sets of values and expectations, our own experience and knowledge, as well as the situational context and use. Thus, we would suggest that quality of service depends on the fitness for the purpose of the user. This is not necessarily luxury or expensiveness, i.e., is it acceptable for this purpose against this set of values, where price is only an indicator of available service levels? Measurement, then, is distinguishing between what is acceptable and what is not, as suggested by Nightingale (1980).

What is marketing's job in terms of quality? For discussion purposes, we suggest that it includes at least the following steps:

1. Determining service levels and passing them on to operations;
2. Communicating quality to consumers, i.e., managing consumer expectations;
3. Providing the opportunity for consumers to purchase;
4. Providing a corrective action mechanism for consumers;
5. Monitoring whether expectations are being met and satisfied.

---

[1] SOURCE: Collins Hall Associates, North Scituate, MA.
[2] SOURCE: Michael Nightingale, Management Consultant to the Hotel & Catering Industries, Palace Road, London.

SPEAKERS

Three people heavily involved in the marketing of services quality are here to discuss these issues today. Bill Crosby is Vice President of Passenger Service for American Airlines. He is reponsible for quality in that organization and, in fact, makes weekly reports on quality achievement to President Robert Crandall who has publicly stated, "Committment to quality is at the cultural core of what this airline is."

Doug Bell is Vice President of Marketing for Holiday Inns. As such, Doug has a high responsibility for the marketing of that company's recently instituted "no excuses" rooms guarantee program, a pioneer effort in the hospitality industry.

Mike Leven is Executive Vice President of Americana Hotels where he started in 1976 as Senior Vice President of Marketing. Mike's work involves the continuous task of where and how to set the service level for a diverse set of hotels and market it to the appropriate target market.

We are extremely pleased to have these people present their comments, which follow.

REMARKS BY WILLIAM E. CROSBY

To help set the stage for our candid - and I hope even spirited - discussion of the marketing aspects of service quality...I want to take a few minutes to talk to you about service as it relates to the airlines in general and to American Airlines in particular.

For instance: How do we define service; what is our overall service objective; how do we measure our service performance; and finally, just how important is service in today's price-oriented world?

As I define it at American...Service quality is doing consistently well those hundreds--even thousands--of little things that satisfy our customers and cause them to return to American again and again.

We recognized the importance of service quality a long time ago. As a highly competitive service business, we realized that if we were to command premium shares of markets and premium load factors we must have a quality passenger service program which is the very center of our overall marketing program. When one considers that more than one-half of our business is repeat business and the fact that our direct sales force can only reach a very small amount of our passengers it becomes obvious how important it is to make every passenger's trip an enjoyable experience. Today, with over capacity in almost every market, any service company that does not realize the importance of service quality is committing suicide.

To understand just how vital a role service skills play at American Airlines, go back to the early 1950's.

We realized that any program was ineffective unless it included specific objectives, measurements, accountability, and most important, was realistic and attainable. We also knew that we must provide a mechanism to provide the resources necessary to accomplish the task being asked of our operating personnel. I am, of course, referring to tying in the budgetary process to a set of standards which are perceivable by our customers and at the same time giving our operations managers not only the tools to do the job but, even more importantly, confidence in the system. Add to this incentives to attain these goals and you have a program which we feel is the very backbone of our marketing plan and complete in every sense.

So, 30 years ago we put together such a program for key areas of passenger service. This includes every area of customer contact: Reservations, Skycaps, Ticket Agents, Flight Attendants, Pilots, as well as non-customer contact people like cleaning personnel, cleaning air terminals, and so forth. Now 30 years later this program is as vital to the corporation's success as it was at its inception.

Despite everything else that's changing in our business under airline deregulation...service continues to be the means of separating one carrier from the others. And we believe our ability to deliver better service than other airlines lends us a unique strength in what has become a chaotic marketplace.

We realize, of course, that some customers are interested only in price--who can get them where they want to go most cheaply. But most are still looking for value--that right combination of price and service quality.

To understand just how vital a role service skills play in the airline business in today's price-oriented world, we must first understand the makeup of the industry.

The airline system that has evolved after four years of deregulation is made up of two distinct types of airlines: One group consists of the established full-service carriers like American that provide all the service the public has come to expect from a major airline--service, I might add, that is provided at considerable cost; the second group is made up of new airlines or regional carriers that might best be categorized as low-cost, point-to-point operators. They are a new breed specializing in very low fares between specific pairs of cities.

These newcomers have little interest in being a part of an integrated airline system. And they are not willing to spend money on the costly services and conveniences that the rest of the full-service airlines provide. They will not, for example, book you on another airline. They will not write you a ticket from Syracuse to San Jose. And they will not transfer your luggage to another carrier. All they do is fly you as cheaply as possible from Point "A" to Point "B."

These airlines are widely applauded for their ability to offer rock-bottom prices. Less attention is focused on the cost structure that makes those fares possible.

Some of the cost difference between the point-to-point airlines and the full-service airlines has to do with wages and productivity. But another part of it is the cost of providing such services as baggage handling, reservations, ticketing, and the like--and of integrating those services with the same services offered by other airlines.

We can offer several flights a day to even fairly small cities and can use our other capabilities--like worldwide reservations and ticketing, seat assignments, one-stop check-in, premium in-flight service, baggage transfers, etc., to offer an overall capability no point-to-point carrier can match.

But, no amount of regulatory change can ever change the fact that our business is a service business. Indeed, this is one of the most significant lessons that can be learned from our experience with deregulation. The standards of service which we established before the enactment of deregulation are serving us well today...and will continue to serve us well in the marketplace of the future.

And just what are our service standards? We have scores of them. For example: Reservation phones should be answered within 20 seconds at least 80 percent of the time; the first cocktail should be served in-flight within five minutes after the seatbelt sign goes off; 85 percent of all our

flights should take off within five minutes of departure time and arrive within 15 minutes of what the timetable promises; aircraft doors should be opened for de-planing within 70 seconds after the plane parks at the gate; the last bag from a flight should be available in the claim area 15 minutes after flight arrival. And so forth.

All of these individual service objectives come together to provide us with American's overall objective which I will now share with you.

At American Airlines, we strive in everything we do to provide "perceptible superior service." That is, service sufficiently better than that of our competitors as to be readily noticeable by most of our passengers most of the time.

And the second part of this overall objective is to get the first part done at a cost that is consistent with sound business practices. In effect, we want to be sure we are clearly number one--and when additional dollars must sometimes be spent to assure that result, we are willing to spend them for very sound business reasons.

To meet this objective, we set high standards for ourselves...and make sure we provide our field management with the tools they need to meet those high standards. For example, we believe it is important to avoid long lines at our ticket counters and confusion in our terminals. This means, we generally have more agents and more passenger service representatives than our competitors, particularly in our major stations.

I am often asked whether American can afford to keep providing good service. I like to answer that question this way: We can't afford not to. I see nothing on the horizon that would cause us to abandon our commitment to service. In a very real sense, we are banking our future on our good service reputation.

Of course, all this does not mean throwing prudence to the winds. To the contrary...we know we cannot adopt every possible suggestion. We know we cannot add sufficient people to handle the highest levels of demand as well as we handle more ordinary levels of demand. And we do not seek to create flying gourmet restaurants on every route. Why don't we? Because the customer doesn't have a need for it and does not want to pay for it.

How do we monitor our service performance and measure how we're doing with regard to our overall service objective? A large part of the answer can be summarized in two words: Constant Checking. To make sure our field management has the tools and resources to get the job done...we keep close tabs on our actual service performance.

Fortune Magazine provided some insight into how we do this in an article last year on service quality. Allow me to quote a key paragraph in that article:

> "The next time you are in an American Airlines lobby, a man with a stopwatch and clipboard may well be hanging around. He's there to see how long it takes you to get your ticket--the company standards say 85 percent of the passengers should not have to stand in line more than five minutes. When you land, you may find another such fellow checking to see how long it takes to get the bags off the plane."

Our employees are held to scores of standards and checked constantly.

If you're a frequent traveler on our airline...you probably have been asked to complete a survey we hand out on our flights every quarter. It asks for your opinion on all

facets of our service--such things as the cabin cleanliness, flight attendant attitude, seat comfort and so forth.
We conduct many other types of surveys...including several
in which we are not identified as the sponsor. And we also
conduct what we call "attitude and awareness" surveys to
gauge how you feel about our company and the effectiveness
of our advertising and promotion efforts.

From our surveys, we learn a lot about who our customers
are and what is important to them. It is our goal that
every trip experience for our passengers must be positive.
We are dependent on our passengers coming back to American
again and again.

We're not in a product business. We're in a service business. A ticket on American Airlines buys the attitude and
ability and expertise of our 35,000 employees. We endeavor to hire the best people we can and we make sure they
get initial and recurring training that we believe is the
finest in the industry. And we seize every opportunity to
remind our employees and ourselves about the importance of
providing good service. We want our customers to know that
they are welcome, that we enjoy the privilege of serving
them and that we are grateful they have chosen us.

The history of service industries affords compelling proof
that leadership and respect are more often gained and held
by outstanding human conduct, personality and service, than
by physical assets. It is unmistakable that with equal or
near equal physical assets such as airplanes, it is the
company with good human qualities and good personalized
service that merits and wins customer loyalty.

Make no mistake about it, this is our...and I suspect every
service company's...principal and most challenging job.

REMARKS BY DOUGLAS H. BELL

I am reminded of a famous story about a General Manager
who in a momeny of frustration commented: "I could run a
much better hotel if I just didn't have to worry about all
these damn people."

Hopefully, the attitude of this General Manager has been
turned to the positive, because those "people" are called
customers - they are the lifeblood of our business.

Customers are also the real decision makers when it comes
to quality:

   ° Customers have expectations of what to expect
     for what they pay; they have a previous exper-
     ience bank of knowledge; they have certain per-
     ceived images of your product.

   ° The customers' expectations cover both the
     tangible physical product, as well as the
     less tangible "service" aspects - the smiles
     of employees, the helpfulness, the friendli-
     ness.

   ° Customers also have alternatives to selecting
     our product. There are always competitive
     product offerings available.

Mid-scale hotel travelers in general expect the fundamentals of lodging:

   ° Clean, comfortable rooms
   ° Convenience of location
   ° Good services - especially reservations

Up-scale travelers are more interested in the service aspects of their lodging experience - naturally, on top of
the good, fundamental product. Budget travelers are more

interested in the price of the product being offered - they
are willing to sacrifice some of the fundamentals.

For the past several years at Holiday Inn there has been a
total committment - also an obsession - with product quality - and the service associated with that product quality.

I should say that as a point of explanation we are a franchised system. Almost 85% of our hotels are owned by franchisees. We are committed to raising the level of the product we sell and the product sold by our franchisees. We
have a complete program in place for raising the level of
that product.

   ° We have refined our standards of operation, taking
     the experiences from our better hotels and trans-
     lating them throughout our entire Holiday Inn
     system.

   ° We also send all of our General Managers through
     a yearly training program at Holiday Inn Univer-
     sity covering both effective operations of the
     hotel at a local level as well as marketing
     programs at a local level.

   ° Our food and beverage managers are similarly
     trained on a yearly basis.

We also utilize a rigorous hotel inspection system to ensure delivery of product quality.

   ° We have 40 inspectors on the road year round
     inspecting our Holiday Inn hotels.

   ° We concentrate our efforts on those hotels re-
     quiring the most assistance in raising their
     level of product quality.

Finally, we have a Guest Assistance Department to handle
and monitor our complaints and importantly to get consumer
feedback:

   ° There is a guest inspection system of comment
     cards in our hotels where we are encouraging
     consumer feedback on our properties.

   ° We also do some independent research to deter-
     mine the quality of stay for our consumers as
     well as the overall perceived cost of that
     stay and some image attribute ratings and in-
     tent to repeat measures.

Lastly, of course, we look at business results to determine
whether or not we are effectively delivering a high quality
product to the consumer.

As a result of all this activity in the area of product
quality, the Holiday Inn system today is a strengthened
one. In the last 5 years, we have added some 250 hotels
to our system. We have also flushed out some 200 hotels.
We have converted 180 hotels to the popular Holidome in-
door recreation concept. We have rebuilt, refurbished, and
remodeled some existing 1,000 hotels.

We have evolved operating systems from our best hotels to
promulgate to all hotels in our system. The systems specify: the one way we run a housekeeping department, the one
way we run maintenance, the one way we run a front desk.

With these changes and improvements in our system, we were
in a superior position to begin marketing these work-a-day
things to travelers. After thorough testing, in January,
1982, we introduced the Room Guarantee Program. We became
the first - and remain the only - hotel chain to guarantee
our consumer satisfaction with the room we sell him - or
he doesn't pay. No ifs, ands, or buts. Every night of the

year, in every room, at every U.S. Holiday Inns. We are, in essence, offering the ultimate in quality service levels with the Room Guarantee Program.

What makes it so significant? Guaranteeing customer satisfaction surely is not a new marketing strategy. Sears has been providing its customers with a guarantee for an eternity it seems.

What makes it significant is that we are guaranteeing our room product - but unlike so many other consumer products, our product quality relies heavily on the service performance of our people. Guarantees are rare in the service business.

We pursued this marketing strategy and program because of the confidence we have in our product. We wanted to transmit that confidence to the traveling public - and to create a unique point of difference for ourselves.

How did we prepare for this dramatic marketing program? First of all, we thoroughly test-marketed in up to 300 hotels. Secondly, we implemented General Manager training, defining the purpose and the procedures of the program. We provided front desk training materials and training. We provided training to our reservation agents, because they would often be carrying the load of customer complaints.

To be successful, it was critical to have all of our employees properly trained.

Once trained, we could then energize our employees around the ultimate statement in service product quality - a guarantee.

Has Holiday Inn's Room Guarantee Program worked? You bet it has!

° Our guest inspection scores continue to improve

° Independent research surveys show our quality ratings posting statistically significant gains since program implementation.

For all of us at Holiday Inn, the Room Guarantee is more than a marketing program. It is marketing service product quality. It is, in fact, a statement about the way we want to do business. We believe in customer satisfaction-and this program ensures it-while helping us to deliver higher levels of service product quality.

REMARKS BY MICHAEL A. LEVEN

Perhaps it is impossible to discuss in a short timeframe all the marketing aspects of service quality in the hotel industry. However, I will try to highlight some points that perhaps are as relevant to our industry as they are to anyone else's sitting here, areas without which we are basically unable to meet our profit objectives in either individual hotel units or in the hotel chain situations.

Service quality in the hotel industry can be defined as "the perception of quality" that is in the mind of the guest or buyer that must be delivered by the company or unit involved. As a survival requisite a hotel corporation or a single hotel unit must, in fact, understand the customers' quality perception and meet that expectation on a consistent basis to allow for enough repeat business and hence, a profitable undertaking.

Service quality from the marketing point of view in our business falls into six different categories--product definition, product creation, delivery standards, product assurances, managerial and human commitment and product profitability.

Product Definition. One cannot define the aspects of the physical product without a program determining the customer need and customer expectation from the very beginning. In that definition would then be the positioning statement engendering the quality levels to the potential guest's Quality Perception".

Product Creation. When it comes to creating hotels from scratch or creating chains or concepts, those creations must be determined based on the service quality level that this product can possibly deliver in its environment vis-a-vis the customer in order to obtain a better result.

Delivery Standards. This is the first non-brick and mortar situation under which service quality falls. An individual unit or company will create standards of delivery from a quality basis. Those standards, of course, are matched to the customer they expect to do business with and they are generally documented and implemented through manuals, inspections, observations, guest responses.

Product Assurances. A number of companies have tried to guarantee that the standards they have set and the expectation the guest has will be met, and if those expectations aren't met that, in fact, they will be satisfied by a guarantee. Holiday Inns and Dunfey Hotels are two organizations that have taken a consumer goods guarantee orientation.

Managerial and Human Commitment. This is the fifth area of service quality and marketing and perhaps is the most important. What we do in our business is try to insure through human resource programs, recruitment, hiring selectivity and training that the right people are selected for the right job and are committed to the standards the company or hotel wishes to execute. However, the head of the organization must personally commit himself to the standards to insure the organization's commitment.

Product Profitability. One can basically assume in the hotel industry if the customer expectation is not met, profits will deteriorate. If the quality standards are selected which are either greatly over or greatly under the expectation of the potential selected consumer, the hotel will not be profitable. If quality standards are, in fact, written, documented, insured, etc., and still personnel are not committed to them, delivery will not take place and hence, customer dissatisfaction.

The hotel industry is abound with dissatisfied customers. In 1977 a research study was done for our company at Washington National Airport which showed at that time that nearly 80% of the business travelers interviewed at the airport would not stay in the same hotel on their next visit to Washington assuming all things being equal, that is, rate, location, etc. Another major corporation, to my knowledge, did a study in the late 70's indicating that 65% of their customers were new customers every night. I don't have any latest data but that data alone would indicate that even though the companies promulgate standards, the performance of those standards on a day-to-day basis is either not perceived by the customer or not delivered to the customer.

One of the important aspects of marketing and service quality is, of course, monitoring that quality. Almost all hotel companies today have programs in place to monitor, either from a firsthand inspection, from a guest commentary, guest letters, guest surveys and focus groups, and all other types of activity, the fact that the standards of the hotel are being maintained or those standards are good enough to meet the perception and expectation of the customer. Unfortunately, probably more work for the majority of hotel companies goes into monitoring quality assurance and quality delivery than pre-planning quality standards.

Many hotel chains have a very diverse group of hotel units. Not all are as blessed as Hyatt or Holiday with hotels that require pretty much similar standards throughout their chain. As a consequence, the standards of quality, delivery, and creativity change from place to place. In my own company, a hotel like the Canyon in Palm Springs, California, has a totally different quality standard than a hotel like the Americana Inn in Springfield, Ohio. Of course, a standard of cleanliness is universal for you are either clean or unclean, similar to the way that you cannot be a little bit pregnant or you cannot be a little bit dirty.

I would assume that most hotel companies, if not all hotel companies, have a cleanliness standard that is universal. Maintenance standards, however, are flexible, personnel standards are flexible, quality of food--the steak you get in Springfield is not the steak you get at the Canyon--all of those types of situations make a mixture-type company such as Americana or Radisson, Amfac, and others more difficult since universal standards are not relevant.

I think this aspect of marketing and service quality is perhaps the most difficult in the hotel industry. Probably the second most difficult is determining exactly the standards of the buyer. Many properties deal, particularly Marriott's, with customers from a low end to a high end and can very well have, just like on an airplane, a millionaire in one room and literally someone on food stamps in another. How can you determine different quality differentiation levels in that situation? Or, more important, how do you train people to delivery quality differentiation levels based on customer demand or customer expectation unless you basically assume that both customers demand a safe flight. If service quality represents a safe flight, then they both demand the same. On the other hand, if a pleasant flight attendant is a service quality does the pleasantness need to change based on the expectation? Example: in many European hotels of very high quality standards the waiter, busboy, maid, etc., are instructed not to talk to the guest under any circumstance. In fact, only captains will talk to a guest in the dining room and on the floor other service personnel standards require that they don't talk to a guest. An American going to a hotel like that would find that the service quality was diminished because of the fact that he expected friendly, warm, hospitable people. So as different standards vary in different properties, whether it be a hotel or an airline or a restaurant, the customers' different standards may all be exhibited in one evening or one day. Imagine the difficulty of trying to train hourly personnel that there are some people that you talk to and some that you don't.

As an independent hotel operator operating one hotel or maybe two, perhaps you can train and hire for different standards based on the customer, in terms of service quality. At any rate, it would appear that unless you have a rather significant standard of product that the ability is severly tested from a human management standpoint. One tends to find a middle ground which undershoots the top quality and overshoots the bottom.

Another concern in terms of quality delivery in the service area is that many hotels will vary their markets rather dramatically depending on the season. Once again, we have a great deal of difficulty when we go from a high season in the winter in Mexico to an off season. The demographics and psychographics of our guest changes dramatically. Yet quality of the product or delivery does not change at all! Many hotels have attempted to solve this problem on a physical basis by having turndown service in high season, better quality chocolates put on the pillow at night in high season, bath beads, shoe mitts and other tangible amenity packages that would yield a higher level of guest quality attitude, instead of delivery human ser-

vice quality that is different from season to season. The physical quality of the product would change from season to season to enhance a basic image of quality.

Many hotels, on the other hand, have tried executive floors which are really the hotel industry's answer to a first-class cabin, I imagine, in an attempt to get more money for a somewhat similar product, but also present a higher level of quality delivery from a service standpoint. A recent Fortune magazine article did some research on these executive floors and felt that they weren't worth the money. Obviously there are a lot of consumers who buy a lot of products that aren't worth the money, for the prestige value alone. Being not a frequent user of those types of floors, I can't make an adequate determination on a personal basis as to whether they are worth it or not, but one would think they are working since more and more hotel companies are placing a number of floors in their units in this higher level category.

Establishing quality standards from a marketing aspect in our business when you are a significant chain ala Holiday Inn, can be done on the front end. When you are not a significant chain you have to establish them as you go for the various units you have.

I would suggest we define those universal standards of service quality and those standards that are variable. In other words, as we view our units in terms of fixed payroll we can also view our units in terms of fixed quality standards and variable standards. Perhaps, it would be a good idea to attempt to define what service quality standards would be fixed and would fit every market and which ones are variable so that they could be plugged in and out in terms of the need of the guest in a particular unit.

I believe the challenge of the hotel industry from a marketing aspect is to perform according to the guest's expectation. We have not done, as an industry, a superb job at this. Certainly we have not done anywhere as well as other service situations such as cruises and airlines that have, in fact, been able for the most part to meet a universal fixed standard level of quality. Some hotel companies like Holiday Inn and Days Inn have been able to market to the consumer a level of quality assurance and, in fact, have delivered for the most part that quality assurance. Their success has led them into a certain long-term future and has extended the product life cycle of many of the units in their chain facilities. Of course, units in these chains have policiesby which they eliminate from their franchises those units that do not meet physical quality expectation levels.

In summary, the marketing aspects of service quality are myriad. The marketing aspects of service quality are, in fact, the key ingredient to the successful hotel venture because a hotel without repeat customers and a hotel without satisfied customers ia a hotel soon to be bankrupt. The challenge is definition of a standard, execution of that standard, delivery of that standard, and monitoring of that standard. Each aspect needs marketing input, marketing planning, marketing research, and marketing manpower. Each aspect needs the flexibility to make objective rather than subjective ego-oriented judgments on customer needs. Perhaps, this is the same almost in every organization. The difference here might be that most hotel organizations deal with a basic fixed standard of quality and what is all on top of that as a variable standard of quality is subject to the boss' usually uneducated guess.

REFERENCES

Nightingale, Michael (1980), "Quality Standards in Tourism." Paper presented at Tourism Society Conference on Quality, Bristol, England, September 19-20.

Quality: The U.S. Drives to Catch Up(1982). Business Week, November 1, 66-80.

IMPRESSION MANAGEMENT IN SERVICE MARKETING: KEY RESEARCH ISSUES

Gregory D. Upah, Young & Rubicam

ABSTRACT

This paper discusses several key propositions relating
to the advertising and other impression-management
aspects of services marketing. A set of key research
questions/issues relating to these propositions is presented.

INTRODUCTION

It is clear that many active researchers and others
interested in Services Marketing believe that the field
has just begun to develop a useful body of knowledge.
However, it also is clear that many of these same people
feel that there already is a substantial amount of conceptual development and middle-range theory which would
greatly benefit from additional thinking and, particularly, empirical research. Specifically, there have
been several hypotheses and propositions put forth
regarding effective services marketing practice. Many
of these propositions flow from the basic assumptions
about differences between goods and services -- e.g.,
tangibility, perishability and degree of interaction
between buyer and seller. In any case, these propositions typically suggest that effective service
marketing -- due to the unique nature of services
themselves -- requires adjustments in degree and kind
for certain aspects of the total marketing effort.

PURPOSE

The purpose of this paper will be to suggest some
research issues which are derived from propositions per-
taining to the unique requirements for effective
"impression management" in services marketing. For the
purposes of this paper, impression management will be
limited to advertising and to the role of physical/en-
viroment cues (e.g., interior decor, architecture,
atmosphere, and the social/physical aspects of
atmosphere). There clearly are other important areas
for research -- many of which are discussed in the other
papers in this session. The impression management area
has, however, been viewed as one in which the need for a
unique services marketing approach is critical.

IMPRESSION MANAGEMENT VIA ADVERTISING

Some of the cornerstone propositions or hypotheses
regarding services marketing deal with the advertising
of services. The central propositions regarding services advertising could probably be summarized as
follows: "Because services are themselves intangible,
service marketers should make special efforts to emphasize the tangible aspects of their service offering
(e.g., symbols, facts, people, and equipment or
facilities)."

This basic proposition can be found in some form in
several sources, (e.g., George and Berry 1981; and
Shostack 1977) including an article I co-authored with
Kenneth Uhl (Uhl and Upah 1982). The basic rationale
for this proposition is that since goods are tangible
and can be seen or touched they are often easier to evaluate than such highly intangible services as legal or
medical services.

Certainly, not all goods are easy to evaluate.
Nevertheless, the consumer of goods often has, in the
good itself, a tangible and useful indication of the
nature and quality of the market offering. As Shostack
(1977) points out, since a service already is intangible, advertising which is intangible-dominant can merely

"dilute the reality" that the service marketer is trying
to portray. By implication, Shostack suggests that this
in turn makes the customer's task all the more difficult, and ultimately leads to less effective marketing
efforts.

This basic proposition appears to have a great deal of
face validity and clearly flows logically from key
assumptions about fundamental differences between goods
and services. However, the exhortation to focus on the
"tangible" in services advertising may be too
simplistic, and may, in fact, be counterproductive for
the development of the very best services advertising.

Before discussing this issue further, it may be useful
to outline the basic benefits of emphasizing the
tangible aspects of a service in advertising.

First, the emphasis on tangible cues may help customers
better understand the nature and character of the
service/service firm. In doing so, these cues may provide the additional "reassurance," and
"permission-to-believe" that cannot be provided by an
emphasis on the intangible service itself. Second, the
emphasis on the tangible aspects of the service may help
customers to better understand the functional benefits
they can expect by using the service. For instance, the
functional benefit offered by H&R Block is a competently
prepared tax form -- one which may afford the taxpayer
his/her maximum tax advantages. For hotel operators,
these functional benefits may be lodging in nicely-
appointed rooms.

There are, however, other aspects of the service which
service firms want, and, arguably need to emphasize. As
George and Berry (1981) point out, a service is a
"performance." Moreover, most all services involve a
substantial amount of personal interaction between the
service firm and its customers. Consider, for instance,
the person-to-person interaction involved in rental car,
lodging, banking, professional and transportation services.

One key question arising from this discussion is that
because services often involve people dealing with
people, shouldn't services advertising "talk" to people
in a personal (as opposed to totally fact-based or impersonal) fashion? Furthermore, aren't such
intangibles as the "personality" of the service firm
likely to be major factors in the customer's choice process and thereby important to emphasize in advertising?
The customer for a service wants to feel "comfortable"
with the service firm. Particularly for such services
as investment, banking and professional services, the
customer would presumably be more "comfortable," with
and reassured by service firms which share or are sensitive to their values, personal goals, etc.

Related to these "personality," and/or "personal" attributes of services advertising is the concept of the emotional end-benefit the service firm is providing. As
Thomas Bloch put it in a speech to this conference,
H & R Block is, in addition to various functional benefits, selling a "feeling" -- a feeling of confidence,
reassurance and satisfaction with the service received.

Can important end-end benefits of the type just
discussed really be communicated by what we might call
strictly tangible-dominant advertising? Can the
tangible and emotional aspects of effective services
advertising be accomplished together? What is the relative impact of services advertising which does both of

these things on "persuasion," "confidence," "interest," "credibility," communication of desired end-benefits and other key factors involved in effective services advertising? These are some key services marketing issues which empirical research could help to resolve.

EXAMPLES OF EACH APPROACH:

For a Fortune magazine article (Fortune 1979) about major advertising agencies, each of four agencies was asked to submit an ad for itself. Young & Rubicam submitted an ad with a dominant visual (a bird soaring across a blue sky and above a mountain range), and a headline and body copy which stated in a brief and fairly general way Y&R's approach to creating effective advertising. In contrast, McCann-Erickson chose to emphasize the facts and figures regarding the number of their clients, offices and years in business as evidence of their capability. The former approach was clearly more intangible-dominant; the latter more tangible-dominant. The question is which basic approach, given the objectives of the advertising and the target audience, is most effective?

There are other examples of services advertising which may strike a balance between the emotional/intangible and the tangible. Arthur Young has used a print ad with a relatively "light" approach to describing corporate operating procedures. The ad makes use of an almost humorous illustration of "a Sherlock Holmes"-like accountant and a headline stating, "We look very hard for what we hope not to find." The ad is signed with the following: "The 582 Partners and Directors of Arthur Young." This ad combines an indication of size, capability and operating procedures with a bit of personality.

Another illustration of this approach can be found in an ad by a regional CPA firm. This firm uses artist renderings of the three partners as the dominant visual followed by a discussion as to how the firm uses its capabilities to go about solving its clients' problems. A different, specific problem is discussed (e.g. real estate, taxes) in each ad in the series. This advertising emphasizes the end-benefits of competent and tailored (to the client's needs) legal services.

CATEGORY-BASED ISSUES IN SERVICES ADVERTISING

The propositions regarding the relative focus on tangible/intangible elements in services advertising raise the need to consider the type of service being advertised. Uhl and Upah (1982) discuss three principal categories of services: people-based (professional services); equipment or facility-based (lodging, transportation) and financial-based (insurance, banking, investments). There are other useful categories which have been developed by others (see, for instance, Lovelock 1981).

These basic categorizations provide the basis for additional propositions for services advertising. For instance, does advertising for people-based services benefit from a definitive (as opposed to incidental) emphasis on people? In addition, does the need for advertising directed at employees (George and Berry 1981) (i.e., in an internal marketing fashion) make such an emphasis even more beneficial? Similar questions/propositions could be and have been developed (Uhl and Upah 1982) for equipment and financial-intensive services.

CORPORATE PRODUCT LINE ADVERTISING

There are still other factors which may play a major role in developing effective services advertising. For instance, one key consideration is whether the service or service firm is just being established or organized. Establishment-Phase advertising may call for a greater emphasis on corporate capabilities ("facts and figures" which establish the firm as a credible, competent service provider). Ernst and Whinney stressed these characteristics in advertising that announced their formation from the original firm of Ernst and Ernst. It may also be the case that existing firms who feel the need for such establishment/capabilities advertising may not need it. Target customers may already perceive the service firm as one that is extremely capable, qualified, etc. Hence, the focus of the advertising may be better placed on illustrating how the capabilities of the firm will be used to satisfy customers. Thus, service firms in this position may be able to forego further "establishment/corporate" advertising; and move toward advertising which reinforces the firm's capabilities but focuses on the key customer benefits to be derived from the firm's services. Clearly, the decision as to which approach is most appropriate should be based on market research data which deals with customer perceptions of corporate capability. A model for implementing this kind of procedure has been suggested by Upah and Uhl (1980).

IMPRESSION MANAGEMENT: IMPACT OF THE IMMEDIATE PHYSICAL/SOCIAL ENVIRONMENT OF THE SERVICE FIRM

"Situation" research in consumer behavior has shown that the social and physical setting in which a product is selected or consumed can have a marked influence on consumers' selection and consumption behavior, and on the degree of satisfaction with the product. In services marketing, the tangible aspects of the services setting have been felt to exert a major influence on how customers perceive the service firm and/or the service firm's personnel. Indeed, the impact of these factors on consumer behavior may be greater for service as opposed to goods marketing.

The role of such factors as interior design, architecture, the effects of crowding, the impact of the nature of the other clientele consuming the service (e.g., others present in the theater, attorneys office, etc.) has only begun to be considered in the services marketing literature. There have been few, if any, empirical studies designed to address these issues. Other researchers in interior design and architecture have, however, devoted considerable effort to considering these factors. There are undoubtedly major contributions to the services marketing literature to be found in the research studies done in these fields.

The techniques used to assess the impacts of these factors must clearly go beyond traditional survey techniques. However, there are some potentially useful methods -- experimental methods, third-person techniques, depth interviews, which could be employed. Some of these methods might serve as a prelude to other studies which might provide more generalizable results. Good illustrations of these special techniques can be found in published studies on situation-related factors in consumer behavior (see, for instance, Belk 1975).

SUMMARY

There are several major avenues for reseach within the impression-management domain of services marketing.

This paper has outlined some of the key research areas and issues dealing with the advertising and service environment aspects of impression management. The propositions to which this empirical research would be directed are ones based on ideas which already have received considerable theoretical support in the services marketing field. However, the services marketing field needs the credibility that empirical research can provide.

There are other elements of the service marketing mix for which tangible (and other) cues may be a critical factor in effective services marketing. As discussed above, the role of these cues in suggesting and/or reinforcing the nature and quality of services is heightened due to the intangible character of the service itself.

One final benefit of this research would be to help to crystallize and further develop the basic propositions that have been suggested. This will provide the additional and needed benefit of further strengthening the base on which growth of the service marketing theory and practice will proceed.

REFERENCES

Belk, Russell W. (1975), "Situational Variables and Consumer Behavior," Journal of Consumer Research, 2 (December), 157-64.

George, William R. and Leonard L. Berry, (1981), "Guidelines for the Advertising of Services," Business Horizons, (July/August), 52-56.

"Here Come the Super-Agencies," (1979) Fortune (April 27), 46.

Lovelock, Christopher H., (1980), "Toward a Classification of Services," in Theoretical Developments in Marketing, C.W. Lamb, Chicago, American Marketing Association.

Shostack, G. Lynn (1977), "Breaking Free From Product Marketing," Journal of Marketing, 41, (April), 73-80.

Ulh, Kenneth P. and Gregory D. Upah (1982) "The Marketing of Services: Why and How Is It Different," Research in Marketing, Jagdish N. Sheth (ed.), 6, Stamford: JAI Press.

Upah, Gregory D. and Kenneth P. Uhl (1980), "A Sequential Approach to the Advertising of Accounting Services," Working Paper.

SEVEN KEY AREAS OF RESEARCH
ACCORDING TO THE NORDIC SCHOOL OF SERVICE MARKETING

Christian Grönroos, Swedish School of Economics,
Helsinki, Finland

Today the demands of the ever-growing service sector has finally been recognized. Even the academic establishment has realized that firms and institutions in the public and private service sectors cannot develop their management, including subareas such as marketing, operations, personnel, and service or product development, without academic research specially geared to the characteristics and problems of service firms and institutions. We do have a range of service firms, which have been successful so far, although they have had to rely entirely on concepts and models from the consumer goods sector, and on their own capabilities. On the other hand, there is a much longer list of service firms and institutions, which have more or less failed to develop their marketing and other business functions in a successful way.

In the future, as competition will increase even more in most service industries, service firms and institutions have the right to demand more assistance from academic research. Without thorough academic research, successfully implemented service marketing will remain a privilage of a rather limited number of firms and institutions in the service sector, whereas the sector as a whole will stay underdeveloped in this respect.

The Nordic School of Service Marketing recognizes at least the following seven key areas of research:

1. The term "marketing" itself is used in an ambiguous way among service marketing researchers. Most researchers, as well as practitioners, seem to be influenced by the marketing mix model of consumer goods marketing theory. According to this model, the marketer is thought of as "a mixer of ingredients", who uses a set of marketing variables, i.e., means of competition, in order to develop an effective marketing program.[1] This tradition sees the marketer as a marketing specialist, who manipulates variables which are marketing variables only. Consequently, marketing becomes, and remains, a function for specialists only, using resources and activities which are thought of as marketing resources and activities only. This view of marketing is, obviously, useful for a manafacturer of consumer goods.

In the service sector, marketing must be spread throughout the organization. Marketing resources can be found in production and operations, finance, personnel, development of technology, etc.[2] This situation is entirely different compared to the situation of manufacturers of consumer goods. Therefore, the term marketing used in the traditional marketing mix sense will probably remain awkward and troublesome in service marketing research and in implications of service marketing by practitioners.[3]

Our hypothesis is that as long as marketing is considered a specialist function only, or mentally thought of as such a function, by researchers and practitioners, no major breakthrought is likely to occur as far as service marketing theory is concerned.

2. There is no generally accepted concept of service quality. Frequently, improved quality is suggested as a means of solving the problems of service firms. Quality is treated as a variable itself. However, this is not the case.[4] In order to be able to change the quality of a service, one has to know the answer to at least two questions: (1) how is service quality perceived by the customers, and (2) in what way is service quality influenced and which resources and activities have an impact on service quality. Today, researchers, as well as practitioners, know very little about the answer to these questions. As a matter of fact, these questions are far too often never even asked.

Our hypothesis is that the mere technical dimensions of a service, which often can be quantitatively measured, e.g., money is transfered on demand from one account to another in a bank, or a consultant produces an acceptable report, in most cases are of minor importance to the service quality as this is perceived by the customers. How the service is rendered by the contact personnel and the physical resources of the firm functionally, i.e., the so-called functional quality of a service, is much more important in most cases. Many times it is the very key to success, according to our hypothesis.

3. Today, service marketing theory does not promote marketing planning and implementation of marketing on a long

range basis. Because of the normally used budgeting systems and follow-up procedures, marketing is often planned and implemented in a myopic way, in order to achieve fast results in the short run, whereas the consequences on a long run basis are not observed. In the long run the results may not be very successful. By then, the manager may, however, have been promoted to another job, and he is not always made responsible for a long run fiasco that may occur.

The reason for this may be that there seems to be no model which explains the development of the contacts between the service firm and its customers over time.

Our hypothesis is that when marketing planning is geared to a customer relation life cycle concept, service marketing theory will be developed in a more market-oriented way and, thus, help service firms and institutions to become more customer-conscious.

4. There is a vast growth potential in internationalization, which has been observed by service marketing researchers to a very limited extent. For instance, banks, hotel and restaurant chains, insurance companies and advertising agencies have gone international, and they have been successful in many cases. Internationalization is one important growth strategy for service firms and institutions.[5] However, there seems to be far too little knowledge of how to internationalize as a service organization, and of how to develop international marketing strategies.

Our hypothesis is that international marketing of services may need new concepts and models which are based on the characteristics of services.

5. Internal marketing is recognized only to a limited extent and when the concept is used, one is likely to use it in too narrow a sense. Service firms and institutions are most frequently very personnel-intensive, and they are likely to stay so in the relevant future. In order to become customer-conscious and market-oriented on an overall basis, the service organization has to influence its employees, especially the contact personnel and managers, in an appropriate direction. Employees that are motivated to perform in a customer-conscious and sales-minded manner are of crucial importance to success.

According to the internal marketing concept - as a complement to the traditional marketing concept - the organization's internal markets of employees can be influenced most effectively and hence motivated to customer-consciousness, market-orientation and sales-mindedness by a marketing-like internal approach and by using marketing-like activities internally. This way the employees' needs for attractive and motivating jobs are met.[6]

Internal marketing is not only a range of marketing tools to be used internally, but it is also a philosophy, involving an active approach to motivation, instead of the traditional, passive approach, according to which the personnel department, in the normal case, tries to make employees motivated by administrative actions. Such passive motivation-oriented programs have failed too often.

Our hypothesis is that the more the internal marketing concept is studied by researchers as a philosophy and implemented as strategic internal marketing management, concerned with management methods, personnel policies, policies of internal training, systems for planning, implementing and controling, etc., the more useful internal marketing will become to pracitioners as a management instrument to be used in order to make the organization market-oriented.

6. Most growing service firms and institutions are organized in the same manner as firms in the industrial sector, which may make the organizations more production-oriented and less close to the market. In the consumer goods sector marketing can be planned and implemented within a separate marketing department and by marketing specialists. Hence, the marketing function of a manufacturer of consumer goods is almost the same as the marketing department in the traditional sense. In the service sector this is not the case. Marketing resources can be found all over the organization in most business functions. Therefore, traditional organizational solutions may not work in service firms and institutions.

Although the marketing department stage is considered the most developed way of organizing for marketing in the consumer goods sector today,[7] this may not be the case for firms and institutions in service industries. Instead, such traditional solutions may turn out dangerous and harmful in the long run. As the marketing department and its marketing specialists are introduced, the rest of the organization working with production and operations, personnel, finance, and technical development, as well as most managers, may choose the easy way of doing their job, i.e., just handling their tasks in a technical sense and forgetting all about the customers. Such a development can be observed in far too many companies.

Our hypothesis is that an organizational innovation, including some kind of a market coordinator, is needed so that service-oriented organizational structures can be developed and successfully implemented.

7. Industrial marketing and international marketing of producer goods, systems and projects can be developed by applying concepts and models of service marketing theory. All firms may be placed on a continuum ranging from pure service firms to pure manufacturers of consumer goods. The frameworks, concepts and models developed at one end of the continuum, for example in the context of service marketing theory, can probably be of considerable value to firms, say, somewhere in the middle of the continuum, but may be not at the other end of it to any greater extent. Typically, firms producing and marketing producer goods, systems and projects are located somewhere between service firms and manufacturers of consumer goods. Hence, it can be argued that industrial marketing is somewhere between service marketing and consumer goods marketing.

In many cases, the customer relation is very broad in scope for firms engaged in industrial marketing. A large range of contact personnel categories may be involved in the customer relation, e.g., persons engaged in training of users, in deliveries, in service and maintenance, in negotiations of technical solutions and in installation at the buyer's premises. In industrial marketing the business functions of a company are typically interrelated to a larger extent than in the consumer goods sector.[8] As a matter of fact, the customer relation and its demands on a holistic view of marketing[9] and on how to organize for marketing is quite similar in the context of industrial marketing as in service marketing.

Our hypothesis is that frameworks, concepts and models of service marketing theory can be applied to industrial marketing and international marketing of producer goods, systems and projects, and that an important cross-fertilization between service marketing and industrial marketing on domestic as well as on international markets can be achieved.

FOOTNOTES

1. The marketing mix concept and the view of the marketer as a mixer of ingredients was introduced by Culliton, J.W. (1948): The Management of Marketing Costs, Andover, Mass.: The Andover Press, and Borden N.H. (1964): "The Concept of Marketing Mix", Journal of Advertising Research, June.

2. See for instance, Grönroos, C. (1982): Strategic Management and Marketing in the Service Sector, Helsingfors, Finland: Swedish School of Economics and Business Administration, and Gummesson, E. (1981): "Marketing Cost Concept in Service Firms", Industrial Marketing Management, No. 3.

3. Compare, for example, Rathmell, J.M. (1974): Marketing in the Service Sector, Cambridge, Mass.: Winthrop Publishers.

4. Compare, for example, Eiglier, P. & Langeard, E. (1981): A Conceptual Approach of the Service Offering, in Hartvig Larsen, H. & Heede, S. (eds.): Proceedings of the E.A.A.R.M. X Annual Workshop, Copenhagen: "It is rather difficult to relate a good service idea to a stable, widespread, well identified customer benefit. And it is extremely difficult to implement the service idea as a well-structured offering of services." (p. 1562).

5. See, Carman, J.M. & Langeard, E. (1978): Growth Strategies for Service Firms, working paper, University of California, Institute of Business and Economic Research, August.

6. Grönroos, C. (1982): Strategic Management and Marketing in the Service Sector, p. 163

7. Compare, for instance, Kotler, P. (1980): Marketing Management. Analysis, Planning, Control, 4th edition, Englewood Cliffs, N.J.: Prentice-Hall, p. 581-583.

8. See, for example, Webster, Jr., F.E. (1978): "Management Science in Industrial Marketing", Journal of Marketing, January.

9. Compare Gummesson, E. (1982): The New Marketing Concept, Stockholm, Sweden: Stockholm Consulting Group, October.

RESEARCH PRIORITIES IN SERVICES MARKETING:
REMEMBER THE LITTLE GUY

Barry Blackman, Blackman Marketing Group, Inc., San Antonio

ABSTRACT

Research most useful to small service businesses differs significantly from the types of research used by large companies. Because small service businesses far outnumber large ones, the author suggests research useful to small businesses is badly needed, and describes the types of information most likely to be widely useful. Problems and opportunities are illustrated with data from a real company history.

INTRODUCTION

I come across so many questions every day I'd like to have answered, participating in a forum like this one feels like winning one of those grocery store shopping spree contests where you can pick up anything you want, and all you want, in three minutes. No matter how much you stuff into the basket, after you race through the check-out stand you can always think of three more things you needed worse.

As a marketing consultant to a variety of service businesses, I'm always looking for "rules-of-thumb" or "guidelines" which will help me make quick, but reasonably accurate, judgments. No matter how big the budget, I'm always short of either money, time, or information. So, as for most consultants, information gleaned from secondary research is frequently the basis for many of my strategic recommendations. Naturally, I'd prefer to be on-target, because the food on my table depends on it.

In my experience, the majority of service businesses are operated as closely-held businesses. Whether organized as a proprietorship, partnership, or corporation, the principals in the business are in a position to adjust compensation, benefits, and overall operations in so many ways, and so often, it's difficult to measure the company's progress quantitatively. Without some quantitative measurement which remains comparable through multiple accounting periods, and which can reasonably compare one business to another, it's impossible to measure a service business' performance impartially.

Find such a measure, and business managers can profit by having a concrete way of telling how well they are really doing. They'll profit by being able to "keep score" and tell whose company is the most successful. This is more helpful than perhaps it sounds, because the most successful business methods practiced by the "winners" can then be copied by the less successful. Consultants and perhaps advertising agencies can profit from knowing the measurement method, because they could use it to prove how much their services are worth, both to present and potential clients.

SEARCHING FOR A SIMPLE, RELIABLE MEASUREMENT OF SUCCESS

Let me illustrate the problem with some real-world data. Before we look at the data, be aware the owner of the business whose data we're using considers the past 6 years to be ones of ever-increasing success. So no matter what our number-crunching shows, the qualitative evaluation by the man who signs the checks is unhesitatingly positive. The business is slightly more than 20 years old. Data for each chart has been disguised using a linear multiplier or

divisor to protect the confidentiality of the client company. All relationships within a chart retain the same proportional nature of the original data.

FIGURE 1

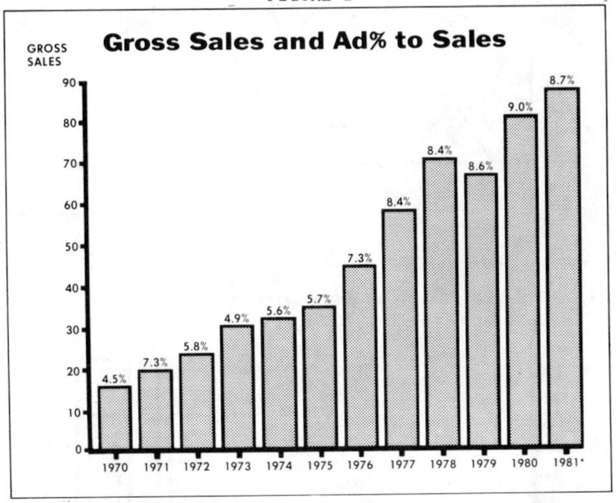

Let's start by looking at Gross Sales. I've included data from a 12-year span. The first 6 years this business operated as most do, without any special marketing guidance. For the latest 6 years, my company has been advising it.

As you can see, in 1976, the first year we began working with the company, there is a significant jump in gross sales compared to the previous years. 1977 and 1978 each show similar increases. Things seem to be fine. Then comes 1979, and the sales trend is broken, resuming in 1980 and 1981 with slightly less vigor. So what happened in 1979 to "distort" results?

Obviously the business owner can't be using Gross Sales as the rule to measure success, because 1979 looks like a step backwards. Actually, in this example, total sales declined in 1979 because management quit providing several types of service. These discontinued services had never been profitable, but had seemed necessary to provide some cash flow during slack seasons. After seeing in 1976, '77, and '78 that advertising could generate adequate volume from service lines which were all profitable, in 1979 several loss-lines were dropped.

Because we know management considers 1979 to have been more successful than any preceding, let's look for the answer in a chart of Before-Tax Profits. Just a cursory glance shows the answer isn't here, because corporate profit for 1979 is barely half of 1978 profits. This drop dramatizes the problem of trying to use Before-Tax Profits as a measure of success for closely-held companies. When we look at a chart of Total Owner Personal Benefits, the corporate profit-drop is explained by a big increase in the primary stockholder's compensation.

While we're looking at the chart of Total Owner Benefits, let's see if it explains success any better than Gross Sales or Before-Tax Profits did. It helped us with 1979, but has a problem with 1976, '77, '80, and '81. Compensation for 1976 and 1977 stayed flat. Personal Benefits in

FIGURE 2

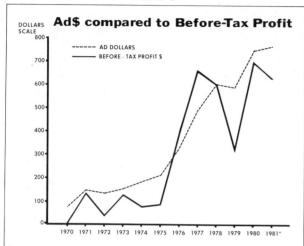

FIGURE 3

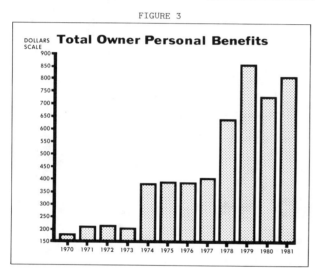

1980 and 1981 actually were less than in 1979. So even owner compensation isn't a reliable measure of success.

Adding Before-Tax Profits to Total Owner Benefits seems a logical next step in trying to achieve a measure which accurately portrays service-business success. To save time and space, I'm not showing the actual plot of those results. To be brief, it still doesn't show ever-increasing success.

MEASURE MUST CONSIDER EXPANSION EFFECTS

In all the measures we've discussed so far, we've made no allowance for the effects of modernizing or expanding the business. In the business we're examining here, detailed planning for growth included computerization and an expanded fleet of service trucks. Major purchases such as these generally cannot be expensed, but must be depreciated over some period regulated by federal tax laws. Although the tax laws allow a variety of depreciation periods, usually a profitable business will depreciate its capital as rapidly as the law allows, to minimize current taxes. In this case, with major modernization and expansion, depreciation amounts to a major expense item in some years.

Further, it is an expense item under management's direct

control, at least in the year of purchase. Assuming management purchases capital goods to "improve", "modernize", "expand", or otherwise make the business "better", at least in its judgment, depreciation reflects another facet of company success. Under United States tax laws, it takes success in a service business to generate deductible depreciation. Normally, there is little incentive to generate depreciation other than to "better" the business and to offset part of whatever profits are subject to taxes.

Perhaps adding Depreciation to Before-Tax Profits and Total Owner Benefits (including dividends and any other special payments) will give us a picture of this company's "consistently-increasing success".

FIGURE 4

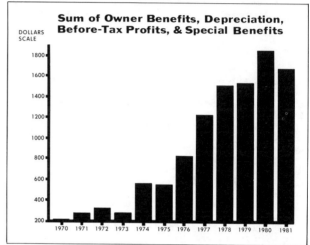

Well, it's not perfect, but this chart does seem to be getting closer. 1976 through 1980 DO show continuously-increasing success, but 1981 declines. Digging into operations that year, we find 1981 the first year this business set up a profit-sharing plan for all employees. The amount distributed in this profit sharing plan was a 5-figure sum which more than accounts for the apparent decline in the sum of Before-Tax Profits, Owner Benefits, Depreciation, and other miscellaneous business benefits.

This is as far as I've taken this inquiry, and it is far from complete. But I believe it illustrates the need to gather information from a variety of service businesses. Data is needed from enough similar businesses in each major service category to spot meaningful patterns. Once gathered, this database could be analyzed to find some relatively simple way of "Keeping Score" on how well a business is doing.

PREDICTING PROFITABILITY

Moving beyond score-keeping, which I believe holds much promise of widespread usefulness, I'd sure like to know more about how to predict profitability from readily-available information about manpower usage. Many service businesses keep such data on purpose, and many others could develop a reasonable facsimile by massaging internal records of pay, sales, and parts purchases.

Because in a service business, the "inventory" is highly perishable, manpower management is imperative for profits. No other commodity is more perishable. If you waste a minute, it's gone forever. . .you can't ever recapture it. Parts, on the other hand, can be stored and sold at any time before they get obsolete. How should a service business balance labor sales against parts sales? Should an effort even be made to relate the two? Would managing this ratio help a business owner manage his profits?

FIGURE 5

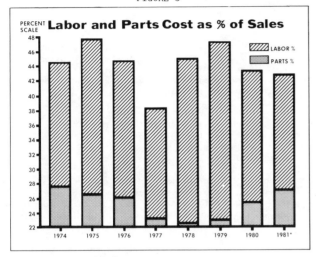

Here is a plot covering 8 years of data for the same company we've been examining. The previous charts showed data for 12 years, but this business didn't organize data collection in a meaningful manner for labor and parts until 1974.

Now compare the Before-Tax Profits chart to the Labor & Parts Cost chart to see if there are obvious relationships. I don't see any. One business philosophy is to make the labor portion of sales as great a percentage as possible, because you're supposed to have much more margin in labor than in parts. Yet looking at our charts, 1978 and 1979 should be super profit years, and they're not. Even when we look at the Sum of Benefits/Depreciation chart, there doesn't seem to be a positive relationship. 1980 has a lower ratio, but significantly better Benefits/Profits. There just doesn't seem to be any consistent pattern.

Now as this Labor and Parts chart is drawn, the Labor and the Parts segments add up to total labor and parts costs as a percentage of gross sales.

Looking at 1974, 75, 76, and 77, there seems to be a pattern. Total Benefits/Depreciation seem to increase when the total cost percentage goes down, and they decrease when it goes up (1974 to 75). But for years after 1977, the relationship falls apart. That's really strange, because what I've illustrated is a case of the age-old Wall Street advice: "To win big, buy low and sell high." As Labor and Parts costs go down as a percent of sales, gross margin increases. Theoretically the business should then be able to keep more. Some years it seems to work that way, other years, it doesn't.

Another relationship which might be meaningful in managing for profits, is the ratio of labor to parts. This measurement might be more comparable between different industries than the Labor and Parts Costs Percentage to Sales. Typically, as parts get more expensive, they are entrusted to more-highly-paid service-providers. An air conditioning service technician gets paid considerably more than a carpet-cleaner, and air conditioning parts are generally more expensive than the supplies a carpet cleaner gets.

Once again, there appears to be a crude relationship in

FIGURE 6

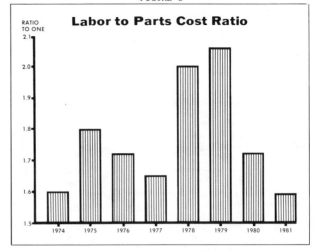

some years, but not others. For 1975, 76, 77, as the ratio of Labor to Parts Cost approaches equality (1;1), Total Benefits/Profits rises. But then in 1978, the ratio jumps up, but so do Total Benefits/Profits.

Which business philosophy should a parts-installing service business follow? Should labor be substantially greater than parts, on the theory you get more margin that way? Or should the business strive to have labor equal to or less than parts. That could mean more sales per serviceman, since the dollar value of parts installed is not directly proportional to the amount of time it takes to install them. These two philosophies lead to vastly different marketing strategies, so knowing which is "right" (meaning "most profitable") is extremely important.

Maybe there is no ONE right philosophy. If not, how do we learn which philosophy is right for THIS business, at THIS time?

Although 8 years is a long time, 8 years worth of data for this one business doesn't seem to be enough to find a dependable pattern. Maybe 8 years of data for 20 similar companies would be. Maybe 50. Pick a number, gather the data, sift and sort it, and let's see what comes up. Find "norms" for the most profitable 20% of firms in a business category, another norm for the median group, and still another norm for the least profitable 20% of the category. With a range of norms, an ordinary businessman can measure his progress. And he can measure it himself without using calculus and differential equations.

CONSIDERATIONS IN MAKING RESEARCH USABLE

Keep in mind most service business don't have IBM 370's and a DP staff to manage their information. What is recorded, is mostly in file folders, or in stacks of service invoices, or in payroll ledgers. If a formula is too complicated to solve in 5 minutes using only pencil and paper, that formula is too complicated to be used by small business. And most service businesses ARE small. If they have a computer at all, it's likely to be an Apple or Osborne. And if that's all they have in the way of computing power, they're certainly not going to be computer programmers.

Keep it simple. Base your investigation on data which can actually be maintained by small business: Sales records, time sheets, purchase records, payroll records, balance sheets, P & L statements. Any measure which depends on gathering data OUTSIDE the business, is unlikely to be widely used. Most service businesses haven't the time, budget, or inclination to pursue such information. Such factors as "Competitive Pressure", "Advertisng Expenditures By Competitors," and "Market Share" are simply unavailable.

In actual small business practice, what the "other guy" spends on advertising matters a lot less than what YOU are willing to invest to promote your own business. Good managers know they can't control what their competition does, so they invest their worrying time worrying about how to improve their own performance.

Take another look at the Gross Sales chart. But this time, look at the little numbers at the top of each bar. Now the heading says "advertising", but that's only because the abbreviation for advertising is shorter than for "marketing". The percent figures include investments for truck-fleet graphic design, telephone direct marketing campaigns, redesign of letterhead and all business forms, and new building signs. It does include radio, newspaper, and yellow page advertising, too, but advertising is only part of the amount.

CHOOSING AN OPTIMUM MARKETING BUDGET

As a marketing consultant, I can't affect the competition's budget. My only influence is on my clients. Look at Figure 1, and remember I began working with this client company in February of 1976. What happened to the advertising percentage to sales? Okay, it went up 28% from 1975 to 1976. In 1977 we raised it again, and again in 1978. Keep in mind we're seeing an increase not just in dollars, but in the percentage of the business' total cash flow allocated to marketing. To convince a business owner to keep channeling more and more of his total cash flow into marketing, something dramatic and very concrete must occur.

Part of the drama shows in Figure 2, the Before-Tax Profits chart. Examine the data for 1976, 1977, and 1978 in both Figure 1 and Figure 2, and compare it to that for previous years. Profits up more than 330% from 1975 to 1976. Profits almost doubling that level in 1977. And this is only part of the story. When you look at Figure 4 data for the same years, you find this business gaining more and more flexibility with every increase in the budget share given to marketing.

Further, when the budget is cut, as in 1979 compared to '78, growth stops. Note that in 1979 the actual dollar-budget for marketing was lower than in 1978. Because advertising media rates went up about 20% from 1978 to '79, this cut represents an effective cut of greater proportions. This combination effect allowed a decline in sales, and a decline in real owner benefits. The Total Benefits/Depreciation chart shows 1979 to be marginally higher than 1978, but not nearly enough to keep up with the double-digit inflation rates of that period.

Back on the right track in 1980 with a bigger budget, more sales, much bigger profits, we obviously haven't reached the point of diminishing return with a 9% marketing-to-sales ratio.

So where is the diminishing-return break-point? Is it 9.2%? Is it 15%? or 20%? If it's really 15% and we plod along raising our percentage by 1/2% a year in trial and error, how much will we miss in potential profits?

Of course there's a lot more to success than a simple percent allocation, because some marketing strategies work, some don't. Some advertising works, some doesn't. Just throwing money at a problem doesn't solve it, unless you're betting on a horse that can win.

IDENTIFYING EFFECTIVE MEDIA & AD CONTENT

Are some advertising media more effective than others for promoting service businesses? If some are more effective which ones are they? What is their relative ranking of effectiveness?

What about communication content? What should marketing materials discuss when promoting a service business? This is not a trivial question. A decent set of answers could help businesses, trade associations, even government regulators make better decisions.

When the Supreme Court of the United States ruled professionals could advertise, the ruling allowed state Bar Associations to set the rules for law practice advertising. In many states, the rules set actually guaranteed ineffective advertising.

Analyzing the content of many advertisements which seem to be effective at acquiring service trial customers could identify a pattern for creating other successful communications. In my experience, one element in such a pattern is the support of any "brags" with concrete "benefits."

I define "brag" to be any piece of information important to the business owner which is not obviously important to most customers. Such commonly-used statements as "in business over 52 years," "largest in the business," and "family owned and operated" have no direct relevance to most consumers, UNLESS a direct personal benefit is explicitly presented to explain it.

Brags tend to occur frequently in small service business advertising, because the business owner is so closely involved with it. When combined with an explanation, a brag can become rational support for a specific claim: "With 52 years experience fixing plumbing problems, you can depend on us to do your job right. . .the first time." "As the largest air conditioning service company in Tulsa, we can get a skilled technician to your home or office the same day you call. . .even on the hottest day of the year." "Because we're family-owned, you get the personal attention you deserve. . .not a high-pressure sales pitch."

What are other effective elements? Are there any commonalities shared by effective service business commercials?

SUMMARY

Most service businesses are small businesses. They don't have access to big computer power to solve differential equations describing a market model, using variables they can't get input for anyway. Some may have desktop computers, but that's about it. Small business managers usually are not educated with a Ph.D. in marketing. They are hands-on-do-ers who learned much of what they know by trial and error. Consequently, to be useful any research must be distilled and massaged into "guidelines," "rules-of-thumb," or other formats readily usable by small business managers. For every airline, surely there are a thousand travel agents. For every national fast food chain, there are thousands more individually-owned hot-dog stands and corner cafes. For every national rent-a-car company, how many independent car repair shops are there? I suggest the most rapid progress in upgrading the marketing effectiveness of service industries can be made by researching topics relevant to small businesses.

THINK BEFORE YOU LEAP IN SERVICES MARKETING

Christopher H. Lovelock
Harvard University

ABSTRACT

There's a tendency among many marketing researchers to overgeneralize about services. The fact is that there are many different types of services and not all of them face the same marketing problems. This paper identifies three problems that are particularly important for certain types of services: (1) selecting and managing customers in those services where customers form part of the product; (2) managing customer relationships in services that experience repeated usage from identifiable customers; and (3) managing asset utilization in capacity-constrained services. In each instance, key research issues and needed date are outlined.

INTRODUCTION

The enthusiastic rush to develop a better understanding of services marketing is welcome (and long overdue). However, I'm concerned lest, in the process, we place too much emphasis on drawing distinctions between goods marketing and services marketing, and not enough on developing good insights for marketing practice in the service sector.

When a new area of application is developed within an established field, such as marketing, there's a natural tendency to highlight the differences between the new and the "old" application areas. The corollary of this is an unfortunate tendency to minimize any differences within the new area, since these inevitably get in the way of impressive generalizations about the distinctiveness of the new field.

OVER-GENERALIZATIONS IN SERVICES MARKETING

A quick review of papers in AMA's first conference on the Marketing of Services (Donnelly and George, 1981) suggests the following short list of well-meaning but potentially misleading over-generalizations in services marketing:

1. Services are intangible
2. Consumption and production of services take place simultaneously
3. Customers are involved in the service production process
4. Services cannot be inventoried--this leads to problems in matching supply and demand
5. It's hard to achieve product consistency in services
6. Channels of distribution for services are short but non-existent

Before anybody remarks that people in glass houses should not throw stones, I will immediately confess to having made many of these over-generalizations myself. However, the more one studies the management of service organizations, the more one is likely to find it necessary to modify earlier generalizations or to preface them by phrases such as "in many instances."

Intangibility

The "intangibility" characteristic has been discussed very articulately by Bateson (1979). Strictly speaking, this generalization is true. Services, as Berry (1980) points out, are "deeds, acts, or performances." They are experiences rather than objects that can be wrapped up and taken home. And yet overuse of statements concerning service intangibility makes me uncomfortable. Certain types of services involve highly tangible acts to either the customer in person or to some physical object owned by the customer. Haircuts, medical care, hotel visits, airline travel, repair and maintenance, lawnmowing and home improvement services all include a number of important tangible elements that would be unwise to overlook.

ible elements that it would be unwise to overlook.

Simultaneous Production and Consumption

The claim that production and consumption of services take place simultaneously holds true for those services that require the customer to be present (physically or mentally) throughout service delivery, since that individual is the object of the service. But it is not necessarily true for services delivered to customers' tangible possessions and intangible assets. The shoe repair product, for instance, is not consumed until the production job is completed and the shoes returned to their owner. Similarly, information retrieval services produce references and abstracts that the customer uses after the search process (production) is completed.

Customer Involvement in Service Production

Since production and consumption of services directed at possessions and intangible assets do not necessarily take place simultaneously, it is also clear that customers may not be involved in service production. What involvement does the homeowner have in the production of lawnmowing services, for instance? Who, other than the janitor, is involved in the production of office janitorial services? Another example is provided by insurance, much of which is sold by mail, with the customer's involvement being limited to filling out an order sheet (policy application) and paying a periodic premium.

Absence of Inventories

The inability to inventory a service is often cited as a direct consequence of the intangibility of servies (Bateson 1979). However, this characteristic is only meaningful for marketing management practice under certain limiting conditions. First, there must be some constraint to the level of service capacity at any given time, and second, there must be periods during which demand exceeds supply. These conditions are not meaningful for many services. Broadcasting, for instance, can supply an infinite number of listeners or viewers within receiving range of transmitters. The supply of insurance for those risks that meet acceptable criteria is theoretically unlimited, although paperwork bottlenecks could lead to delays in issuance of policies. However, most insurance policies are written for extended periods of time and are not strongly seasonal, so that the demand for new or renewed policies does not fluctuate sharply and rarely results in bottlenecks.

Lack of Product Consistency

Difficulties in achieving product consistency in services are often cited as resulting from the simultaneity of production and consumption, and as being compounded by the presence of the human element inherent in many services. However, as noted early, production and consumption often don't take place simultaneously in services delivered to consumer possessions or assets. Further, the trends toward self-service and replacement of service personnel by machines (such as automatic teller machines in banks) are eliminating or at least minimizing the variable human element in many service businesses.

Short or Non-existent Distribution Channels

Finally, we come to the oft-repeated statement that channels of distribution tend to be short or non-existent for services. Shortness may imply either limited geographic distance or a limited number of intermediaries. Neither situation is necessarily true any more. Physical distribution channels exist primarily for repair and maintenance services, where an item must be returned for servicing. Sometimes this involves taking the item to an appointed dealer who then ships it a considerable distance either to the original equipment manufacturer (OEM) or to a specialist repair firm approved by the OEM. Electronic channels of distribution are assuming increasing importance in the financial services and information industries. Plastic debit cards can be used to withdraw cash from almost any bank, thousands of miles from the institution in which one's own funds are deposited. Brokerage firms in the U.S., such as Merrill Lynch, that offer cash management accounts must use an intermediary bank to handle checking and credit/debit card transactions for their customers since government regulations forbid them to engage directly in banking transactions themselves. In the lodging and transportation industries, tour bookings frequently involve two levels of intermediary: wholesale tour brokers put together travel and hotel packages and sell these through retail travel agents to individual travelers. Similar packaging and distribution procedures can also be found in the entertainment and restaurant industries.

Needed: Greater Specificity

In short, many commonly-heard generalizations about service marketing do not hold true across a wide range of service industries or situations. My plea to researchers is to be more specific in the future when drawing conclusions about services. I regard this as the first and most important research priority in services marketing.

DISTINGUISHING BETWEEN DIFFERENT TYPES OF SERVICES

If it is unwise to generalize about the entire array of services, then what are useful ways of distinguishing between different types of services? Historically such research as there was into services marketing tended to concentrate on individual industries. However, such an approach fails to generate the insights that might come from focusing on specific classes of services that share common problems and extend across industry boundaries.

In an earlier paper (Lovelock, 1980), I examined a dozen different schemes for classifying services. I concluded that the most basic classification scheme concerns the nature of the service act: at whom or what is this act directed? And is this act tangible or intangible in nature?

As shown in Figure 1, these two questions result in a four-way classification scheme, involving (1) tangible actions to people's bodies, such as airline transportation, haircutting, and surgery; (2) tangible actions to goods and other physical possessions, such as air freight, lawn mowing, and janitorial services; (3) intangible actions directed at people's minds, such as broadcasting and education; and (4) intangible actions directed at people's intangible assets, such as insurance, investment banking and consulting.

Sometimes a service may seem to spill over into two or more categories. For instance, the delivery of educational, religious, or entertainment services (directed primarily at the mind) often entails tangible actions such as being in a classroom, church, or theatre; the delivery of financial services may require a visit to a bank to transform intangible financial assets into hard cash, and the delivery of airline services may affect some travelers' mental state as well as physically moving their bodies from one airport to another. But in most instances the principal service act is confined to one of the four categories, although there may be secondary acts in another category.

Most services research has focused on tangible services to people's bodies and intangible services to customers' intangible assets. Research in nonbusiness marketing provides insights from education and the performing arts (Kotler, 1982), although these have yet to be fully incorporated into the broader context of services marketing. However, relatively little attention has been directed at

Figure 1: UNDERSTANDING THE NATURE OF THE SERVICE DEED

Who Or What Is the Direct Recipient of the Service?

	PEOPLE	THINGS
What is the Nature of the Service Deed? **TANGIBLE ACTIONS**	Services directed at people's bodies ·Health Care ·Passenger Transportation ·Beauty Salons ·Exercise Clinics ·Restaurants ·Haircutting	Services directed at goods and other physical possessions ·Freight Transportation ·Industrial Equipment Repair and Maintenance ·Janitorial Services ·Laundry and Dry Cleaning ·Landscaping/Lawncare ·Veterinary Care
INTANGIBLE ACTIONS	Services directed at people's minds ·Education ·Broadcasting ·Information Services ·Theatres ·Museums	Services directed at intangible assets ·Banking ·Legal Services ·Accounting ·Securities ·Insurance

the wide array of tangible services directed at customers' physical assets.

As I demonstrated earlier in this paper, many of the generalizations commonly made about services marketing do not apply to services in all four cells. One of the values of this classification scheme is that it can serve as the basis for more focused research in marketing. For instance it helps to answer the question: Does the customer need to be physically present during service delivery? Possible answers include:

    (a) throughout service delivery;

    (b) only to initiate or terminate the service transaction (e.g., dropping off a car for repair and picking it up again afterwards);

    (c) not at all (the relationship with the service supplier can be at arm's length through the mails, telephone, or other electronic media).

Only tangible services delivered to customers' bodies require these customers to remain present throughout service delivery. Let's look at some of the marketing implications and use these to help identify some research needs for such services.

CUSTOMERS AS PART OF THE SERVICE PRODUCT

If customers need to be physically present during service delivery, then they are basically entering the service "factory" (whether it be a train, a hairdressing salon, or a hospital at a particular location) and spending time there while the service is performed. Their satisfaction with the service will be influenced by the interactions they have with service personnel, the nature of the service facilities, and also - perhaps - by the composition of and behavior of other customers using the same service (who become part of the service product). Questions of timing and the convenience of the location assume great importance when a customer has to be physically present.

Dealing with a service organization at arm's length, by contrast, may mean that a customer never sees the service facilities at all and may not even meet the service personnel face-to-face. In this sort of situation, the outcome of the service act remains very important, but the process of service delivery may be of little interest, since the customer never goes near the "factory." Increasingly, there are moves to get customers out of the factory, thereby reducing services that formerly entailed a high level of personal contact to low contact status. Bank-by-mail and automatic tellers in remote locations greatly reduce the need for customers to visit bank offices; and broadcast educational services and telecommunication hook-ups between teachers and students can eliminate the classroom.

However tangible services directed at people's bodies will continue to require the customer to be present during service delivery. When receipt of the service is shared with other customers, then these people become part of the service product.

Management Issues and Research Needs

All organizations need to think carefully about what customers to target, but services for which customers become part of the product itself should devote special care not only to customer targeting decisions, but also to managing customer interactions with the organization. Among the issues to be addressed are:

    1. Which are the most appropriate customers for the service organization, given its current positioning and the image that it seeks to convey?

    (2) Assuming it can attract the desired customers, how can management get them to behave in ways that are consistent with (a) the desired image, and (b) operational considerations?

What types of information do service organizations need to help them address issues and to develop appropriate strategies? A useful starting point would be to survey customers of several service businesses within each of several different service industries to determine their views on the following points:

    o How important as a product attribute are other customers of the organization? Are other customers a determinant attribute for some services?

    o Against what criteria do customers evaluate each other?

    o Are there significant perceived differences in other customers across different usage situations (e.g. time of day or season, purpose of use, group versus individual use)?

    o Do customers perceive themselves as having their behavior "managed" by the service organization? If so, in what ways? And do they feel positively or negatively about being encouraged/required to behave in specified ways?

MANAGING ASSET UTILIZATION

For many service organizations, life is a continuing alternation between feast and famine. Capacity is constrained and cannot easily be increased or decreased significantly in the short run. Yet customer demand for the service varies widely, equalling or exceeding capacity at peak periods and falling far below it in periods of low demand. This situation is found most commonly in services that entail tangible actions (see Figure 1), requiring either the customer or the customer's physical possessions to be present in the "factory" during service delivery.

In such organizations marketers are faced with a twofold task:

    1. Smooth demand over time so that demand matches capacity (this may not be possible in service organizations subject to random demand fluctuations, such as births in a hospital obstetrical unit).

    2. Ensure that the organization's assets are used in ways that will maximize the return on investment at that point in time by focusing on the most profitable customers.

Success in these endeavors requires close interactions between marketing and operations managers, willingness to use the full array of marketing mix elements--not just pricing alone, and good market information. Let's consider the relevant issues for researchers.

Research Issues and Data Needs

Many capacity-constrained service organizations use percentage of capacity sold as a measure of operational efficiency. For instance, transportation services talk of the "load factor" achieved, hotels of their "occupancy rate," and hospitals of their "census." But, by themselves, these percentage figures tell us little of the relative profitability of the business attracted, since high utilization rates may be obtained at the expense of heavy discounting to attract customers from price-sensitive market segments.

What is needed, then, is a measure of the extent to which the organization's assets are achieving their full revenue-generating potential. This must take into account the relationship between the average price actually obtained per unit of service and the maximum price that might potentially have been charged - what might be termed the price efficiency rate. By multiplying the capacity utilization rate by the price efficiency rate, we can derive an index of what I call asset revenue generating efficiency (ARGE). For example, a hotel has 400 rooms with a maximum posted price of $100 each. If only 70 percent of rooms is occupied one night - 140 at $100 and 140 at $60, then the price efficiency rate is 80 percent and the ARGE is (80x70)=56 percent. Another way to arrive at the ARGE is to divide total revenues received ($22,400) by the theoretical maximum revenues that could have been obtained by selling all rooms at the highest price ($40,000).

The value of the ARGE approach to performance measurement is that it forces explicit recognition of the opportunity cost of accepting business from one segment when another might subsequently yield a higher rate. Of course, the decision to accept or reject business shouldn't be based on the flip of a coin. Rather, that decision should represent a realistic estimate of the probabilities of obtaining the higher rated business, together with a recognition of any incremental costs involved.

The issues for researchers fall into two groups. First, it is important to understand the determinants of demand: why does demand vary over time? Is there a predictable cycle to the level of demand? Are there variations in demand over time between segments and, if so, what causes these? Second, the marketer needs to develop an understanding of how best to manage demand, which entails attracting the right segments at the right time at the right price. Decisions must be made on the extent to which

profitability should be traded off against capacity utilization. Some services, such as theatre or sports, project a greater aura of success and enjoyment if their capacity is fully sold, others provide greater consumer satisfaction if they are not operating at capacity. Research can help answer these questions as well as helping marketers to evaluate alternative strategies for achieving the desired result.

Data need to be collected on the following topics:

o The nature of demand curves for different segments under situation specific conditions In many instances, we can expect wide variations. For example, the levels of demand for hotel or transportation services at different prices tend to vary between business travelers and tourists also by day of the week and by season, yielding multiple demand curves for these services.

o The impact on demand of non-price variables (product features, communications, location, timing of delivery) and how these vary by segment

o Attitudes toward reservations and actual observed reservation behavior

o Attitudes toward queuing and actual observed behavior

o Current composition of the customer base by segment, over time.

Based upon experience and research insights, prices can be set that reflect the demand curves of different market segments. At the same time, "selective sell" targets (Fig.2)

Figure 2

Setting Capacity Allocation Sales Targets Over Time
(Hypothetical Example of Allocating Hotel Capacity to Different Segments)

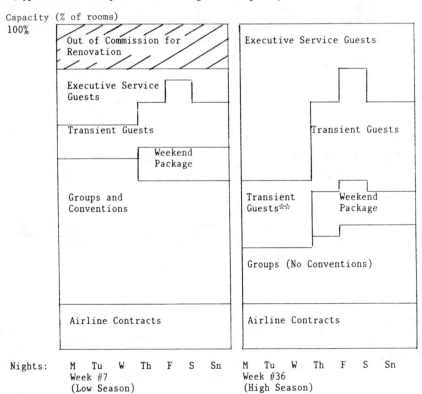

TIME

can be assigned to advertising and sales personnel, reflecting how management expects to allocate available capacity among different market segments <u>at a specific point in time</u>. These allocation decisions by segment also constitute vital information for reservations personnel, since it tells them when to stop accepting reservations from certain segments. To simplify their task, different segments can be assigned different phone numbers or mailing addresses for making reservations.

An example of how capacity might be allocated by a hotel over separate weeks in the high and low seasons is shown in Figure 2, which allocates available room capacity to different categories of guests, with day-of-the-week and week-of-the-year variations. These allocations represent forecasts of the customer mix that might potentially be obtained, based upon an analysis of demand levels for various segments and an assessment of competitive activity. Prices can be assigned to each category, also reflecting demand-and-supply analysis for different days of the week and different seasons of the year.

MANAGING RELATIONSHIPS WITH CUSTOMERS

The final area of research that I would like to discuss concerns what Leonard Berry (1983) has called relationship marketing, which requires efforts to cement the relationship once a new customer has been attracted to the organization and to transform indifferent customers into loyal ones.

In some instances, a de facto relationship exists between the service organization and the customer; in other instances it has to be created. To determine the potential for relationship marketing, we need to ask two questions:

1. Does the service organization enter into "membership" relation with its customers or is there no formal relationship?

2. Is service delivered on a continuous basis over an extended period or is each transaction recorded and charged separately?

There is a large category of services that customers cannot use unless they have previously signed up with the service organization--"joined the club," as it were. Examples include most financial services (banking, stockbroking and insurance) and public utilities requiring connections to a building (gas, electricity, and telephone). Once signed up, the customer has continuous access to the service--an access that is either denied to non-members or else is not available on the same terms. Other examples include college enrollment and membership in mutual or professional organizations, such as the American Automobile Associaton or the American Marketing Association.

The marketing advantages of being a membership organization are significant, since a great deal of information is collected about customers and their behavior in the normal course of doing business. There is excellent potential for direct mail communications, since the customer's name and address are known, as well as for segmented marketing strategies based on actual usage behavior. Unfortunately, not all membership organizations take advantage of their situation.

Services, that do not have the built-in "membership" requirement of those cited above may wish to seek ways of creating an ongoing relationship with their potentially most profitable customers. One way to do this is to offer incentives for bulk purchases of what would otherwise be discrete service units. Examples include theatre series subscriptions, prepaid medical plans, monthly commutation tickets on public transportation, and so forth. Although such incentives often include price discounts, other bene-

fits (such as product enhancement) may be appealing to customers, too. Where the price is being borne by a third party, such as an employer paying for hotel and transportation expenses, then ways have to be found of appealing to the traveler who make the actual choice between alternative suppliers. For instance, hotel chains have established clubs offering benefits for frequent users and airlines offer discounts on future flights to frequent fliers (see Berry, 1983).

Research Issues and Data Needs

All service organizations that expect to serve customers on a repeated basis should be examining their operating records to determine what information they collect about customers in the normal course of doing business. Are these data retained? If so, are they stored in a format that makes it easy to access and analyze them in ways that are meaningful for marketing decision-making? If the data are being collected but not used by marketers, how might they best be analyzed and used for building and cementing relationships with customers? What additional data about customer characteristics and usage behavior could easily be collected and stored on an ongoing basis?

The challenge for service organizations that do not currently have a membership relationship with customers is how to develop one. Among the areas requiring research are:

o What factors currently influence consumer choice between competing suppliers

o Is there a strong motivation for customers to use a mix of service suppliers for different transactions within the same service industry, or could a full-service organization realistically supply all needs?

o What benefits would a customer wish to receive in return for bringing all his/her business to a single service organization? Is there significant segmentation among customers in terms of the benefits desired?

o How can our organization develop meaningful membership benefits that will be hard for competing organizations to copy?

CONCLUSION

Services marketing at this point is beginning to mature as a field of study. We should be moving away from trying to determine what is "different" about marketing in the service sector and towards undertaking research that offers insights to practising managers. The key to this latter approach lies in avoiding overgeneralizations about services and instead focusing research efforts on specific marketing problems that are faced by specific categories of services.

REFERENCES

Bateson, John E.G. (1979), "Why We Need Services Marketing," in O.C. Ferrell, S.W. Brown, and C.W. Lamb (eds), Conceptual and Theoretical Developments in Marketing. Chicago: American Marketing Association 131-46.

Berry, Leonard L. (1980), "Services Marketing is Different," Business (May-June), 24-29.

Berry, Leonard L. (1983), "Relationship Marketing," in G.Upah (ed), Proceedings, Services Marketing Conference. Chicago: American Marketing Association.

Lovelock, Christopher H. (1980), "Towards a Classification of Services," in C.W. Lamb and P.M.Dunne, Theoretical Developments in Marketing. Chicago: American Marketing Association, 72-76.

INTRODUCING MARKETING INTO SERVICE ORGANIZATIONS: A CASE STUDY

Neil M. Ford, University of Wisconsin-Madison
Ruth J. Dumesic, Williams, Young and Hebert, Madison, Wisconsin

ABSTRACT

This paper examines a case history of the introduction of a marketing program into a public accounting firm. As late as 1979, this industry only seriously began to examine the possibility of using marketing concepts to increase or retain market growth. This paper discusses the techniques utilized to integrate marketing into a service organization that did not have a formal marketing plan.

INTRODUCTION

In 1979, when the ban was lifted on advertising and other forms of solicitation, many CPA firms began examining various marketing principles and techniques (Upah and Uhr, 1981). Unfamiliar with basic marketing principles, many firms sought outside consultants for assistance in formulating their marketing programs.

Although the consultants were able to identify strategies to initiate marketing programs, three obstacles confronted the professional organization that hindered successful implementation of their marketing plans.

The first obstacle reflected the historical nature of professional accounting firms. Historically, providers of professional accounting services, and other professional services as well, felt that "hanging up the shingle" was sufficient to attract customers. Marketing activities, if they existed at all, tended to be more passive than active, emphasizing pricing, service capabilities (product) and market (distribution). Selling, advertising publicity and promotion were ignored and, in fact, were deemed unprofessional. When marketing activities were first initiated, they were introduced as "practice development" concepts to avoid the negative connotation of marketing. The first obstacle involved reversing this negative attitude towards marketing to gain the necessary support of management.

A professional service organization, such as a CPA firm, is often structured around the specialized, technical skills of its staff. The professional mix within the organization can result in the branching of operations into independent directions based on these technical abilities. This structure can lead to a lack of coordination among the various areas of specialization constituting the second obstacle to introduction of a marketing program. Clients needing services from different areas, e.g., tax and data processing, find that their tax specialist is not knowledgeable about the firm's data processing services. Moreover, the tax specialist fails to "sell" the client on the firm's data processing capabilities and is unlikely to mention the client's needs to the computer group. These independent talents can result in divergent groups of clients. A marketing plan that focuses on common firm needs may not satisfy the specific requirements of each group. Each specialized area may have its own system of operation and, therefore, needs its own plan. The second obstacle facing the marketing program is integrating these independent operations.

The third obstacle is coordinating and controlling the marketing program, once it has been defined. Professional service organizations often become frustrated with marketing because of the lack of a full-time coordinator. The marketing responsibility is usually delegated to a manager who has some "spare" time to oversee the program. Too often, the program is neglected when client work is pressing. No one person is ultimately responsible for coordinating the marketing program. As a result, marketing is implemented on an "as needed" basis. Although recognized as important for securing growth, marketing planning is often hindered because of this "part-time" status and it looses top management's support. Also inherent in this arrangement is the perception that marketing only takes place at the management level. Marketing must be coordinated throughout the entire firm. The need for a full-time, internal coordinator is not often apparent and hinders the marketing program.

OBJECTIVE

To introduce a marketing program into a professional service organization, such as a CPA firm, one must address these obstacles when defining strategies. Historical data addressing these issues is almost non-existent. The first objective of introducing a marketing program into a service organization becomes twofold: (1) to design operating systems that will support the marketing program to coincide with the existing technical procedures, and (2) to delegate responsibility for monitoring and controlling all marketing efforts. Organizations that can address these two issues may achieve the competitive edge needed for continued growth through a successful marketing program.

BACKGROUND

A CPA firm, servicing local, state and national clients, experiencing the frustrations of defining, implementing and controlling their marketing program, took an unprecedented step by hiring a full-time marketing professional. The responsibility of this person was to define and identify marketing strategies and coordinate the program internally. Before developing marketing plans and strategies, the marketing coordinator had to develop a detailed understanding of the firm's marketing mix, as well as capabilities, personnel expertise, client base, and operating structure.

The marketing director spent the first few months researching the literature, observing firm activities, attending seminars, reviewing correspondence, observing client meetings, discussing successes and failures of past marketing activities, monitoring operations, and identifying the various requirements associated with the firm's clients. This observation period allowed the marketing coordinator to identify the current marketing mix and examine the informal marketing system operating within the firm.

Three key weaknesses kept appearing during this observation period: (1) the support or commitment to marketing activities had been diminishing at the management level and was nonexistent at the staff level; (2) an internal communication system between the areas of specialization did not exist, resulting in duplicative marketing efforts and the loss of important client data exchange; and (3) an operations system to support marketing efforts did not exist, resulting in inadequate follow-up or post-activity procedures and the loss of potential prospects.

DEVELOPING A MARKETING SYSTEM

The marketing professional's first step was to define a plan that addressed the firm's specific marketing problem areas and tackle the previously identified obstacles against initiation of a marketing program into the CPA firm. Table I shows that these problems and obstacles were related. This relationship was important in determining the marketing program.

Gaining Management Support: The marketing program's first objective was to address marketing's negative perception, to generate a positive attitude, and to gain management support. Management must participate in marketing activities, but initially only to the degree so as to not interfere with their professional commitments. The marketing professional's first responsibility in developing a marketing program was to define, in advance, management's participation in the stated activity including time, costs, etc. Through the approval process for the marketing program, management was able to adequately analyze the proposed activity. Once approved, management gave the marketing program the necessary support. Predetermining management's responsibility, coupled with a successful marketing program, increased motivation and enhanced a positive marketing attitude.

TABLE 1 -- DEVELOPING A MARKETING PROGRAM

Industry Obstacles	Firm Problem Areas	Program
1. Changing negative marketing attitude	Management support	Increase motivation; enhance positive marketing attitude
2. Integrating independent operations	Firm communcation system	Develop internal communications system
3. Coordinating and controlling marketing program	Operational marketing support system	Analyze, design, integrate system into present operations

Once the strategy for increasing motivation and gaining support had been established, the next step was to develop marketing programs that satisfied the subsequent areas of concern. The first program established a two-way communication vehicle (1) to inform the staff of client and firm activities, and (2) to obtain information from the staff regarding client data or marketing opportunities. A second strategy analyzed, designed, and implemented the systems which supported the firm's marketing programs. Both plans incorporated the motivational concept identified earlier.

PROGRAM I: INTERNAL COMMUNICATIONS

Professional services organizations often view marketing as external firm activities consisting of advertising and brochures (Denney, 1982). Little attention was given to an internal marketing program. The objective of this program was to provide the staff with a communication vehicle that will enhanced their ability to communicate with clients through increasing the staff's knowledge of the firm's operation.

To introduce the on-going marketing program, an in-house staff meeting was held. The basic firm operating structure was reviewed first, focusing on the firm's areas of specialization and services available to clients (Dumesic and Ford, 1982). Knowledge of the firm's operating structure was important in providing staff with the necessary information to market the firm's services to clients. Once the structure was understood, the staff was given instructions on how to refer clients to other specialty areas within the firm. To expedite this objective, staff members also were informed of the scope of firm services. The objective of this initial program was to define the firm's goals and open up firm-wide communication.

PROGRAM II: BUILDING THE MARKETING FOUNDATION

Step 1: Identifying Common Needs

A professional service organization is composed of a number of individuals, each with a specialized skill. Ideally, the organization offers full service to a client. More commonly, each professional targets their efforts toward a particular market. The end result is an organization of specialists, each with their own group of clients. The first step in building a system to support a firm marketing program is to identify common marketing needs.

Personal interviews were conducted within each area of specialization. The interviews were designed as a mini-marketing audit (Kotler, 1975). Each manager was asked the same series of questions about the following areas:

1. Target Markets
2. Market Growth
3. Services Offered to Markets
4. Market Needs
5. Marketing Efforts Utilized
6. Marketing Tools Required
7. Firm's Strengths and Weaknesses
8. Department's Strengths and Weaknesses

After all the interviews, the responses were categorized under each heading. This procedure allowed identification of common needs, and also identified the professional's specialized needs.

Step 2: Designing Support Systems

Step one identified three key elements: (1) the firm's strengths and weaknesses, (2) present and future opportunities, and (3) marketing needs. It was evident from the results of these interviews that two marketing programs for this firm required immediate attention: (1) some external activities to gain exposure in the targeted market and to simultaneously demonstrate to the staff the firm's marketing commitment, and (2) an internal operations system to support marketing programs.

To achieve both programs simultaneously, five specific objectives were set. A committee was established to meet each objective. Each committee consisted of top management and was chaired by a key executive. A set of objectives and guidelines were given to each committee. A progress report was given at the monthly management meetings by each committee. The philosophy of including all of management was twofold: first, they were made aware of the systems that have succeeded or failed in the past and secondly, their involvement with design of the systems, ensured their likely support of the systems they had designed.

The committees formulated to meet the needs identified in Step one include:

Committee I: Advertising/Literature
Goal: To develop a brochure or literature and an advertising campaign which meets the firm's overall goal.

Committee II: Correspondence
Goal: To design an internal procedures system that improves external communications

with both current and prospective clients to reflect personalized and individual attention.

Committee III: Community Involvement
Goal: To design a program which increases visibility and increases the firm's professional reputation.

Committee IV: New Clients/Key Prospects
Goal: To systematize internal procedures which controls and monitors progress for proposing services to new and/or present clients.

Committee V: Client Retention/Referrals
Goal: To develop an internal program which enhances retention of current clients and encourages referrals.

SIX MONTH'S RESULTS

The marketing program, as described in this study, has been in operation for six months. During this period, the following objectives have been accomplished:

Internal Communications

Following the in-house marketing program, two major programs have been developed to enhance internal communications. The first is a weekly, internal newsletter routed to all employees, which includes information such as:

- New clients
- New/modified services
- Staff activities
- Technical updates
- Firm marketing activities update
- Marketing news (articles designed to improve staff selling expertise)

The second program is to incorporate, with the staff's technical training sessions, the elements of marketing technical services. Actively integrating marketing with technical knowledge prepares the staff to more effectively market accounting services. Recognizing and matching client needs with firm capabilities and services is emphasized during these training sessions. Each in-house technical training session includes a discussion of the marketing implications of technical capabilities.

Building the Marketing Foundation

As a result of the five committees, the following systems have been designed to support the firm's marketing programs:

Internal

A. Correspondence Manual: A manual of various sample correspondence has been provided to the staff. This manual will encourage more personalized contact with current and prospective clients by providing a marketing tool that is convenient and that displays a professional firm image. This time-saving instrument encourages more client contact.

B. Log of Requests for Proposals: A review of the system for responding to Requests for a Proposal (RFP) indicated that there was (1) no centralized procedure, (2) no method for tracking success or failure, and (3) no follow-up procedure. A system was developed on a form designed to monitor RFP's (see Exhibit I). The data from the form is entered on the firm's computer and routed weekly to the staff, indicating changes, updates and the status of each RFP.

C. Speaker's List: A census of the topics/subjects that are currently available to present to clients or prospects has been compiled. Also topics that management would like to develop have been identified. From these lists (see Exhibit II), a speaker's bureau will be circulated to clients, prospects and community service organizations for reference. "Topics to be developed" can be evaluated at future management meetings.

D. Membership Directory: Members of a service firm often are active in outside organizations on a variety of levels. A census of organizations has been compiled and rated by the participants for (1) their level of activity within the organization, and (2) the level of potential client referrals. This listing shows the exposure of the firm outside the immediate business environment. The ratings give direction for expanding the firm's exposure within the community.

E. Key Clients' List: A listing of the top 20 clients has been compiled for each manager. A program for monitoring these clients has been developed to assure that proper attention is given to the clients who represent 80% of the firm's practice.

F. Firm Prospect List: A program for prospective clients requiring joint departmental marketing efforts has been designed and implemented. A "firm prospect form" was developed to record important prospect data and track marketing efforts (see Exhibit III). This data is reviewed at management meetings, where strategies are identified and results recorded. A "Firm Prospect List" was also designed to communicate, firm-wide, the joint activities and status of the prospects.

External

A. Monthly Client Newsletter: The firm's correspondence to clients was upgraded from the professionally prepared excerpts used previously to articles written by the staff, identifying needs and informing clients on important issues.

B. Advertising Campaign: A goal of the firm was an advertising campaign. The committee interviewed agencies and selected the agency that best matched its requirements.

FUTURE IMPLICATION

Knowledge of client needs is often missing in a specialized service organization. Thus, one of the first requirements is to establish a data base which identifies client needs as well as past successes and failures to meet these needs. This data base, if expanded to include competitive service offerings and their prices, market segmentation and service availability, will be instrumental in developing a formal marketing program.

Introduction of a marketing program will receive faster acceptance if the firm can focus on readily observable results. Examples include media advertising, the development of brochures, publicity and emphasis on individual staff accomplishments (new accounts). This is important because it demonstrates that a marketing program can make a positive contribution to the firm.

The marketing program must constantly be monitored to insure that the initial enthusiasm is not lost. The staff must be given marketing objectives and be evaluated according to their accomplishments. Their performance evaluations have to be structured to cover not only their technical accomplishments but also their marketing efforts. This infers that the individual marketing goals will need to be established.

CONCLUSION

This partial case history describes activities that, no doubt, are very routine for many companies that have been marketing-oriented. Even in these companies, however, the marketing concept was not an overnight phenomenon. It took time to develop. The speed with which a firm becomes marketing-oriented is a function of personal attitudes. In this case, strong support from the firm facilitated the process. Indeed, active involvement by top management gave a sense of direction to other staff members.

Implementing a marketing program into a service organization is a full-time activity that requires the support of the entire management team. To avoid the frustrations of diminishing marketing efforts, the marketing program must have a firm foundation on which to rest. Observations in the firm studied showed both an improvement in communications and an enhanced marketing attitude. Since these initial efforts did not concentrate directly on increasing business, the bottom line effect cannot be evaluated. Increased marketing awareness and effort on the part of the firm should lead to achieving the overall goals of client retention and growth. After all, a firm cannot expect external marketing successes until the marketing concepts and programs have been accepted internally.

EXHIBIT I -- NOTICE OF REQUEST PROPOSAL RECEIVED

Instructions:

This form should be filled out the SAME DAY a Request for Proposal, either written or verbal, for approximately $2,000/or 60 staff hours, is received.

Fill out the top half and route the entire form to the office manager. After it is logged in, the form will be returned and should be kept with the proposal. The lower half should be completed and returned to the office manager two days prior to: (1) the date the proposal is submitted (via hand or mail) or (2) the date a no thank you letter is sent.

```
------------------------------------------------
Date RFP Received _____ By (Initials) _____
Check one: ___ Potential Client: _____
           ___ Current Client: _____
Key Individual: _____ Decision Maker: _____
Kind of work: _____
Geographic location of work: _____
Industry type _____ Approx. size ($ or Hrs.) _____
Due date of proposal _____ Dates of work _____
Source _____ Comments _____
```

* *
Partner Review (Initials) _____

GENERATE PROPOSAL

Reason for submitting _____
Team assigned to respond (initials) _____
Fee Proposed: _____ Date Proposal Out _____
Follow-up: Was proposal accepted by client? _____
           If not, reasons for rejection: _____

DECLINE PROPOSAL

Reason for not submitting _____
No thank you letter mailed _____ Date

EXHIBIT II -- SPEAKERS' LIST

TOPICS/SUBJECTS NOW AVAILABLE TO PRESENT	LENGTH	PRESENTER
General:		
Opportunities in Accounting	30 min.	
Career Opportunities in Accounting	15 min.	
Banking:		
Accrual Accounting for Banks	60 min.	
Acctg. Treatment for Res. for Bad Debt	60 min.	
Business:		
Organizational Development of Closely Held Businesses	30-40 min.	
Starting a New Business	60 min.	
How the CPA Can Help the Small Business	15 min.	
How the CPA Can Help the New Business, Growing or Mature Company	25 min.	
Government:		
How to Get Into Government Work	45-120 min.	
Unified Eligibility Audit (CETA)	120 min.	
Head Start (CAP Agency) Rules & Regulations	1-2 days	
Nonprofit:		
How to Write a Good RFP	60 min.	
Financial Procedures for Nonprofits	90-120 min.	
NPO Board Training (Rights & Resps.)	90-120 min.	
NPO Financial Mgmt. (Budgeting, etc.)	4-8 hrs.	
Ramifications of Getting in Business	4-8 hrs.	
Tax:		
Estate Planning Basics	60 min.	
Sale of Personal Residence	60 min.	
Income Tax Treatment of Installment Sales	60 min.	
Personal Tax Planning	30-60 min.	
Real Estate Taxation Update	60 min.	

****

TOPICS/SUBJECTS NOW AVAILABLE TO PRESENT	LENGTH	PRESENTER
General:		
Personnel Mgmt. in Med.-Sized CPA Firms	4 hrs.	
Anything in Mgmt. or in the Financial Field		
Personal Financial Planning	30-60 min.	
Business:		
New Acctg. & Taxation Issues for Targeted Industries		
Developing & Operating Budget & Cash Flow Projections		
Small Business Financial Planning	Both a 1 day & 30 min.	
Trade Association Acctg. & Taxation		
Acctg. & Taxation for Construction Companies		
Acctg. & Taxation for Retailers		
Capital Sources for Closely Held Businesses	30-60 min.	
Government:		
Nonprofit:		
Internal Control in NPO's		
Tax:		
Tax Shelters		
Divorce Tax Planning		
Economic Recovery Tax Act- 1982 Effective Provisions		
How to Accumulate Funds for a College Education in Pre-Tax Dollars		

EXHIBIT III -- FIRM PROSPECT FORM

Form #: _____

Name of Organization: _____
Address: _____
_____
Telephone: _____
Type of Business: _____

Size:
    Net Worth:
    Gross Profits: _____
    # of Employees: _____
    Annual Sales: _____
    Total Sales: _____

Current Data:
    Auditor: _____
    Lawyer: _____
    Banker: _____
    Other: _____

Key Contacts:
    1. _____
    2. _____
    3. _____
    4. _____

Services Required: _____
Action to Date: _____
_____
_____
_____
_____

REFERENCES

Denney, Robert (1982), "Marketing Accounting Services: How to Prepare a Marketing Plan," WG&L Accounting News, (April), 3-5.

Dumesic, Ruth J. and Neil M. Ford (1982), "Internal Practice Development--An Overlooked Tool," The Practical Accountant, forthcoming.

Kotler, Philip (1975), Marketing for Nonprofit Organizations, Englewood Cliffs, NJ: Prentice-Hall, Inc., 56-74.

Upah, Gregory D. and Ernest B. Uhr (1981), "Advertising by Public Accountants: A Review and Evaluation of Copy Strategy," Marketing of Services, James H. Donnelly and William R. George, eds., Chicago: American Marketing Association), 95-98.

MARKETING IN HIGHER EDUCATION: ENABLING CONSTRUCTS

Linda Delene, Western Michigan University, Kalamazoo

ABSTRACT

This paper identifies and links eight enabling constructs
which the author suggests are essential to acknowledge and
consider if marketing is to be successfully incorporated
into the mainstream of higher education, one nonprofit industry beginning serious use of marketing. The eight enabling constructs are: (1) recognition of marketing's
relationship to organizational management; (2) recognition
of the limitations of marketing; (3) recognition of the
limited understanding of the marketing concept; (4) recognition that use of marketing in the nonprofit sector is
essentially different and not well understood; (5) recognition of the commonalities in marketing which transcend
applicational differences; (6) recognition of the nature
of organizational management and decision-making processes
in higher education; (7) recognition of the lack of business education and training of senior academic officers;
and (8) recognition of the need to incorporate marketing
in existing administrative structures. Particular attention is paid to the preliminary development of educational
performance measures to determine strategic marketing
effectiveness. The paper concludes by suggesting that
"logical incrementalism" will be the most congruent method
for the full incorporation of strategic marketing in higher education.

INTRODUCTION

Increasing numbers of institutions in higher education are
using marketing in some fashion. While exact numbers are
unavailable, the proliferation of seminars, books, the
discussions about marketing at higher education conferences, the advertisements of marketing consultants, and
the growth of related literature in academic journals all
attest to the growth of interest and the use of marketing
in the nonprofit sector of the economy (Rados, 1981 and
Kotler, 1981). The issue addressed in this paper is whether the "boom" in nonprofit marketing will be replaced by
a "bust" atmosphere of disappointment and frustration because enabling constructs for the successful adoption and
incorporation of marketing in higher education were un-
recognized, unknown, or simply glossed over as minor
matters. The recognition and consideration of these enabling constructs for successful incorporation of marketing is more crucial now than when earlier marketing applications in higher education focused on admissions and public relations. The environmental constraints facing many
institutions of higher education (fewer students, poorer
students, excess capacity, diminished federal support,
greater competition, unionized labor forces, etc.) require
the most intelligent choices in the years ahead. Marketing can measurably assist in institutional management
when these eight constructs are consciously taken into
consideration by *both* marketing professionals and educational officers and staff.

Eight enabling constructs are identified and discussed,
suggesting why each is essential for the successful incorporation of marketing. Fundamental in nature, related in
terms of relative sequence, and specific for higher education, the explicit acceptance of these constructs should
insure that individual colleges and universities will benefit from marketing *intentionally*. Of course, marketing
professionals already realize that some of these constructs are essential to *all* successful uses of marketing.
The thesis here is that these enabling constructs are

paramount for the successful development of marketing in
higher education because the *context* of application is so
different. The potential for misunderstanding and failure
will be greatly enhanced unless marketing professionals
recognize the limits of their understanding about the nature of higher education institutions. Likewise, an aura
of "rising expectations" about marketing by educators
could result in empty promises rather than productive programs.

Enabling Conditions

Enabling Construct 1: Recognition of marketing's
relationship to organizational management, especially
strategic planning. It is imperative that marketers do not
create a scenario wherein marketing is viewed as a substitute or replacement for educational or academic management.
Avoiding the emerging controversy about marketing's "place
in the sun," careful use of the concepts and analytical
tools with which we have substantial experience, that is,
market segmentation, definition of target markets, positioning and perceptual mapping, and the product life cycle
(Biggadike, 1981) would be the most credible course.

Secondly, when considering this construct in higher education, marketers need to concentrate on the central strength of a "futures' orientation" and the consequent holistic
environmental scanning so intrinsic in strategic marketing
(Wilson, 1978, and Resnik, Sand, and Mason, 1981). Marketing's framework for assessing the future, determining
trends relevant to a particular institution through the use
of such tools as cross-impact analysis, provides a solid
basic rationale for its use in higher education. Colleges
and universities have, for the most part, developed forward planning systems which have fundamentally focused on
enrollment patterns and trends. What is needed in these
institutions is for marketers to add the dimensions of
determining the emerging or changing target markets and
their respective needs which are masked by simple extra-
polation of numerical data. It is in the university planning process that visibility must be given to emerging
markets by resource allocation to academic program development -- primarily for those markets consciously selected
for long-term cultivation and need satisfaction.

Enabling Construct 2: Recognition of the limitations
of marketing. Many educational institutions, like other
nonprofit organizations, face a press of environmental
issues which are threatening their survival. Changing perceptions about the value of a college education; fewer and
poorer students; older, mostly tenured faculties; inconse-
quential financial resources in many instances; and, un-
changing mission statements and state charters in the midst
of dramatic demographic shifts -- all are illustrative of
problems which cannot be markedly improved at the *individual* college or university level by the application of
strategic marketing. This is particularly true if one
institution faces several of these problems simultaneously.
We must not "over-sell" marketing to those who, in retrospect, could have benefited most from strong marketing
programs begun years ago. This scenario, of course, will
not hold true for all colleges and universities. And, for
institutions with a stronger environmental position and
fairly substantial resources, marketers must reiterate that
positive changes from marketing applications are usually
somewhat slow in developing, cumulative, and often expen-

sive. This is principally prevalent in environments where competition for the few students has accelerated and where academic program differentiation is not meaningful to those students. For those stronger institutions, when faced with the costs of implementing marketing plans and programs, an experimental design approach (Emshoff and Carroll, 1980) may be useful in determining the initial effectiveness of marketing.

In any case, for developing effective working relationships with colleges and universities, marketers need to make *prudent* predictions about marketing's power when addressing institutional issues -- or we could incur a revival of the notion of "hucksterism" in our profession. Finally, the concerns about marketing performance in the for-profit sector (Webster, 1981) may be replicated in the higher education sector. *If* marketers are "risk aversive," then few marketers may possess the creative, entreprenurial characteristics so necessary to facilitate change in one of the country's oldest (1636), most traditional industries, higher education. It is an industry which is *not* characterized by change.

Enabling Construct 3: Recognition of the limited understanding of the marketing concept. This remains a perennial problem for marketers and is now occurring in the nonprofit sector as well (Andreason, 1982; Lovelock, 1981: Kotler, 1981). This is a two-fold issue. First, the marketing concept has been variously defined and interpreted by marketers. Different phrases such as "managing exchanges," "meeting customer needs and wants," and "satisfying needs and wants with a bundle of benefits" all reflect the essential need determination and want satisfaction of defined target markets, central to the marketing concept. Marketers understand this. However, very few educators believe students can or are best prepared to determine how to satisfy their educational wants and needs. Layers of institutional policies and requirements generally determine the constitution of educational programs and often with little, initial student understanding for their rationale. Intrinsically, educational programs, and student passage through an institution, are complex undertakings. Marketers would probably argue that determining what those career or educational aspirations mean in terms of particular curricular offering and the provision of accurate information about such programs to prospective students is really what is involved. It is in this communicating with students that educator's and marketer's perceptions may be divergent and in conflict. Additionally, marketers as a group have not been noted for their consistent long-term view and have often concentrated on "customer satisfaction in the short-run" (Resnik, Sand, and Barry, 1981, p. 29). Now marketers, increasingly involved in marketing for colleges and universities, are building work which requires use of the marketing concept in long-term contexts and in very traditional institutions.

Enabling Construct 4: Recognition by marketers that services and nonprofit marketing is not simply an elementary translation of various techniques from one sector of the economy to another; rather that the differences between for-profit and nonprofit marketing are many, complex, sometime subtle, and not yet well understood. This is especially true when considering the use of marketing in colleges and universities, where general business methods and practices have long been suspect and are usually adopted reluctantly.

The cogent assertions by Lovelock (1981) of some fundamental differences between goods and services marketing warrant serious consideration and further elaboration, coupled with appropriate empirical research, by those genuinely engaged in developmental efforts in this field. For example, the notion that consumers or clients of services marketing are often engaged jointly with the service

organization in the actual creation of the product connotes an experiential dimension lacking with more traditional notions of product. Further, the absence of inventories and the general lack of channels, specifically with reference to roles and assistance normally provided by channel intermediaries, places major additional, highly focused performance responsibilities on service organizations.

Additional basic differences which are likely to emerge between goods and services marketing include the following: (1) *primary* dependence on direct mail and personal reference groups as major promotion tools rather than mass media; (2) variable cost-price patterns, based primarily on ability to use the service rather than on ability to pay; and, (3) comprehension that apparent conflicts in institutional programs and statements of objectives stem from dual authorizatins, i.e., charter by a state, political, or philanthropic agency, and often subsequent use by other societal groups. Developmental work on such differences will occur while other marketers are operationally directing marketing programs in nonprofit organizations. Each needs to be an ongoing contributor to this developmental work on differences -- perhaps in forums historically shunned -- so we collectively can effect a more positive, productive incorporation of marketing into the "third sector" of the economy.

Enabling Construct 5: Recognition of the commonalities in marketing which transcend application differences, fundamentally with reference to various marketing processes such as strategic (market) planning, competitive analyses, positioning, and market definition through segmentation. While the theoretical base in marketing may not be as well defined as in other social sciences, there is a core commonality in marketing which centers on its explicit definition of target markets and their needs satisfaction (Enis and Roering, 1981). Basically, we need to recognize that the *context* in which we are developing marketing applications is somewhat "strange" from a traditional point of view but the *content* of our work remains constant, requiring explanation in different terms but with the same expected outcome, that is, the further integration of organizational behavior to satisfy markets with accordingly defined resource allocation patterns.

Enabling Construct 6: Recognition of the different organizational structures, history, purpose, and decision-making processes in colleges and universities. Organizational structures in large universities tend to be highly decentralized with somewhat autonomous collegiate units while small colleges tend to have more centralized structures with little unit or department autonomy. Most colleges and universities, quite unlike for-profit firms, share an academic history with associated mores and behavior that go back to 1100, about the time of the establishment of the first university, the University of Bologna. The regular appearance of academic dress, processionals, use of governance councils, and the relative caste system of tenured and non-tenured faculty remain firmly in place some 700 plus years later. While some organizational changes certainly have occurred, the basic practices of participative discussions, the seeking of consensus, diffusion of responsibility, and extensive consultation which precedes recommended decisions, characterize most internal operations and decisions. Persuasion is more important to decision-making than administrative logic in higher education.

The purpose of these institutions remain fairly clear in the broad sense with differentiation dependent upon historical bases associated with institutional age; denominational boards of control; geographic expansion of the U.S., especially in the 18th and 19th centuries; and, current levels of institutional endowments. Statements of purpose have often been developed into lists of objectives, which remain the initial basis on which to develop marketing

strategy. Given the centrality of institutional objectives in development of strategic marketing, and lacking
the normative for-profit measures of successful programs,
e.g., ROI (return on investment), market share, sales volume, etc., it is apparent that different criteria for
measuring the "success" of marketing and programs in higher education are necessary.

Using the framework for determining the effectiveness of
marketing (Hulbert and Toy, 1977) the following preliminary performance criteria for colleges and universities
can be developed. Use of these criteria reflects the
assumption that effective, appropriate marketing programs
can positively affect these educational performance measures. The more traditional marketing or financial criteria are noted primarily for illustrative purposes and to
prompt further the delineation of normative measures of
effectiveness for marketing in higher education.

TABLE 1

PERFORMANCE MEASURES: ORGANIZATIONAL LEVEL
MARKETING IN HIGHER EDUCATION

Traditional For-Profit Firms	Colleges and Universities
Market Share	Applicant Pool Yield
Sales Volume	Institutional Enrollment
Sales Variance	Enrollment Variance[1]
New Product Development	New Academic Programs (Majors/Minors)
Inventory Levels	Teaching Loads[2]
Production Capacity	Physical Space Utilization
Corporate Image	Unsolicited Student Inquiries
Repeat Purchase Behavior	Attrition Patterns
Price Structure	Financial Aid and Scholarships
Sales Quotas	Recruitment Goals
Investment Intensity	Gifts and Grants
Quality Control	Accreditation
General Financial Strength	Endowment Level

[1]This is *the* fundamental measure which indicates institutional knowledge of target markets.

[2]This would be an inverse relationship, i.e., the higher
the teaching load, the lower the inventory of available
services.

These comparative indices for measuring marketing's effectiveness in colleges and universities are "primitive" at
this writing and require study and research for full determination. Finally, while the recent, initial work on
the differences between state-owned and private organizations as these pertain to marketing strategy is quite useful (Capon, 1981), it makes a central assumption which is
doubtful, i.e., "specific objectives of state-owned enter-
prises can be wider ranging than for private corporations
because of this potentially unlimited cash availability
(p. 12). While that paper was *not* focused on colleges
and universities as "state-owned corporations" it may
contribute to the notion that governmental-related organizations and agencies have greater resource availability
than do for-profit corporations. This is rarely, if ever,
true.

Enabling Construct 7: Recognition of the lack of
business and managerial training generally found among
senior officers of educational institutions; and, the
fundamental differences between governing boards in for-
profit and nonprofit organizations. Most presidents,
chancellors, and provosts have qualifications for admin-

istrative positions based upon a background of *professional*
education and training, for example, as a chemist, American
literature scholar, mathematician, botanist, and so on.
Few have been formally educated for managerial work involving millions of dollars, labor management, fund raising,
and trustee and community relations. Their ability to meet
job responsibilities (in most cases!) with success is an
abiding testimony to "on-the-job-training" and the adapt-
ability of people. Nonetheless, marketers need to be sensitive to the fact that, as a group of managers, their
knowledgeability about typical business functions (marketing in particular) is vague, limited, and ill-defined.
Also, the historic antipathy between marketers and finance
and accounting professionals could surface as unknowing
Presidents turn to finance or business officers for an
explanation or evaluation of recommended marketing plans.
This powerful, informal reference source, usually sought on
matters related to the for-profit business sector, must be
understood in advance if the development of effective marketing is to move forward in higher education institutions.
This is particularly true in medium and small size colleges,
as opposed to major universities, because resources tend to
be fewer and their use severely reviewed.

Furthermore, the significant differences between Boards of
Trustees behavior, composition, size, service continuity
and value systems (Unterman and Davis, 1982) and corporate
Boards of Directors must be understood if productive relationships are to mature between practicing marketers and
administrative officers of colleges and universities.
These nonprofit Boards of Trustees will, I believe, look
with a fairly jaundiced eye upon the arrival of marketers
on campus - partly because they too misunderstand the
marketing concept; and secondly, because traditional constraints on trustee involvement in operational matters in
higher education have been entrenched and widespread.

Enabling Construct 8: Recognition of the need to
incorporate strategic marketing into extant structures and
decision-making systems, rather than to pursue the "add-on"
approach. The outright addition of marketing officers into
the administrative structure of colleges and universities
(Kotler, 1979) seems unwarranted and basically unnecessary
at this stage of incorporating marketing into the mainstream of academia. This "add-on" approach would serve to
isolate the function; make its costs more visible when it
will be (initially) a support function and provide developmental assistance to other functions; and would increase
the size of the institution's administration when most
colleges and universities lack either the resources or a
political climate conducive to apparent expansion. While
such an approach may be warranted when the utility of marketing in higher education is generally demonstrable and
affordable, such an outright, initial approach will probably generate more suspicion and resentment than short-term
benefits could offset. In reviewing the contemporary external environment facing most institutions, except for a
very few select ones with abundant resources and no major
threats to institutional programs, many colleges and some
universities are wrestling with basic questions of purpose
and long-term solvency. Further, the "add-on" approach
could vitiate the marketing concept *per se* and suggest that
marketing is someone else's responsibility.

Fundamentally, if the incorporation of marketing is to be
widely replicated, at least partly through emulation of
those colleges and universities which have been successful
with marketing, then the reported "market-oriented institutional planning" (Kotler, 1979, p. 39) *approach* seems the
preferred method for such incorporation. Most institutions
of higher education have fairly sophisticated planning and/
or institutional research offices, which would seem to be
ideal *loci* for the incorporation of marketing's functional
tasks. Staff in these positions, with necessary specific
formal training, could integrate the marketing functions
and evidence the marketing orientation which they may

already possess given the nature of their normal tasks, e.g., planning, assessing environmental issues, collecting data for definition of students (target markets), and already "housing" primary responsibility for enrollment forecasting. This blend, given available talented people, would integrate the forward planning, the analysis of markets, the determination of competition with the assessment of student preference and enrollment patterns. Over time, such an arrangement would likely culminate with the use of full-time, formally trained marketers. Further, this integrative approach would avoid the fanfare and resentment associated with the addition of new functional offices and staff in a time when other, traditionally established and legitimately perceived, units are being forced to abolish or harvest programs, personnel, and supporting services.

SUMMARY

None of the foregoing should be construed as implying that it is inappropriate to develop plans, programs, and conceptual frameworks for marketing in higher education. The reverse is the belief of the author. The challenge is to do so with greater sensitivity, recognition of the significant differences in patterns of institutional operation, and with conscious perceptions of the limitations of both marketing and the institutions involved. Marketing, for effective incorporation, does not require the addition of new systems, large staff, or expensive support services. Most fundamentally, it is a systematic assessment of future alternatives with an appreciation of historical roots and given philosophical and resource limits. I believe it will be achieved through a process similar to that described below:

> ...strategic decisions do not lend themselves
> to aggregation into a single massive decision
> matrix where all factors can be treated rela-
> tively simultaneously to arrive at a holistic
> optimum. ...of equal importance are the "process
> limits." i.e., the timing and sequencing of
> imperatives necessary to create awareness,
> build comfort levels, develop consensus, select
> and train people, etc. -- which constrain the
> system, yet ultimately determine the decision
> itself. It is virtually impossible for the
> manager to arbitrate all internal decisions,
> external environmental events, behavioral
> and power relationships, technical and
> information needs, and actions of intelligent
> opponents so that they can come together at
> any precise moment (Quinn, 1977, p. 13).

This approach of "logical incrementalism" is more congruent with the nature of colleges and universities than the usual separate functional placement of marketing in for-profit companies. Hopefully, marketers will be satisfied with incremental developments. The flash point of properly incorporating marketing in higher education may come because both parties involved in this exchange have expectations which are short-term and immediate. The incorporation process will not be without error and we must seek to maximize past lessons to meet the promise of the many future developments open to the use of marketing in higher education.

REFERENCES

Andreasen, Alan R. (1982), "Nonprofits: Check your Attention to Customers," Harvard Business Review, 60 (May-June), 105-110.

Biggadike, E. Ralph (1981). "The Contributions of Marketing to Strategic Management," The Academy of Management Review, 6 (October), 621-632.

Capon, Noel (1981), "Marketing Strategy Differences Between State and Privately Owned Corporations: An Exploratory Analysis," Journal of Marketing, 45 (Spring), 11-18.

Emshoff, James R. and Carroll, Vincent P. (1980), "The Use and Abuse of Marketing Experiments: Organizational Initiatives," Sloan Management Review, 22 (Fall), 23-35.

Enis, Ben M. and Roering, Kenneth J., "Services Marketing: Different Products, Similar Strategy," in James H. Donnelly and William R. George, eds., Marketing of Services (Chicago, American Marketing Association, 1981), 1-3.

Hulbert, James M. and Toy, Norman E. (1977), "A Strategic Framework for Marketing Control," Journal of Marketing, 41 (April) 12-20.

Kotler, Philip, Marketing for Nonprofit Organizations, Prentice-Hall, Inc., Englewood Cliffs, N.J., 1981 (Second Edition).

_____(1979), "Strategies for Introducing Marketing into Nonprofit Organizations," Journal of Marketing, 43 (Winter), 37-44.

Lovelock, Christopher H., "Why Marketing Management Needs to be Different for Services," in James H. Donnelly and William R. George eds., Marketing of Services (Chicago American Marketing Association, 1981), 5-9.

Quinn, James Brian, "Strategic Change: Logical Incrementalism," in Management Preview: Strategies for the 80s, (Cambridge, Mass., Alfred P. Sloan School of Management, 1979), 3-17.

Rados, David L., Marketing for Non-Profit Organizations, Auburn House Publishing Co., Boston, Mass., 1981.

Resnik, Alan J., Sand, Harold E., and Mason, J. Barry (1981) "Marketing Dilemma: Change in the '80s," California Management Review, 24 (Fall), 49-57.

Unterman, Israel and Davis, Richard H. (1982), "The Strategy Gap in Not-For-Profits," Harvard Business Review, 60 (May-June), 30-40.

Webster, Frederick E., Jr. (1981), "Top Management Concerns About Marketing: Issues for the 1980s," Journal of Marketing, 45 (Summer), 9-16.

Wilson, Ian H., George, William R., and Soloman, Paul J. (1978), "Strategic Planning for Marketers," Business Horizons, 21 (December), 65-73.

CONCEPTS AND STRATEGIES FOR DENTAL SERVICES MARKETING

Peter M. Sanchez, Villanova University

ABSTRACT

A rapidly changing environment in the dental services profession has raised the need for the application of marketing technology in this area. This paper provides concepts and strategies for the dental service profession.

NEW FORMS OF DENTAL SERVICES COMPETITION

One of the most significant changes occurring in the dentistry field today is the rapid proliferation of "retail" or "department store" dentistry (Business Week, 1981). Dental facilities can now be found in non-traditional locations such as Sears, Montgomery Ward, regional chains and pharmacies like Peoples Drug Stores in Washington, D.C. It is estimated that this fast growing industry (approximately $100 million at present) will capture 25% to 35% of the dental market by 1990.

While the precise nature of these retail dental locations varies considerably, they do have several things in common. First of all, they are characterized by the heavy use of such marketing tools as advertising, promotional pricing, and high-traffic locations in malls and department stores. Secondly, they seem to attract the consumer interested in convenient, quality dental care at a reasonable price. Most present consumers of these new dental services have never visited a dentist before while many visit the dentist only irregularly.

OVERSUPPLY OF DENTISTS

Recent American Dental Associations statistics indicate that there are approximately 120,000 dentists currently practicing in this country. Projections show that this number will increase by 24% in the next decade, with the country's population increasing by only 9%.

While there are still spot shortages of dentists in some parts of the country (primarily rural areas), urban areas are currently glutted. More and more dentists are being graduated every day and they are not neatly distributing themselves across the country. Most tend to concentrate in urban areas where they end up competing in a shrinking market.

CHANGING CONSUMER BEHAVIOR PATTERNS

The average dental patient of years past probably looked upon his dentist with awe. To him, or her, the dentist represented a figure of authority whose judgment and opinions were never to be questioned. Consultations were typically one-way communications, that is, from the dentist to the patient. Dentist loyalty was high, except in rare cases of obviously poor dental treatment. Charges, scheduling of appointments, and other aspects of the dental experience were never questioned but rather accepted as a part of the price one had to pay for not taking care of his teeth.

Today, however, the practicing dentist finds himself dealing with an increasingly sophisticated and educated consumer. Consumers have become more knowledgeable about available alternatives in the dental field. They are now asking questions, demanding information, and in general are being more aggressive in pursuing a level of treatment they perceive to be satisfactory in light of the cost of treatment (Holtman, and Olson, 1976).

A second behavioral factor dentists must contend with these days is the increased number of women employed in the work force. With fewer working mothers in the past, appointment scheduling was less of an important factor than it is today. The working mother with children is under severe time constraints and in general has become more and more convenience-oriented in the purchase of goods and services.

Changing lifestyles are also having an impact on the manner in which consumers seek dental care. While today's consumer perhaps has more discretionary income than he did in the past, he also has a wider range of alternatives upon which to spend this income. Several vacations a year, a tennis club membership, and a private school for the children are examples of what have evolved into almost necessities for many consumers. Dental care, unfortunately, is reviewed as a deferable expense by many consumers and so the dentist ends up competing with much more sophisticated marketers in non-related fields. For most people cost is not the reason for deferring dental treatment but rather it is an excuse (Kegeles, 1963). Given the choice of a vacation in the Bahamas or a trip to the dentist, most consumers would opt for the former.

DILEMMA OF THE SOLO PRACTITIONER

The overwhelming majority of dentists in this country are engaged in individual, private practices. These solo practitioners are likely to feel the greatest impact from the changing dental marketplace. For them, this new environment presents pitfalls as well as opportunities.

The greatest threat to the survival of the solo practitioner will come from the competitive pressures presented by retail dentistry and the oversupply of dentists. Competition will likely be fiercest in urbanized areas. To survive in this increasingly competitive environment, the solo practitioner can no longer rely simply upon delivering quality dental care but rather he must seek to differentiate himself from competition. In short, solo dentists must now learn to market themselves in order to find a competitive advantage. In the final analysis, most dentists do deliver good quality dental care, but most consumers cannot perceive the quality of dental care they receive.

BUILDING A DENTAL SERVICES MIS

Fortunately, the nature of most dental practices permits the development of a solid research base for marketing planning which is neither costly nor time consuming. The foundation of such a data base is the existing patient files and records. Contained within these records is a wealth of information which can serve as a starting point for a dental services marketing information system (MIS). Most dental practices routinely gather patient basic demographic information on patients such as age, occupation, income etc....as well as pertinent medical and dental history. In the course of treatment and billing, patient records are also consistently updated and therefore will reflect patterns of visitation and reasons for seeking dental care (preventive measures vs. dental problems, e.g.).

With a systematic procedure for compiling, editing, and coding this information combined with the advent of low cost computer technology, it is within the means of most dentists to have at their disposal at least a crude marketing information system.

While a specific plan for the operational implementation of an MIS is beyond the scope of this paper, some initial recommendations can be made. Demographic information on each patient should first of all be coded to include at least age, occupation, and income. Occupation and income are widely used measures in determining consumer social class membership, the significance of which is discussed in the next section of this paper.

Patient records should also be coded to reflect patterns of office visits. For example, patients visiting the office less than once per year could be grouped into one category. Those visiting the office one to two times per year would be in another category, and those visiting three or more times per year could be grouped in yet a third category.

The patient's reason for an office visitation should also be coded. An obvious category would be first of all to code a particular visit as being either a routine check-up or problem oriented. Further coding of problem type visitations would depend on the nature and extent of a particular dental practice, but could be as elaborate as necessary to yield desired information. The significance and potential uses of the information made possible through such an approach is the subject of the next sections.

MARKET SEGMENTATION-FOCUSING THE DENTAL SERVICES STRATEGY

In moving towards a marketing orientation, there are several strategies which can be implemented immediately by the solo practitioner at relatively little expense. Ironically, these inexpensive strategies also are likely to have the greatest impact on the consumer of dental services.

The first of these strategies includes the orientation of the practitioner's services towards the dental patient. This goes beyond simply learning the patient's name and showing an interest in his or her problem. But rather it includes recognizing the patient's needs beyond that of a physical nature. All dental patients have similar physical needs, that is the need to receive high quality dental care, be it merely a preventive checkup or an extensive root canal. Most dentists can supply this physical based need. What becomes important then is also satisfying needs of a non-physical nature. As discussed earlier, the majority of dental patients are unable to differentiate dentists on the quality of dental work performed. Judgments concerning quality will, however, be made on the basis of a broader set of experiences undergone while visiting the dental office. This will include everything from the encounter with the receptionist to evaluation and follow up.

While patients find difficulty in articulating specific reasons for satisfaction or dissatisfaction with a particular dentist, they nevertheless do walk out of the office with an overall perception of how they have been served. This perception ultimately affects whether or not the patient will continue to utilize the services of a given dentist. It will also affect what the patient communicates to other potential patients of the dentist. In this regard, probably nothing is more damaging to a dentist's reputation than a poor recommendation from a former patient.

The emotional or non-physical needs of the dental patient are not directly observable, but rather must be inferred from indirect measurements. Demographic data such as age, income, and occupation included as part of a patient's dental records in the MIS can yield crude, but useful measures of a patient's social class. A patient's social class, in turn, holds clues regarding emotional needs.

Although the concept of social class is far more complex than will be elaborated in this paper, the concept is nevertheless useful to the solo practitioner in attempting to focus his marketing effort as well as providing input to the makeup of his marketing strategy. Because the various social classes tend to group themselves geographically, the typical solo practitioner will find himself dealing primarily with one social class rather than several. This enables a given dentist to tailor his practice in terms of the needs of the social class he is serving.

Figure 1 depicts three potential social class segments, their emotional needs, and appropriate communicative strategies. The upper class segment is comprised of those individuals in our society who have acquired considerable wealth by virtue of successful professional careers. They tend to be older, high income people living in the best neighborhoods. While they still engage in conspicuous consumption, they are secure in their social standing in society. They can best be described as having "arrived" at success. This social class segment, having fulfilled most of their lower order physical and material needs, is motivated by higher order needs such as the need for self-actualization and the need for self fulfillment. As a whole, this group makes up about five percent of the population.

The middle class segment consists of those people who have attained moderate success in our society. They are, for the most part, active, striving people attempting to move up the social ladder. This group tends to be younger, and educated, with respectable incomes. They are not as secure in their social standing as the group above them and for this reason, much of their consumption behavior is dominated by the need for further achievements. They tend to view themselves as important. Consequently this group is highly motivated by esteem needs such as the need for recognition and the need for reputation. This group is the second largest group among the social segments, making up about fifteen percent of the population.

The lower class segment of society includes both white and blue-collar workers with limited skills and education. This group tends to be more secure in their social standing than the middle class. Limited aspirations and more of a tendency to live for the present dominates much of the consumptive behavior for this segment. As a whole, this group represents what might be typified as the "average" American. They exemplify the core of respectability, conscientious work habits, and adherence to culturally defined norms and standards. Moreover, this segment tends to be home-oriented, less prone to experimentation, and less confident in their ability to make choices. Generally speaking, this group is motivated by lower order needs such as the need for security, pain-avoidance, and order and structure in the environment. This social class segment is the largest in society, making up about sixty-five percent of the population.

As discussed earlier, the predominant social segment a dental practitioner is serving should be discernible from existing patient records. Knowledge of the social segment being served enables the practitioner to begin developing marketing strategies which will satisfy the particular needs of the market segment. Included in Figure 1 is a combination of verbal and non-verbal communication variables which the solo practitioner can employ to communicate need-satisfaction to appropriate market targets. Atmospherics refer to communicative variables such as office location, design, and layout. Communicative appeals

FIGURE I

POTENTIAL MARKET SEGMENTS BY SOCIAL CLASS

Social Class	Motivating Needs	Atmospherics	Communicative Appeals	Dentist--staff--patient Interaction
Upper	Self-actualization Self-fulfillment Independence from environmental demands Realization of self-potential	Elegance Taste Success Tradition	Aesthetics Vanity Cosmetics	Deference Respect
Middle	Esteem Achievement Adequacy Reputation Attention	Modern Complete Conspicuous Quality	Prevention Rationality Convenience	Tolerance Sympathy Attentiveness Importance
Lower	Safety Security Pain-avoidance Order Structure Affiliation-affection	Sterile Tidy Modest	Problem Pain-avoidance Fear Economy	Firmness Direction Conversation Familiarity

include the rationales for dental treatment that may be built into messages directed to each of the segments. The dentist-staff-patient interaction variable refers to the manner in which the dentist and his entire staff should orient their interaction with patients in each market segment.

A marketing strategy directed towards the upper class segment, for example, should include first of all an office location in the better sections of a given community. The office should be located in a free-standing structure or in a building which connotes success and experience. A modern, brand new office building, for example, would be inappropriate for this segment. The interior design and furnishings of the office should likewise communicate a quiet elegance indicating that the dentist practicing here is a successful, experienced practitioner much like the successful professionals he is treating. Furnishings and decor should be of the highest quality and styled in a traditional mode.

In communicating with this segment, the practitioner should emphasize the long-range benefits of appropriate dental treatment. As a whole, this group is particularly receptive to appeals that will enable them to age more gracefully, and to look and feel better in the process. Success has given this segment the opportunity to be less concerned with the world around them and more concerned with their own well-being. The aesthetic and cosmetic aspects of dentistry should be emphasized with this group.

The upper class segment is quite used to being treated with deference and respect as a result of their social position. In their interactions with this group, the dentist and his staff should proceed accordingly. Within reason, it is not inappropriate to attempt to cater to every whim of this group.

In contrast, a marketing strategy aimed toward the lower social class segment, should emphasize surroundings and demeanor that this segment is comfortable with. For example, office location should be in a modest section of town obviously as close as possible to the neighborhoods in which the group lives. Office furnishings and decor should match as closely as possible the type of surroundings one would expect to find in the homes of this segment. Furniture should be modest, sterile, and tidy. As a whole, this group may be fearful of the cost of den-

tistry. Modest atmospherics will communicate an affordable fee structure. Reading material in the waiting room should be appropriately downscaled to match the desires of this group. Since this group is visually oriented, the inclusion of a television set in the waiting room would also be appropriate.

Appeals that this group is receptive to are primarily problem-oriented. For example, they will understand and relate to a message couched in terms of pain-avoidance as they possess a deep seated fear of dentistry. Thus, anything that can be done to alleviate that fear will gain acceptance. Likewise the consequences of not receiving adequate dental treatment should be related to this group in terms of potential future complications leading to additional unnecessary pain and expense.

In interacting with the lower class segment, the dentist and his staff should understand that this group prefers order. They are not confident of their ability to make choices, particularly in an area such as dentistry. This, combined with a respect for professionals in general leads this segment towards treatment characterized by firmness and direction. They are used to taking orders; confronting them with alternatives in the dental office would make them feel insecure.

Because this group is also motivated by needs for affiliation and affection, the dentist and his staff should attempt to communicate an atmosphere of warmness and friendliness. While this group realizes that they are not on the same social level as the dentist, they also have the need to feel that the dentist is a friend.

BUILDING THE DENTAL SERVICES PRACTICE

In addition to revealing clues concerning social class, an analysis of patients' records also will likely turn up wide variations in the frequency of visits to the dental office. Typically, patients can be grouped into regular, moderate, or low patterns of visitation (Holtmand and Olson, 1976). There is little need to worry about patients falling into the regular category, other than implementing the recommendations suggested in the previous section. Patients falling into moderate or low patterns of visitation however represent opportunities for building the dental services practice.

131

In spite of the well advertised benefits of regular dental examinations, preventive dental care is still widely under-utilized. Consumption is particularly low among lower social strata populations (Kriesberg and Truman, 1960; Pointer and Mobley 1969). Even among middle class groups, where purchase of preventive measures is more routine, saturation has by no means been reached. This phenomena is characteristic of the purchase of preventive health care services in general, as is the difference in purchase patterns among social classes (Nikias, Fink, and Shapiro 1975).

Historically, irregular purchase of preventive dental care was attributed to low purchasing power. More recent evidence however, suggests that free or low-cost checkups are relatively ineffective in attracting consumers to the dental office (Holtman and Olson, 1976). Even prepaid dental insurance plans covering the entire cost of preventive care but a lower percentage for treatment have failed to live up to their expected impact (Kegeles 1963).

Alternative approaches to undertaking reasons for wide variations in the purchase of preventive dental care have focused on other variables such as "fear" (Hassett 1978) and working class "dental fatalism," (Summett 1970). One study concluded that important motivating factors for seeking preventive dental care include lack of anxiety about dental treatment and aesthetic concern for one's teeth (Kegeles, 1963). The primary focus of the majority of these studies has been on reasons for purchase versus nonpurchase of preventive dental care, hence their usefulness in terms of managerial significance is limited.

A more recent study (Gelk and Gilley, 1979) utilizing contemporary consumer behavior theory takes a significantly different approach in dealing with the same problem. Rather than trying to understand reasons for purchase or non-purchase, this study examined the general hypothesis that promotional activities directed at problem recognition and ease of buying can substantially increase consumption of the six-month dental checkup. Briefly, two experimental sample groups selected from dental practices in the Houston area were sent the usual six month reminder postcards informing them that they were due for a checkup. One group however also received phone calls to schedule appointments while the other group was left to call on their own. Results indicated that the group receiving phone calls was much more likely to agree to an appointment and also adhere to it. More specifically, the results show practically no blue-collar patients returning for preventive care without the phone call, and show only one-third of the middle-class patients returning without the call. Because of the limitations of the study, there is no basis to generalize the results. However, the effectiveness of telephone calls in scheduling preventive checkups substantiates the conventional marketing wisdom that it pays to make something easy to buy. In this case of preventive care slightly more aggressive promotional and marketing tactics may be much more effective than traditional passive tactics such as reminder postcards.

DEVELOPING NEW MARKETS FOR DENTAL SERVICES - REPOSITIONING THE PROFESSION

One constraining factor which limits the market for dental services is how dentists view themselves and how dentistry is perceived by consumers. While there are no supportive statistics, it is probably fair to say that the old "drill em, fill em, and bill em" philosophy is still prevalent among dental practitioners even today. Technically, dentists are trained in a holistic approach to the oral cavity. Yet in practice and in communicating what they are capable of doing, dentists for the most part have too narrow a focus on only the teeth. This myopic orientation to the concept of dentistry undoubtedly carries over to the consumers' image of the profession. Again no supportive statistics exist, but it is probably fair to say that the average consumer sees dentists as caretakers of teeth rather than as caretakers of the oral cavity. This limits the perceived benefits of dentistry on the part of the consumer. Likewise it limits the ways in which dental services will be utilized by the consumer. For example, if consumers view dentists as being concerned only with teeth then consumers will preceive benefits only in terms of the health of their teeth. Relatively few, and then only the well educated, will make the correlation between healthy teeth and a healthy body. This limited perception may explain in part the lack of a wider acceptance of preventive dentistry and the continuing prevalence of a problem orientation in seeking dental services (Kleinknecht, et al, 1976).

In order to broaden the market for dental services, the profession must first broaden its role to encompass a more holistic orientation to the practice of dentistry. This involves more than merely technical training. More importantly, it involves repositioning the image of the profession in the eyes of the consuming public.

Repositioning dentists as caretakers of the oral cavity with a mouth-face orientation will enable the profession to supply a broader range of perceived benefits to consumers. To accomplish this, the profession must communicate and establish the importance of the mouth as the entrance for everything which will ultimately affect the health of the body. Consumers should be brought to appreciate the correlation of oral care to nutrition, physical health, and physical appearance. This not only moves dentists upstream with other health care providers, but also serves to give consumers a variety of reasons to purchase dental services beyond that of having healthy teeth.

An excellent example of this type of positioning strategy is currently being pursued by the American Association of Orthodontists. Faced with a dwindling supply of teenage consumers in their traditional market, orthodontists are now hoping to attract a larger share of adults in need of orthodontia. Statistics indicate that about half of the general population is in need of some type of orthodontic treatment with about 25% of those having severe problems. In attempting to reach this market, orthodontists have found that a large segment of adults will seek such treatment primarily for cosmetic reasons. Motivators here appear to be career enhancement and the general desire to look younger and better (Advertising Age, 1979).

SUMMARY AND CONCLUSIONS

Changing dental services marketplace variables as well as prevailing consumer attitudes towards dentistry highlight the need for marketing in the dental services profession. This paper has explored several of these changes. Concepts and strategies well within the reach of most dental practitioners have been developed.

REFERENCES

Summet, Clifton O. (1970), "How Does Dentistry Face Up to
Urban Needs?" Journal of the Missouri Dental Association, 7-11.

Gelb, Betsey S. and Gilley, Mary C. (1979), "The Effect of
Promotional Techniques on Purchase of Preventive Dental
Care," Journal of Consumer Research, 6, 305-308.

Hassett, James (1978), "Why Dentists are a Pain in the
Mind," Psychology Today, 60-5.

Haltman, A.G., and Olson, E.O. (1976), "The Demand for
Dental Care: A Study of Consumption and Household
Production," The Journal of Human Resources, 11, 546-
60.

Kegeles, Stephen (1963), "Some Motives for Seeking Preventive Dental Care," Journal of the American Dental
Association, 67, 110-8.

Kleinknecht, R.A., Klepac, Robert K., and Bernstein, D.A.,
(1976), "Psychology and Dentistry: Potential Benefits
from a Health Care Liaison," Professional Psychology,
7, 132-6.

Kriesberg, Louis and Treiman, Beatrice R. (1960), "Socio-
Economic Status and the Utilization of Dentists'
Services," Journal of the American College of
Dentists, 27, 147-65.

"Moving the Dentist's Chair to Retail Stores," Business
Week, Jan.19, 1982, 56.

Neher, Jacques, (1979), "Orthodontists Hope to Pull in
Adults with First Drive," Advertising Age, 135-6.

Nikias, M.K., Fink, R., and Shapiro, S., (1975), "Com-
parisons of Poverty and Non-Poverty Groups on Dental
Status, Needs, and Practices," Journal of Public
Health Dentistry, 35, 237-59.

Pointer, M.B., and Mobley, E.L. (1969), "Dental Status
and Needs in a Poverty Population of North Nashville,
Tennessee," Journal of Public Health Dentistry, 29, 239-
45.

MARKETING THROUGH FACILITIES DESIGN

Hank Sherowski, Wendy's International

ABSTRACT

The article entitled "Marketing Through Facilities Design"
is an interesting insight of how Wendy's uses its building
and equipment design as a marketing tool. It traces the
original concept on through the most recent changes and
how the "Old Fashioned" selling umbrella was retained
despite a total revised image.

For two days we have examined the problems and opportunities involved in the marketing of services. This
morning we are looking at the role design plays in that
process.

I would like to preface my remarks with the fact that I
am not a marketing person. I am an architect...an architect who, for the last 11 years has been directly involved in the growth of Wendy's International and in supporting the marketing efforts of that company...supporting
them through design and building engineering. This morning I would like to share with you some personal thoughts
on design as they are applied to marketing, as well as
some of the experiences we have been through at Wendy's
over the past few years.

As marketing people, I'm sure that you are aware design
is quite subjective. While there certainly are standards
of design, what is perceived as "good" by one person may
be distasteful to the next. Not only is it subjective,
but it's success must be measured against the goals at
hand. For example, the design elements of a fast food
restaurant cannot be fairly compared to the universe of
all commercial buildings or even all restaurants. It is
obvious that one does not design a contemporary continen-
tal restaruant the same as a fast food store featuring
hamburgers and chili.

So the test of design, is whether or not it accomplishes
a very specific set of goals that contribute to the suc-
ess of the business. Design must not only fit and be
appropriate for the product or service, it must totally
support the image and marketing effort of that product or
service.

Another key factor of design is that it is, indeed, a
process...a constantly changing thing. This is sometimes
hard to accept. Our perceptions of the so-called "classic" designs would seem to indicate the opposite. The
Eames chair is a good example. Since its inception it
has been considered a classic design...and it is. But
that does not mean that the design of chairs stopped
there. It continued...a few more classic designs have
appeared...and the design evolution continues today. So
you can see that design is a fluid process. At its best
it involves continual evaluation and refinement.

How does this relate to marketing a fast food company?
Let us go back eleven years to the very first Wendy's
store...the beginning of the concept.

When it began the Wendy's concept was unique.
It presented a totally new image to the public, unlike
any other fast food operation at that time.

If we look at the molecular model of a service business
as proposed by Synn Shostack, we see the outer-most
circle represents the image of the entity. The next cir-

cle is the cost and price...the pricing strategy.

The Wendy's approach to both image and pricing was almost
unheard of in the fast food business of eleven years ago.
The primary concern of image development was for a quality product served in pleasant surroundings. The pricing
strategy supported this notion. The product was more
expensive. But we soon found out that people were willing
to pay for a superior product. The image developed at
that time worked and continues to work today...it is a
major part of Wendy's success.

Throughout the history of Wendy's design has played an
important role in both developing and maintaining the
Wendy's image...in effect, directly supporting the marketing effort. For example, it we examine some of Wendy's
Marketing positions..."Hot n' Juicy", "Old Fashioned",
and so forth, we can see how physical design of the stores
has helped support those. The physical layout and selection of equipment for the food preparation areas are all
designed to support the idea of using fresh ingredients.
The simple fact that food is prepared on a grill in full
sight of the customer may seem to be an insignificant
item, but is actually an important design factor that
helps reinforce the idea of fresh ingredients prepared to
the customer's order.

These and other design elements all work together to support our marketing and reinforce the Wendy's image. But
that does not mean that we have not changed. From the
original concept to the present image update we have constantly worked at refining, testing and developing our
design to better support our image. That fact points up
what I mentioned earlier...change. For in order to develop and maintain a consistent image in the mind of the
public, we have had to change.

A good deal of the change we have gone through was brought
about by our own success. Wendy's was the first fast food
chain to put major emphasis on the interior of the store
...making it attractive and comfortable. We were the
first to carpet our dining rooms and we pioneered the
pick-up window. Those elements of design were part of a
very successful package of service elements that supported
a very good product. The formula worked, and Wendy's went
through a dizzying period of growth. During that time,
quite frankly, design lost some of its importance. The
original concept was working and most of our efforts were
spent merely building stores...keeping up with that rapid
growth.

But our business was changing. I would like to think that
Wendy's had a major impact on those changes. Our success
made us a target. Other fast food operations began upgrading their dining rooms. More and more had carpeting
and the all formica interiors began to disappear. Pick-
up windows became the norm. You can guess what was
happening...the competition was using our own design
elements to help change their image, while our image
was gradually becomeing diluted. We were no longer quite
unique as we had been.

That was the point we began to realize that to maintain
the image we wanted...that we had so carefully developed,
we had to change. And a major part of the change was
design related.

Before I begin with a discussion of those changes and how they helped refine our image and support our marketing effort, I should make the point that we were fortunate in anticipating change. At the time we began development of our new image store and graphics, our sales were still strong. We were growing steadily and profitability was good. There was really no hard financial indication that we needed to change...it was more of an intuitive decision than one based on hard fact. We sensed the competition catching up to us in terms of design and customer comfort. We made design changes before we had to make them. We have tried to anticipate the next ten years of Wendy's growth.

Let's review the physical design aspects of the typical Wendy's store and examine how they support the marketing effort and our overall image.

Wendy's began with the "Old Fashioned" theme as a cornerstone. We were fortunate that, even during our periods of very rapid growth, we were able to maintain this theme. Although the details and materials incorporated in the store design were not authentic "turn of the century" decor, they were unique enough to make an impression on the public and help establish an image.

For example, one element that immediately identified a Wendy's was the hanging beads. From an architect's or designers standpoint, they were atrocious...a strange combination of pink, green and yellow. Yet, because they were used consistently, they quickly became, for better or worse, an integral part of the "Old Fashioned" decor.

There were other old fashioned elements. The tables with a newsprint top, the tiffany lamps. By the way, these are all handmade, authentic art glass. We have installed over 50 thousand of these over the last ten years. When we introduced the salad bar in the late seventies, we retained the tiffany effect in its canopy and designed it to fit the old fashioned formula.

With the selling umbrella of "Old Fashioned" ingrained in both the marketing strategy and the mind of the consumer, it should have been easy to decide which direction the re-design of our building would take. Surprisingly, it wasn't. As with several of our competitors who experienced very successful image changes, it seemed logical that a total, fresh, new contemporary look would have the most impact on our customers. This direction would have made economic sense because laminates and plain carpeting are much less expensive than creating an "Old Fashioned" atmosphere.

So we began doodling...toying with ideas and new designs. But the more we designed the more we learned that a sudden change of direction was not the proper course. We knew we had to sharpen our image to the consumer, but we soon realized that our existing design elements were working very well. They only needed to be refined and strenghtened, not replaced.

Another major area that we addressed during this period of change was the operational aspect and size of our units. Do we offer more generous seating arrangements and booths, or do we continue the elbow rubbing cafeteria seating arrangements of the old stores?

Again, the original philosophy of building small, compact units probably played an important role in our rapid growth. From its inception, Wendy's has had and still has the best return on investment ratio in the business.

In examining this problem, once again, design had to support company philosophy and marketing...so we stayed

with a winning formula and developed several even smaller stores than the current standard.

Our marketing people and our franchisees realized a need for some way of tapping marginal and specialized marketing areas. Areas that could not possibly support the investment and overhead required for a full size store. So we designed a series of very specialized units to address these needs. These include a compact, small town store, a walk-up/pick-up facility and a drive-up only facility. About 20 of these stores have been built and opened on a test basis, and it appears the philosophy of "less is more" may again prove to be true.

Another aspect of a quick service restaurant that at first glance may not appear to have much impact from a marketing point of view is the service and preparation area. Yet, in our case, I feel these aras have indeed played an important role in what the customer perceives as quality. As I mentioned earlier, of the major chains, only Wendy's prepares the product within full view of the customer. It would be easy to re-arrange the configuration of the cooking area to hide the preparation process. It might even be easier to design a store that way. Equipment could be more compactly arranged and we wouldn't have to worry about the condition of the grill surface or the look of the cook's apron.

But, again, this design that we have is really a marketing tool...a marketing tool supported by store design. The customer sees his sandwich being made just for him. That reinforces our "prepared the way you want it" concept. By seeing it taken off the grill surface, he gets the impression that it is, indeed "hot and juicy". By seeing the crew hustling to prepare his sandwich, there is a "human" element. "Someone" is preparing his lunch, not an automatic cooker.

As we began our re-design efforts we carefully evaluated all of the design elements of the existing stores and essentially listed those elements that we felt we should keep and develop and those that should be eliminated or totally changed. All of these decisions were based on the simple premise...does the design element support the Wendy's image and marketing thrust? By the way, the colored beads lost.

We began the interior upgrades by taking the old elements and improving their quality. Paneling was replaced with real oak bead board. New sculptured panels replaced the old acoustic ceilings. The beads were replaced with stained glass cameo panels.

With the salad bar in place in every store, we increased the emphasis on the product by creating a gazebo enclosure. We made the salad bar a major design element...giving it more legitimacy and importance.

This kind of reinforced presentation has almost doubled the percentage of salad bar sales. I still marvel at the number of major chains that have attempted to introduce a salad bar served out of a wheeled portable unit sitting in the corner of the dining room. The kind of permanence and emphasis we have placed on it can be the strongest marketing tool in the store. A clear cut example of how design can support a marketing effort.

Although the interior details and layout play an important part of the dining experience, the exterior appearance and signage are the elements that attract attention and likely have the greatest impact on sales. Every marketing person in the world knows the success story associated with the golden arches. Not only do they attract attention on the highway, but they are the only terrain feature you can identify at 20 thousand feet.

The re-imaging of the exterior of our stores began with signage and graphics. After almost a year of consultants and in-house design work on abstract shapes, contemporary script logo and colors, we (you guessed it) went back to the elements and logo that contributed to our success.

Essentially, all of the elements remain unchanged. They were a major part of our image and had good recognition. The problem with our old signage was the lack of a distinctive shape. So, the old elements were retained, but repositioned to create that new shape. The cameo was pulled to the top to create an easily identifiabile profile that, while not as bold as the arches, is much more recognizable than the original rectangular box.

Another aspect of our signage I feel has had a positive impact on our success is the name itself, "Wendy's". Back in the early seventies when R. David Thomas formulated the concept, almost everyone who knew the business advised him that the name was inappropriate and meaningless. It was an era when the market was being saturated with Burger Kings, Burger Chefs, Borden Burgers, Etc., yet through foresight, or instinct, he saw the advantage of an unusual name and apparently he was right. Sometimes we wish his daughter's name was "McWendy" or O'Wendy to give us more flexibility in identifying individual products but we think just the wholesome aspect of the red haired, freckled cheeks and old fashioned pigtails has worked very well.

Just using this girl in the cameo and the word, "Wendy's", we have created a brighter, uncluttered graphic that really lends itself to all areas of our image. Within the next few months, the logo will be extended to all paper products, name badges, corporate logo or anything using the corporate name.

We completed our re-design project with the most expensive aspect of an image change, the building. If there was an element that had little or no relation to the "Old Fashioned" image, it was the building. Although the brick was a turn of the century material, our profile and fascia exuded the true fast food image of the sixties. It apparently wasn't bad enough to scare away customers. Business flourished whether we used turquoise, white or yellow. In fact, the gaudy colors and shiney plastic told the public, "Hey, there's a fast food place". But with the additional new menu items, breakfast and so forth, we no longer want a building that screams "fast food".

For overall building design, we went through several prototypes to capture the old fashioned design elements.

The first prototype had a real copper roof with rounded awnings and a number of architectural details. It was eye catching, but it was expensive and the design did not lend itself to a retrofit...going back and changing the first 2,000 or so Wendy's stores.

The second prototype was a simplification of the first, using less expensive materials in some cases, but keep the overall flavor. It incorporated a system that could be easily retrofitted to existing stores.

The final was a combination of the first two. It incorporates a bit more detail such as dentals, crown mouldings, and lighting packages. This new image store has been adapted to our small specialty and pick-up only stores and is now the standard image being built across the country.

An architectural feature of the building that might be of interest from a marketing point of view is the glass storefront. The early buildings all had wall to wall glass to showcase the tiffany lamps, tables and chairs

from the street. We've always felt it was advantageous to expose the inside activity and the dining atmosphere while at the same time allowing the customer to watch the world go by. This I feel is more important where you have a high percentage of customers eating alone. On the new store, the glass has been narrowed for energy efficiency, yet they are held as low as codes permit to achieve this showcase effect.

We have established a five year timetable to have all stores retrofitted with the new look. Early testing in a half dozen or so markets has shown that the new look is well perceived by our customers and has had an initial positive impact on sales.

Analyzing these subtle changes as a whole, it may be questionable if we really have altered our image at all. We have certainly strengthened it and refined the design elements of the original stores to support the marketing thrust of Wendy's. The customer will never get the impression he is a totally different Wendy's, but it will be obvious he's in a totally new environment.

Our experience in design and in managing a design change has been a pleasant one. We have been lucky. Sometimes designers in the corporate situation feel like Rodney Dangerfield...we got no respect. But design in a service industry or any other for that matter is essential. It is essential to support the image of the product or service, to help define and sharpen that image and to support the overall marketing goals of the company.

MODELING SERVICE PROCESSES

Richard B. Chase, University of Arizona, Tucson

ABSTRACT

Descriptive modeling of service systems has lagged manufacturing in both product and process design. This paper
examines the notion of blueprints for services as put
forth by Shostack, and reviews some other models which
might be used for process design. A more general design
model, developed by the author, is also discussed.

INTRODUCTION

In her provocative article, "How to Design a Service,"
Lynn Shostack called for service system designers to
develop blueprints for services in much the same way
engineers go about designing manufactured products. Her
thesis was that blueprinting and the preliminary modeling
which attend it provide the service marketer "...a system
that can lead to the kind of experimentation and management so necessary to service innovation and development"
(Shostack 1981, p. 229). While I am in strong agreement
with the desirability of having sharper tools to design
and analyze services as noted by Ms. Shostack, my experience in attempting to model both manufacturing and service production systems leads me to question the adequacy
of the engineering blueprint for direct application to
services. In this paper, I will point out the conceptual
and practical difficulties of applying the traditional
industrial engineering models which go hand-in-hand with
the blueprint (or might be used as the blueprint), and
comment on sociotechnical models which could be of use in
designing a service blueprint. I will also present the
service modeling approach that I have been developing for
the past four years. I hasten to add that my approach is
not offered as a blueprint but rather as a way of concep-
tualizing, and then designing a service production system.

Blueprints and Industrial Engineering Models

A blueprint for a service constitutes a set of dynamic
procedures carried out in a specified sequence. In this
sense, it differs from a manufactured product blueprint
in that while the latter specifies the process (e.g.,
"grind outside diameter to plus or minus .002 inches"),
it doesn't provide the sequence to be followed in executing the steps. This function is typically performed by a
route sheet. Thus, while the notion of a blueprint for
services is a worthy target, we get into immediate trouble when we propose a direct application of the traditional manufacturing tool to services. Now while we can
get around this issue by adopting a broader definition of
blueprint to include specifications and routings, we run
up against a critical conceptual problem when we try to
draw analogies between the materials which the blueprint
says we must transform. In manufacturing, our materials
may be highly unstable or fragile, but they don't talk
back to the worker who is running the process. To put it
another way, it is the customer, through his infinite
variability, that eliminates the application of manufacturing type blueprinting to services.

What about other engineering models for services? In a
1975 paper, I discussed the utility of industrial engineering models for mapping factories as sociotechnical
systems--that is, systems composed of hard technologies
and people. After going through the traditional I.E.
mapping tools (flow process charts, operations sheets,
man-machine charts and the like) I concluded that none of
them provided "...more than superficial, one-dimensional
views of the relationship between a) the worker and the
technology, b) the worker and other workers, and, c)
between technology and work groups." (Chase 1975, p.
48). From there, I moved to a presentation of what
appeared to be richer models drawn from the sociotechnical literature.

Sociotechnical models include in some way the interaction
between the worker and/or work group and elements of the
physical "hard" technology which is used in the transformation process. Indicative of the general tenor of these
admittedly diverse models are Herbst's "task dependency
matrices" (which employ symbols to indicate task relationships between individuals or work groups), and
Meissner's "categories of analysis" (which provides a
classification of work situations along 12 dimensions such
as "distance between work centers").

In reviewing these models in light of Shostack's insight
about the need for explicit modeling of service processes, it is my belief that one or more of them can be
modified or redefined for this purpose. In fact, the
flow chart model that Shostack proposed (1981, p. 226),
which includes a quality dimension as well as time specifications, offers an excellent foundation upon which to
add aspects of the sociotechnical models. I would suggest that an enriched model must explicitly account for
the inevitable variability of the customer input, and the
reciprocal interdependence which exists between the customer and the server. I would also suggest that perhaps
several models are needed to accurately reflect the subtle differences between standardized and customized services, between automated and non-automated services, and
between those which entail much or little boundary span-
ning between high and low customer contact units.

Customer Contact Model

The customer contact model was proposed as a way of classifying service organizations along a dimension which
would have operational meaning for marketing and operations (Chase, 1978). The essence of the model is that
the critical feature which distinguishes one service
system from another, and units within a given service
organization from other units within that system, is
degree of direct contact with the customer during the
creation of the service. The implications of this for
operations management were discussed in Chase (1981), and
implications for organization theory are discussed in
Chase and Tansik (1983).

A Contact-Based Design Methodology

The methodology, currently being applied to a large savings and loan company, consists of five steps which lead
to a development of an ideal branch office "contact profile." This profile indicates the degree of matching
between the services provided by the branch and contact
required with the customer. The objective is to maximize
sales opportunities by enhancing contact with big depositors and at the same time reducing operating costs by
limiting contact with smaller depositors. At a broader
level, the objective of the methodology is to provide a
mechanism for developing a service marketing strategy.[1]

_____

[1] This methodology was presented at the conference
and is available as a working paper.

137

CONCLUSION

Process design for services represents a fascinating challenge to academics and practitioners alike. It calls for an eclectic group of skills ranging from engineering to behavioral science to perform the analysis function, and calls for a balanced mixture of theoretical and pragmatic thinking to perform the synthesis function. Conferences such as this one seem to me to capture the spirit of the quest and provide an ideal venue for continued innovation.

REFERENCES

Chase, Richard B. (1975), "A Review of Models for Mapping the Sociotechnical System," American Institute of Industrial Engineers Transactions, 7 (March), 48-55.

_____ (1978), "Where Does the Customer Fit in a Service Operation?," Harvard Business Review, 56 (November-December), 137-42.

_____ (1981), "The Customer Contact Approach to Services: Theoretical Bases and Practical Extensions," Operations Research, 29 (July), 698-706.

_____, and David Tansik (1983), "The Customer Contact Approach to Organizational Design," Management Science, forthcoming.

Shostack, G. Lynn, "How to Design a Service," in Marketing of Services, 1981 AMA Special Conference on Service Marketing Proceedings, James H. Donnelly and William R. George, eds., Chicago: American Marketing Association, 221-229.

EMERGING THEMES AND DIRECTIONS FOR SERVICES MARKETING

Gregory D. Upah, Young & Rubicam, Inc.
Leonard L. Berry, Texas A&M University and
G. Lynn Shostack, Bankers Trust Company

ABSTRACT

This paper presents some of the key ideas, perspectives and issues raised at the 1982 Services Marketing Conference. The authors -- members of the Conference Program Committee -- cite major, enduring ideas about services marketing management, as well as some relatively new ideas and perspectives, discussed at the meeting.

INTRODUCTION

The 1982 AMA Services Marketing Conference proved to be an excellent forum for an exchange of ideas among business people and academicians from throughout the world. Several "new" ideas and ways of thinking about services marketing were expressed. In addition, attendees found that many of their existing ideas and concepts/principles about services marketing were reinforced and echoed by others.

Indeed, it can be suggested that a consensus as to the validity of several key services marketing concepts developed during the conference. In addition, there was some degree of agreement as to the key issues and unanswered questions which warrant further investigation.

The purpose of this paper is to provide an overview of key services marketing themes which emerged at the conference. This overview is not intended to be a summary of all of the ideas expressed. Readers are encouraged to read the detailed discussion of these issues in the papers included in this volume.

For the purposes of this overview, we have categorized our assessment of key themes according to whether they had a positive (what is) or normative (what should be) focus and whether the concern was largely internal (for example, organizational or operational issues) or external (for example, attracting/retaining customers, economic issues). Figure I illustrates this arrangement.

Figure 1

	Internal Focus	External Focus
Normative Focus		
Positive Focus		

INTERNAL/NORMATIVE THEMES

A theme from the first AMA services marketing conference held in 1981 was the importance of internal marketing -- i.e. using marketing approaches to encourage employees to be more "service minded." This theme carried over to the 1982 conference. However, there were several additional aspects of internal marketing discussed during the most recent conference. These included: the role of customer-oriented advertising in promoting desired employee behavior toward customers and in building employee morale; and the need to consider "hiring" decisions along with training programs as a strategy to develop effective public contact personnel.

Organization and location of the marketing function in service firms continued to be a tipic of interest and discussion. A number of alternatives were presented, including critical examination of the merits and disadvantages of centralized versus decentralized marketing. Langeard suggested that marketing specialists frequently confuse the purposes of the marketing department and the marketing function and fail to encourage the diffusion of marketing practice in the field. George and Kelly wondered if the existence of a marketing department communicated to others in the firm that they did not need to practice marketing. Gronroos pointed out that it is particularly important for service firms to integrate the marketing function since different parts of the organization may be involved in interacting with and delivering service to the customer. For instance, airline customers encounter reservationists, cabin attendants pilots, skycaps, ticket and boarding area personnel, and the staff of airline clubs. Any of these personnel can influence the customer's degree of satisfaction with the service.

The importance of understanding "service quality" and the need for programmed service design to ensure efficient delivery of desired levels of service quality was stressed in a variety of sessions. Several speakers pointed to the need for service firms to carefully determine how their customers "define" service quality. Thomas Bloch of H&R Block illustrated this point in his explanation of his firm's decision to convert from a "walk-in" service system to an appointment-based system. Appointments, presumed to be a desirable way to minimize waiting time, proved inconvenient and undesirable to many customers who wanted service whenever they were "ready" to take their tax information to the preparer's office.

In a similar vein, a contrast was made between functional and technical service quality. The essence of this argument was that, though it is important that a service be performed in a technically correct way (technical quality), the manner in which the service is provided (functional quality) may be the critical determinant of perceived service quality and customer satisfaction. In other words, a technically correct bank procedure delivered by a bored or unsmiling teller (or one continuing to chat with a co-worker during the transaction) may result in the customer leaving the bank dissatisfied.

Taking a formal "management" approach to service quality was stressed by Munder, Rothman, and others. Munder emphasized setting quality standards, communicating them throughout the organization, using them as a basis for monitoring service performance, and, in general, using various means to build quality achievement into the "reward" system and quality awareness into the corporate culture. Rothman pointed out the importance of insuring that service quality is good before promoting the service if profitable market share gain is the objective.

Still another theme in the internal/normative category was the stress placed on service firms investing in behalf of innovation. Langeard stated that it was a mistake to think of R&D as strictly for manufacturing companies. McGill noted the importance of pushing decision-making authority down to the lowest possible levels in the organization...where people understand customers' problems. Youngclaus discussed three steps in being innovative: recognizing sources for innovation, nurturing an innovative environment, and eliminating policies and personnel that get in the way of innovation.

EXTERNAL/NORMATIVE THEMES

Two major though not independent themes of the discussion falling into the external/normative category were "relationship marketing" and impression management. The central idea behind relationship marketing is the use of formal marketing programming to retain existing customers. "Relationship marketing," according to Berry, is "attracting, maintaining, and in multi-service organizations -- enhancing customer relationships." Emphasizing existing customer retention, in addition to new customer attraction, may promote less restrictive and more efficient use of marketing resources. Customer losses in a given period can often offset customer gains. Furthermore many firms may find it less costly and more beneficial to retain existing customers than attract new ones.

Impression management obviously covers a very broad area. Most everything that service firms do, say or show can lead to favorable or unfavorable impression formation. The focus on impression management at the conference centered on three prominent areas: (1) the unique requirements for effective services advertising; (2) the multiple communications roles of the services salesperson; and (3) the influence of "atmospherics" associated with the service in shaping perceptions of the nature and quality of the service being offered.

Services advertising continued to be seen as an important tangible cue to customers as to the nature and quality of the service being offered. Papers by Firestone and Upah suggested that a major consideration for the advertising of services involves the need to merge a focus on the tangible aspects of the service (e.g., symbols, facts, equipment or people) with key intangibles -- the personality of the service firm and the "world or domain" in which this firm operates. It was pointed out that because service transactions often involve extensive person-to-person interaction that this personal aspect of a service be recognized in advertising. Futhermore, a service is very much a process. Service delivery necessitates the direct involvement of the service organization -- often multiple facets of the organization. A service is not merely a product to be taken off the shelf. As such, efforts to communicate the nature of the service firm and to reassure customers that the firm shares their values, goals, etc. may be a critical element of advertising programs.

George and Kelly suggested that personal selling of services requires impression management at various levels including establishing a reasonable level of expected performance in the prospect's mind, tangibilizing the service (for example, showing pictures of the service outcome), emphasizing organizational image attributes, and encouraging references external to the organization.

George and Kelly, McGill, and other speakers all stressed the critical nature of sales training.

The importance of interior decor and architecture in impression formation and management was stressed by several speakers. Due to the intangible nature of services, aspects of the service firm's physical environment can become key indicators to customers of the nature and quality of the services they will receive or have received. Accordingly, atmospherics need to be managed in the context of a service firm's marketing plan. As Sherowski of Wendy's put it: "Design supports marketing objectives." The impact of physical environmental factors, though difficult to quantify, nevertheless merits investigation. The development of innovative approaches to help to further understand the role of physical environment in services marketing is a key research area to be pursued.

INTERNAL/POSITIVE THEMES

A third major area of inquiry focused on describing and categorizing the internal/intrinsic aspects of services. Into this area principally fell a continuation of Lovelock's efforts to develop taxonomies for services. Lovelock has, for instance, classified services in terms of: the object of the service -- whether the service is directed toward the "person" (e.g. medical services) or the "property" of the customer; (e.g. auto repair) the extent to which customer/provider relationships are discrete (e.g. a ticket to an opera) or on-going/continuous (a full subscription to the opera); and whether the service is highly equipment- or facility-intensive (e.g. hotels, air travel) or people-intensive (e.g. legal, medical services). These classifications have several implications for services marketing. They include: the nature and cost of the service delivery system; the means by which customers are reached or retained -- e.g. direct mail is easier to use when there is a continuous or membership relationship with customers, and the relative focus on the people or equipment of the service provider in advertising, respectively.

The major benefit of these classification efforts is a better understanding of the similarities and differences in the requirements for, and challenges, to, effective service marketing practice across service industries. Moreover, such taxonomies once fully developed will serve as a basis for developing and refining key propositions for effective service marketing practice in various service industries. This same descriptive orientation applies to the process involved in defining and fostering service quality. The key dimensions of service quality (e.g. times that services are offered, time taken to provide services, manner in which personnel provide services, how customer problems/complaints are handled, etc.) must be defined and categorized for various types of services. This descriptive approach also applies to understanding and categorizing the various aspects of physical setting, architecture and interior design that impact on customer perceptions of services. For instance, customer reception areas/ waiting rooms, and the location and layout of payment areas may all be dimensions of the physical environment which impact customer satisfaction with medical, dental, and even auto repair services. Building location and architecture may be key factors influencing perceptions of legal and investment banking firms.

EXTERNAL/POSITIVE THEMES

Several of the presentations and discussions at the conference centered on understanding customer behavior for services. As already mentioned, understanding customers' perceptions of quality, and the role of physical setting in impression formation, were seen as key inputs to managerial decisions in the areas of quality control, service design and overall impression management. There were several presentations devoted to helping understand other aspects of customer behavior for services. Parasuraman and Zeithaml focused on the differential perceptions of service providers and clients with respect to key benefits/attributes sought.

Their paper again points to the need for firms to ensure that their decisions regarding service design and quality control are not contrary to key customer expectations. Smith and Houston pointed out the benefits of understanding the selection and acquisition of a service from the customer's perspective. The development of "scripts" for the process and steps used by customers to acquire a service provides assistance in, and perhaps the basis for, more effective and efficient service design.

Bateson showed that there is a substantial segment of consumers of a variety of services for whom "self-service" is an intrinsically attractive service delivery system. In addition, Bateson suggests that there is evidence that the attractiveness of self-service may carry over from one service to another. Further efforts to understand how the desirability of self-service differs by service and customer type continues to be a major priority for further research efforts.

Another external/positive theme stressed by Edvinsson and Nandorf and echoed by Langeard was the significance of service exporting to the balance of payments of many industrialized countries. Generally, political leaders in the United States and elsewhere are unaware of just how much net services exporting "pays" for net goods importing and, as a result, give insufficient attention to important policy and strategy issues.

Finally, as Gene Kelley pointed out in his luncheon address to the conference, any assessment of services marketing must include the continued recognition of the growing importance of services in the U.S. and world economy. Several forecasters point to the critical impact of knowledge/information services in the 1980's -- what Kelley refers to as technoservices. These services (e.g. relying on advanced computer and telecommunications technology) are not labor-intensive but highly equipment-intensive. Moreover, they offer the promise of subsantial increases in productivity in decision-making and delivery of goods and services -- an interesting contrast from the charge (recently disputed by many economists) that services have been the less productive sector of the economy.

CONCLUSION

Services marketing must retain its focus on services -- whether they be pure services or the service component of industrial products. This need to continue to develop a body of knowledge for services marketing (as distinguished from goods marketing) was perhaps the central theme at this second AMA Serices Marketing Conference. This commitment to services marketing as a specific field of study and practice should continue to fuel the kind of rapid progress made in recent years.

SUMMARY

This paper has presented an overview of key themes and issues discussed at the Second AMA Services Marketing Conference. A summary is presented in Figure 2. Clearly, the most impressive aspect the conference was the quality of ideas expressed, and the progress the field has made in the short time since the first AMA services marketing conference was held. To fully appreciate this aspect of the conference, we recommend the papers and presentations themselves, all of which are reproduced in this volume.

Figure 2

SUMMARY OF KEY THEMES

	Internal Focus	External Focus

Normative Focus	. Internal Marketing
	. Improving Service Quality
	. Quality Control
	. Service Design
	. Organization of the Marketing Function
		. Relationship Marketing
		. Impression Management
		  - Advertising
		  - Personal Selling

Positive Focus	. Taxonomy of Services
	. Understanding the Dimensions of Service Quality
	. Dimensionalizing the Physical Services Environment
		. Customer Evaluation
		  - Benefits sought
		  - Processes/Steps in Buying
		  - Perceptions regarding "Self-Service"
		. Industrial Goods/ Services Marketing Parallels
		. Services Exporting

APPENDIX
SELECTED SERVICES MARKETING BIBLIOGRAPHY
William George, Vivanova Unwersty

Baranoff, Seymour and Donnelly, James H., Jr. (1970)
"Selecting Channels of Distribution for Services."
Handbook of Modern Marketing. Edited by Victor P. Buell.
New York: McGraw-Hill Book Company.

Bateson, John E. G. (1979). "Why We Need Service
Marketing." Conceptual and Theoretical Developments in
Marketing. Edited by O.C. Ferrell, Stephen W. Brown,
and Charles J. Lamb, Jr. (Chicago: American Marketing
Association), Pp. 131-146.

Berry, Leonard L. (1980) "Services Marketing Is Different".
Business (May-June), pp. 24-29.

Berry, Leonard L. (1981) "Perspectives on the Retailing
of Services" in Theory in Retailing: Traditional and Non-
Traditional Sources. Edited by Ronald W. Stampfl and
Elizabeth C. Hirschman. (Chicago: American Marketing
Association), p. 9-20.

Bessom, Richard M., and Jackson, Donald W., Jr. (1975)
"Service Retailing: A Strategic Marketing Approach."
Journal of Retailing. (Summer), pp. 103-110.

Brundage, Jane and Claudia Marshall. (1980) "Training as
a marketing management tool." Training and Development
Journal (November) p. 7]-76.

Carlson, Edward E. (1975) "Visible Management' at United
Airline." Harvard Business Review. (July-August), pp.
90-97.

Chase, Richard B. 91978) "Where Does the Customer Fit in
a Service Operation?" Harvard Business Review, pp. 8.

Cooke, Blaine (1970) "Analizing Markets for Services."
Handbook of Modern Marketing. Edited by Victor P. Buell.
New York: McGraw-Hill Book Company.

Crosby, Philip. B. (1979) Quality Is Free. NY McGraw-Hill
Book, Co.

Czepiel, John A (1980) Managing Customer Satisfaction in
Consumer Businesses. (Cambridge, MA: Marketing Science
Institute Report #80-109).

Daltas, A. J. (1977) "Protecting Service Markets with
Consumer Feedback," Cornell Hotel and Restaurant
Adiministrative Quarterly, 18 (May), pp. 73-77.

Davidson, David S. (1978) "How To Succeed In A Service
Industry... Turn the Organization Chart Upside Down."
Management Review (April), pp. 13-]6.

David, Duane L. (1978) "An Empirical Investigation Into
the Marketing of Consumer Services: Toward the
Development of a Typology of Services Based on Attitudes
Towards Search." Unpublished Ph.D. dissertation,
University of Kentucky.

Davis, Duane L., Guiltinan, Joseph P., and Jones, Wesley
H. (1979) "Service Charisticics, Consumer Search, and the
Classification of Retail Services." Journal of Retailing
(Fall), pp. 3-23.

Dearden, John. (1978) "Cost Accounting Comes to Service
Industries," Harvard Business Review, (September-October),
pp. 132-140.

Denney, Robert W. (1981). "How to Develop and Implement
A Marketing Plan for Your Firm." Practical Accountant
(July), p. 18-29.

Donnelly, James H., Jr. (1976) "Marketing Intermediaries
in Channels of Distribution for Services." Journal of
Marketing. (January), pp. 55-57.

Eiglier, Pierre, et al. (1977) Marketing Consumer Services:
New Insights. Cambridge, MA: Marketing Science Institute.

Enis, Ben M. and Roering, Kenneth S. (1981). "Services
Marketing: Different Products, Similar Strategy" in
Marketing of Services. Edited by James H. Donnelly and
William R. George. (Chigago: American Marketing Association)
p. 1-4.

Feldman, Sidney P., and Spencer, Merlin C. (1971) "The
Effect of Personal Influences in the Selection of Consumer
Services." Consumer Behavior. Edited by Robert Holloway,
et al. Boston: Houghton Mifflin Company.

Fuchs, Victor R. (1968) The Service Economy. New York:
Columbia University Press for National Bureau of Economic
Research.

George, William R. (1972) "Marketing in the Service
Industries." Unpublished Ph. dissertation, University of
Georgia.

George, William R. (1975) "Service Firms -- A Marketing
Holdout?" Proceedings: Southern Marketing Association.
pp. 49-51.

George, William R. and Barksdale, Hiram O. (1974)
"Marketing Activities in the Service Industries." Journal
of Marketing, (October), pp. 65-70.

George, William R. and Berry, Leonard L. (1981) "Guidelines for the Advertising of Services." Business Horizons
(July,August), p. 52-56.

George, William R., and Murray Richard M. (1975) "Marketing Practices of CPA Firms." The CPA Journal (October),
pp. 33-36.

George, William R. and Solomon, Paul J. (1980) "Marketing Strategies for Improving Practive Development." The
Journal of Accountancy (February), pp. 79-84.

George, William R., and Meyers, Thomas A. (1981) "Life
Underwriters Perceptions of Differences in Selling Goods
andServices" CLU Journal (April), p. 44-49.

Gotlieb, Jerry B. and Schwartz, Bill N. (1982) "How a CPA
Firm Can Anazyze the Market for its Services" Ohio CPA
Journal (Winter), p. 11-15.

Granger, C. H. (1977) "Growth Strategies in Service Bus-
ness." Management Review 66 (April), pp. 5-12.

Gronroos, C. (1978) "A Service-Oriented Approach to Marketing
of Services." European Journal of Marketing. (8).

Gronroos, C. (1979) "An Applied Theory For Marketing
Industrial Services" Industrial Marketing Management (8)
p. 45-50.

Gronroos, Christian (1980) "Designing A Long Range
Marketing Strategy for Services" Long Range Planning
(April), p. 36-42.

Gummesson, Evert. (1978) :Toward a Theory of Professional
Service Marketing" Industrial Marketing Management (7),
p. 89-95.

Gummesson, Evert (1979) "The Marketing of Professional
Services -- An Organizational Dilemma" European Journal of

Marketing (Vol. 13, #5)

Gummesson, E. (1981) "Marketing Cost Concept in Service Firms", Industrial Marketing Management (]0) p. 175-182.

Guseman, Dennis S. (1977) "The Perception of Risk In Consumer Services -- A Comparison With Consumer Products". Unpublished D.B.A. dissertation, University of Colorado.

Hardin, David K. (1970) "Marketing Research for Service Industries." Handbook of Modern Marketing. Edited by Victor P. Buell. New York: McGraw-Hill Book Company.

Hempel, Donald J. and Laric, Michael V. (1979) "Marketing Productivity Analysis: Strategic Implications for Consumer Services." Conceptual and Theoretical Developments in Marketing. Edited by O.C. Ferrell, Stephen W. Brown, and Charles W. Lamb, Jr. (Chicago: American Marketing Association, pp. 554-566.

Hoffman, Arthur W. (1981) "How Advertising Helped A New CPA Rirm Build Its Practice." Practical Accountant (Octover), p. 52-56.

Hollander, Stanley C. (1979) "Is There A Generic Demand for Services?" MSU Business Topics (Spring), pp. 41-46.

Hostage, G.M. "Quality Control in a Service Business." Harvard Business Review (July/August), pp. 98-106.

Jenkins, Kenneth M. and Justin Shimada. "Quality circles in the service sector." Supervisory Management (August 1981), p. 3-7.

Johnson, Eugene M. (1970) "Arg Goods and Services Different: An Exercise in Marketing Theory." Unpublished Ph.D. dissertation, Washington University.

Johnson, Eugene M. (1970) "The Selling of Services." Handbook of Modern Marketing. Edited by Victor P. Buell. New York: NcGraw-Hill Book Company.

Judd, Robert C. (1964) "The Case for Redefining Services." Journal of Marketing. (January),pp. 58-59.

Judd, Robert C. (1968) "Similarities or Differences in Product and Service Retailing." Journal of Retailing, (Winter), pp. 1-9.

Keeney, Ralph L. and Nair, Keshavan, (1976) "Setting Goals in a Professional Service Firm," Long Range Planning (June), pp. 54-58.

Kelly, J. Patrick and George, William R. (1980) "Perceptions of the Personal Selling Function in Service Marketing: A field Study." Marketing in the 80's: Changes & Challenges. (Chicago: American Marketing Association), pp. 244-247.

Kelly, Patrick and George, William R. (1982) "Strategic Management Issues for Retailing of Services." Journal of Retailing (Summer), p. 26-43.

Kessler, Ellen Terry. (198]. "Advertising Accounting Services: How Effective Has It Been?" Practical Account (July), p. 37-44.

Konrad, Evelyn. (1968) "An R&D Approach for Service Industry." Business Horizons. (October), pp. 73-78.

Kotler, Philip and Connor, Richard A. (1977) "Marketing Professional Services." Journal ot Marketing (January), pp. 71-76.

"Kramer Urges Service Firms to Audit Employees' Performance." (1975) Marketing News. (January 31), pp. 9.

Legum, Lynn and George, William R. (1981) "Analysis of Marketing Management Practices of Dance Companies" Journal of the Academy of Marketing Science (Winter/Spring), p. 15-26.

Levitt, Theodore. (1972) "Production-line Approach to service." Harvard Business Review. (September-October), pp. 41-52.

Levitt, Theodore. (1976) "The Industrialization of service". Harvard Business Review. (September-October), pp. 63-74.

Levitt, Theodore. (198]) "Marketing intangible products and product intangibles." Harvard Business Review (May-June), p. 94-102.

Lewis William. (]976) "An Empirical Investigation of the Conceptual Relationship Between Services and Products in Terms of Perceived Risk." Unpublished Ph.D dissertation, University of Cincinnati.

Lovelock, Christopher H. (1981) "Why Marketing Management Needs To Be Different For Services." Marketing of Services. Edited by James H. Donnelly and William R. George (Chicago: American Marketing Association), p. 5-9.

Mapel, Eugene B. (1970) "The Marketing of Services." Handbook of Modern Marketing. Edited by Victor Pl Buell. New York: McGraw-Hill Book Company.

Matteis, Richard J. (1979) "The New Back Office Focuses On Customer Service." Harvard Business Review (March-April), pp. 146-159.

Mizerski, Richard W. and, Weinberger, Marc G. (1978) "Casual Attribution with Goods Compared to Services." Proceedings: Southern Marketing Association, pp. 146-149.

Murray, Richard M. and George, William R. (1978) "Managing CPA Personnel - A Marketing Perspective." The CPA Journal (July), pp. 17-22.

Parker, Donald D. (1960) The Marketing of Services. Seattle: Bureau of Business Research, University of Washington.

Rathmell, John M. (1966) "What is Meant by Services?" Journal of Marketing, (October), pp. 32-36.

Rathmell, John M. (1974) Marketing in the Service Sector. Cambridge, MA: Winthrop Publishers, Inc.

Regan, William J. (1963) "The Service Revolution." Journal of Marketing, (July), pp. 57-62.

Researchers Can Help Sell Services, But The Questions Deffer." (1975) Marketing News. (January 31), pp. 8.

Sandeman, Graham (1981) "Implications of the Molecular Marketing Model in the Design of Retail Concepts." Marketing of Services. Edited by James H. Donnelly and William R. George (Chicago: American-Marketing Association) p. 230-235.

Sasser, W. Earl (1976) "Math Supply and Demand in Service Industries." Harvard Business Review, (November-December), pp. 133-140.

Sasser, W. Earl and Arbeit, Stephen P. (1976) "Selling Jobs in the Service Sector." Business Horizons. (June), pp61 65.

Sasser, W. Earl, R. Paul Olsen, and D. Daryl Wycokoff. (1978) Management of Service Operations Boston: Allyn and Bacon.

Schlissel, M.R. (]977) "Pricing in a Service Industry," MSU Business Topics, 25 (Spring), pp. 27-48.

Schneider, Benjamin (1980) "The Service Organization: Climate is Critical" Organizantional Dynamics (Autumn), pp. 52-65.

Shaw, John C. (1978) The Quality-Productivity Connection in Service Sector Management NY: Van Nostrand Reinhold Co.

Shaw, John Co., and Cappor, Ram. (1979) "Quality and Productivity: Mutually Exclusive or Interdependent in Service Organizations?" Management Review (March), pp. 25-28, 37-39.

Shostack, G. Lynn. (1977) "Breaking Free From Product Marketing." Journal of Marketing 41 (April), pp. 73-80.

Shostack, G. Lynn. (1979) "The Service Marketing Frontier." Review of Marketing 1978. Edited by G. Zaltman and T. Bonoma. Chicago: American Marketing Association pp. 373-388.

Shostack, G. Lynn (1981) "How To Design A Service." Marketing of Services. Edited by James H. Donnelly and William R. George (Chigago: American Marketing Association), p. 221-229.

Skigen, Michael R. (1981) "Advertising of a Limited Budget: A Small Firm's Experience." Practical Accountant (october). p. 57-61.

Swan, John I., I. Frederick Trawick, and Maxwell G. Carroll. "Effort of participation in Marketing Research on Consumer Attitudes Toward Research and Satisfaction with a Service" Journal of Marketing Research (August 1981), pp. 356-363.

Swinyard, William R. (1977) "Marketing Segmentation In Retail Service Industries: A Multiattribute Approach." Journal of Retailing (Spring), pp. 27-34, 92-93.

"Three AT&T Research Projects Show Variety of Methods Used" (1975) Marketing News. (January 31), pp. 9.

Thomas, Dan R. E. (1978) "Strategy is Different in Service Businesses," Harvard Business Review, (July-August), pp. 158-165.

Uhl, Kenneth P. And Gregory Upah (1983). "The Marketing of Services: Why and How is it Different" Research In Marketing. Edited by Jagdish N. Shith.

Unwin, Stephen. (1975) "Customised Communications: A Concept for Service Advertisint." Advertising Quarterly 44 (Summer), pp. 28-30.

Upah, Gregory D. (1980) "Mass Marketing is Service Retailing: A Review and Synthesis of Major Methods" Journal of Retailing (Fall), p. 59-76.

Weinberger, Marc G. (1976) "Services and Goods: A Laboratory Study of Informational Influences." Unpublished D.B.A. dissertation, Arizona State University.

Weinberger, Marc G. and Brown, Stephen W. (1977) "A Difference in Informational Influences: Services vs. Goods." Jorunal of the Academy of Marketing Science (Fall), pp. 389-402.

Wilson, Aubray. (1972) "The Marketing of Professional Services. London: McGraw-Hill Book Company (UK).

Winter, Elmer L. (1970), "How to License A Service." Columbia Journal of World Business. (September-October), pp. 83-85.

Wittreich, Warren. (1966), "How to Buy/Sell Professional Services." Harvard Business Review. (March/April), pp.71-86.

Woll, Milton. (1975) "Planning for the Next Decade -- Merchandising Services." Stores. (May), pp. 60.

Wyckham, R.G. Fitzroy, P.T.: and Mandry, G.D. (1975), "Marketing of Services -- An Evaluation of the Theory." European Journal of Marketing of Services Vol. 9 Number 1, (Spring) pp. 59-67.

Education Essentials and the Marketing of Higher
Education
    Larry H. Litten

The Marketing of Higher Education: A Multimarket, Multi-
service Approach
    Michael J. Houston

Five Myths About Marketing and Public Health
    Jary Jane Rawlins Schlinger

A Marketing Framework for Assessing the Failure of New
Health Services
    Mary Ann Stutts
    Debra Low

Moving From Concept to Action: Strategic Barriers in
Health Care Marketing
    Roberta N. Clarke

Health Care Marketing: Issues for Future Development
    Eric N. Berkowitz

Intermediary Strategies for Non-Profit Organizations
    Alan R. Adnreasen

The Public Schools as Untermediaries
    Karen F.A. Fox

The Teaching of Nonprofit and Public Marketing
    Mary Joyce
    Kathy Krentler

SERVICES THEORY

Tactical Service Marketing and the Process of Remixing
    Martin L. Bell

Some Organizational Problems Facing Marketing in the
Service Sector
    Christopher H. Lovelock
    Eric Langeard
    John E. G. Bateson
    Pierre Eiglier

Analysing the Customer/Firm Communication Component of
the Services Marketing Mix
    Bernard H. Booms
    Jody L. Nyquist

Federal Trade Commission Activities in the Service Sector:
Recent Experiences and Potential Future Directions
    Ronald Stiff
    Patrick E. Murphy

Services Marketing: The Challenge of Stagflation
    Dennis Guseman
    Peter L. Gillett

How Consumer Evaluation Processes Differ Between Goods and
Services
    Valarie A. Zsithawl

Toward a Consumption/Evaluation Process Model for
Services
    Raymond F. Fisk

The Advertising of Consumer Services and the Hierarchy of
Effects
    Robert F. Young

Risk Perception and Risk Reduction in Consumer Services
    Dennis S. Guseman

Goods vs. Services Marketing: A Divergent Perspective
    James R. Brown
    Edward R. Fern

A Matrix Approach to the Classification of Marketing
Goods and Services
    Martin L. Bell

Implications of Human Capital Theory for the Marketing
of Services
    Nikhilesh Dholakia
    David Dilts

Concept Testing for Services
    Patrick E. Murphy
    Richard K. Robinson

How To Design a Service
    G. Lynn Shostack

Implications of the Molecular Marketing Model in the
Design of Retail Concepts
    Graham Sandeman

International Marketing - An Integral Part of Marketing
Theory
    Christian Gronroos

CLOSING PRESENTATIONS

Marketing of Services: Meeting of Different Needs.
    Neil E. Beckwith
    Thomas J. Fitzgerald

Service Evaluation
    Robert Krughoff